§H $2.95 A

PATHWAYS OF BUDDHIST THOUGHT

PATHWAYS OF BUDDHIST THOUGHT
Essays from *The Wheel*

Edited by
The Venerable Nyanaponika
MAHATHERA
and selected by M. O'C. Walshe

BOOKS
10 East 53d St., New York 10022
(a division of Harper & Row Publishers, Inc.)

Published in the U.S.A. 1972 by:
HARPER & ROW PUBLISHERS, INC.
BARNES & NOBLE IMPORT DIVISION

ISBN 06 4952215

Printed in Great Britain

For Christmas Humphreys

15. 2. 1971

PREFACE

The following essays are all taken from the Wheel series of publications which have been issued during the past ten years by the Buddhist Publication Society, Kandy, Ceylon, under the editorship of the distinguished German scholar-monk, the Ven. Nyānaponika Mahāthera. This remarkable series of inexpensive, well-printed paperbacks has set an entirely new standard for mass-distribution Buddhist literature, and indeed there are probably few Christian or other religious publications of a similar character to compare with it. The series embraces simply-written but authoritative essays on many aspects of Buddhism, together with selections from the Pali scriptures in new translations, commentaries, and so on. It is supported by a parallel series of even smaller and cheaper 'tracts' called Bodhi Leaves which maintain the same high quality.

It may be objected by some that, excellent though they are, these publications present only one aspect of Buddhism—the teachings of the Theravāda school of Ceylon, Burma and Thailand, ignoring almost totally the riches of the Mahāyāna schools of Zen, Tibetan Buddhism and the rest, to which so many Western people find themselves drawn. But it is being increasingly realized today, as Western interest in Buddhism grows and deepens, that it is almost impossible to gain an adequate grasp of these 'developed' or 'expanded' Buddhist teachings without a fair grounding in Theravāda principles, which can, in truth, be regarded as 'Basic Buddhism', containing as they do all that we can know of the authentic doctrines laid down by Gotama the Buddha (c. 563–483 BC) himself. As such, this teaching represents a complete system in itself which can well substantiate its claim to provide the answer to the problem of life that faces all men, in modern times no less than in ancient India. Those who wish to make their own comparisons between the schools of Buddhism may do so, and in the essay by Dr Burns will find some tentative approaches to such a comparison.

The title of this volume is taken from that given by the editor to the little collection of posthumous essays by the English Bhikkhu Ñānamoli, who devoted most of his energies during his relatively short monastic career to translation work, his most substantial memorial being his classic version of Buddhaghosa's *Path of Purification* (Colombo, 1956). The essays here reprinted are as found after his death, some in an unfinished state, but showing a lively and original mind at grips with some of the most fundamental problems of life—and death. Then come some important essays from distinguished scholars on philosophical and ethical aspects of Buddhism, and one of these scholars, Dr Jayatilleke[1], is also the author of a brief but brilliant discussion of Buddhism in relation to modern science, which follows. The next two selections, by the general editor of the series himself, deal with the fundamental Buddhist practice of mindfulness, and with the much-misunderstood topics of *anattā* or egolessness and the goal, Nibbāna or Nirvana, and the volume concludes with a long essay by Dr Burns, an American psychiatrist resident in Thailand, who approaches the question of Nirvana from a different angle as well as pointing out a possible approach to the Zen experience of *satori*.

I cannot refrain from expressing the hope that the reader who has studied this selection will find his appetite whetted for more from the same source. Any such reader who cares to send £2 or $5 a year to the Buddhist Publication Society, P.O. Box 61, Kandy, Ceylon, may become an Associate Member of the Society and as such will receive all future publications and lists of those in print.

November 1969

M. O'C. WALSHE

---

[1] Died July 1970

PUBLISHER'S NOTE

Since this book is a compilation of writings by different authors, there are certain variations in style of transliteration. We have decided to preserve the individual style of each author, and this may account for any apparent inconsistencies in spelling and phraseology.

CONTENTS

CONTENTS

I. PATHWAYS OF BUDDHIST THOUGHT

THE VEN. NANAMOLI THERA[1]

---

1. BUDDHISM: A RELIGION OR A PHILOSOPHY?

Sometimes the question is heard: 'Is Buddhism a religion or a philosophy?' And sometimes the answer comes readily: 'It is a religion.'—'But why?'—'Well isn't religion a matter of observances? And the Eightfold Path is largely observance, with Right Speech and so on, so Buddhism is a religion, like any other.' Or it may come just as readily: 'It is not a *religion*, it is a philosophy.'—'Why?'—'Because it doesn't rely on blind faith but emphasizes understanding. It is the way of Reason. And isn't Right View philosophy?' Or someone may say: 'It is neither a religion nor a philosophy, it is an Ethico-philosophical System.' Who is right? Are they all right? or some right? or none?

We may remember to have read somewhere that Religion is a matter of emotions and that philosophy is rational. If we fly to the dictionaries for help, we may well come away in this case more uncertain than before—to define 'Buddhism' and 'religion' and 'philosophy' from the dictionaries is no easy matter (but if we once begin to inquire from them what exactly the word 'is' implies, we shall find ourselves soon in a pretty tangle, as anyone can see for themselves if they like to try).

But if we are not sure what we mean by 'religion' or 'philosophy' (let alone the word 'is'), can we attempt to answer the question at all? But even suppose we do agree on a meaning for

[1] Written in June 1957.

those two words, are we right in supposing that the question is rightly put—put in such a way that some correct answer is possible if it can be found? Are, in fact, all religions and philosophies each just *a* religion and *a* philosophy among a crowd, and is Buddhism *necessarily* one among this crowd? What then, would be the unique Olympian point of view able to survey all those religions and philosophies, and able to class them and pigeon-hole them so readily and neatly?

There used to be a recognized type of question in ancient Greece which committed the answerer equally, whether he replied affirmatively or negatively. One was 'Do you use a thick stick when you beat your wife? Answer yes or no.' Now whether the answer was 'yes' or 'no', the retort came: 'So you *do* beat your wife, then.' There are many questions of that type, and some of them not at all evidently so.

Why not pause—there is no hurry—before plumping for a one-sided answer and take a quick glance at the way in which the Buddha handles and presents his whole teaching. One thing among many others to be noticed here is that he is careful to spread a *net* with which to intercept all speculative views. This is the *Brahma-jāla*, the 'Divine Net', which as the first discourse of the whole *Sutta Pitaka*, forms as it were a kind of filter for the mind, or to change the figure, a tabulation by whose means, if rightly used, all speculative views can be identified, traced down to the fallacy or unjustified assumption from which they spring, and neutralized. This 'Net', in fact, classifies all possible speculative views (rationalist or irrationalist) under a scheme of 62 types. These 62 types are not descriptions of individual philosophies of other individual teachers contemporary with the Buddha—a number of those are mentioned as well elsewhere in the Suttas—but are the comprehensive net (after revealing the basic assumptions on which these speculative views all grow) with which to catch *any* wrong view-points that can be put forward. (Ultimately, these must all be traceable to the contact of self-identification in some form, however misinterpreted, but that cannot be gone into here.)

But why bring in this here, though? it may well be asked.

Because, instead of accepting the question 'Is Buddhism a religion or a philosophy?' and attempting an answer straight off, we can step back for a moment. We can ask ourselves if, by replying 'It is a philosophy', we may not be making out that the Buddha was actually teaching one of the types of wrong view catchable in the 'Divine Net', against which that 'net' should protect us. Then the Buddha denounces ritualism (*sīlabbata-parāmāsa*) as a vain waste of time bound to lead to disappointment. So if we mean just 'practice of rites' by religion, or if we mean unjustified and unverifiable emotional beliefs, if we say 'Buddhism is a religion', should we not be implying that Buddhism teaches the very rite-ridden blindness of gullible credulity that the Buddha himself so plainly denounces?

There is, of course, no end to the arguments that can be churned out on both sides, the dialectic goes on oscillating with no resolution, till cut short by sheer weariness, or till some eloquent plea lulls us into thinking the matter is settled once and for all. Or we may just accept one side and forget about it for the time. But it will be reopened again for sure sooner or later, and the dialectic will resume its pendulum-swing. With the best will in the world, though, and the most tireless patience and brilliant dialectic skill, is there really anywhere to be got to, any solution to be found, on these lines? What are we to do, then?

In the *Anguttara Nikāya* the Buddha divides questions into four kinds. Some can be answered unilaterally (yes or no). Some have to be analysed before answering. Others must be dealt with by a counter-question (making the questioner produce material out of himself that shows him for himself how things are). And lastly there are some that cannot be answered at all (they are like that mentioned above about thick and thin sticks; for they make the answerer affirm an assumption, whatever he replies). These must be entirely set aside.

Now a *question*, as long as it remains a question, is a *dialectic*, and when it is answered, the dialectic is unilaterally resolved.

In his fourfold classification of questions (dialectics), the Buddha may be taken to be communicating how to treat dialectics. Now there are two forms of communication. They have been called the 'didactic' and the 'existential'. The first says, in fact, 'this is like this; this is what has to be done', while the second tends to set forth the basic elements of a situation and leave it to the other to discover for himself the act-of-discovery that can be made on the basis of those elements set forth. Didactically one can tell someone how to cook a dish by communicating the recipe, but the satisfying of hunger and the discovery of the cooking and how good the dish is in the eating can only be communicated existentially—it must be lived.

Now to return to the four types of questions and ways of communicating answers, as communicated to us by the Buddha: first, any question is a dialectic. Now the first type of question is answerable didactically. It is the kind of dialectic where both sides are already evident, which can and ought to be resolved by a unilateral answer (the authority for such a resolution being always accurate observation without forgetting what has been accurately observed). Examples of such unilateral decisions would be: choosing giving and not avarice, choosing kindness and not hate and anger, choosing unilateral keeping of the five precepts unbroken (since the Buddha observed that breaking them entails pain, such being the observable nature of existence for a Buddha who sees how it is), and so on. The highest form in which this unilateral decision is expressed is in the form of the Noble Eightfold Path, in choosing the Right and rejecting the Wrong. (N.B.: regarded in this way the Path appears, not as an 'observance' or a 'rationalist scheme' or a 'duty' but as a *practical way to end suffering*.) This is a didactic communication which communicates the unilateral resolution of a dialectic for a clear reason without mystification.

The second type of question—that answerable after analysis —can be regarded as a dialectic, one side of which is hidden or partly hidden, and both sides of which need bringing clearly to light, one whose *ambiguity* should be *displayed* didactically. Whether it can then be answered, or partly answered, unilaterally is here of secondary importance. The important thing is not to 'buy a pig in a poke' by answering unilaterally a question one has not yet fully understood. The *doubleness* of the dialectic

16

involved, until it has been brought to light by analysis, lurks concealed and can be harmful and mislead. Such a question would be: 'Does the Buddha condemn all asceticism?' Before answering, the main debatable points involved should be clearly displayed.

The third type has to be dealt with by a counter-question. It makes the questioner dig out of his own mind the elements that prompt him to ask it. These, when thus brought to light *by himself*, give him the opportunity for his discovery how he went wrong in formulating his question. He can discover for himself that the supposed dialectic of his question is fictitious and that the truth lies elsewhere. This is not a didactic communication at all but an existential one. The questioner is not told didactically what to do, he is existentially given the opportunity to *discover* for himself. (What is *discovered* may be didactically communicable, but the act-of-discovery is not.) The Buddha's teaching—that of the four truths together—is at heart an existential communication, in this sense. (An example would be the *Gaṇaka Moggallāna Sutta—Majjhima Nikāya* 107.)

The fourth type of question which must be avoided, is that which traps the answerer, either purposely or unwittingly, into affirming an unjustifiable assumption, whether he answers negatively or affirmatively makes no difference. (It is well recognized in logic how a denial necessarily implies the prior affirmation of what is denied or negated.) The best examples of such questions are the set of four: 'Does the Tathāgata exist after death?', 'Does he not exist after death?', 'Does he both exist and not exist after death?', 'Does he neither exist nor not exist after death?', none of which the Buddha consented to answer. 'Was it because he was an agnostic?' some people have asked. But that very question shows that the existential communication has failed in the questioner; for besides the fact that to describe the Buddha (the 'Awakened One') as 'agnostic' is rather a quaint contradiction, the point is overlooked that the four questions about the Tathāgata existing after death or not all contain an assumption which the answers yes and no alike affirm—they are all ultimately begged questions.

B

We may seem to have by now wandered rather far from the original query: 'Is Buddhism a religion or a philosophy?' But two things have come to light. The first is that if we answer in too much of a hurry one way or the other, we may unwittingly be making out that Buddhism 'is' either one of the speculative views which are caught by the Buddha's own 'Divine Net' (the *Brahmajāla*), or that it 'is' one of the ritualistic observances of blind faith condemned by the Buddha as bound to disappoint. The second is that, before undertaking to answer, we may ask ourselves which of the four types of questions this question falls under.

Yet before we start doing that, which might well involve us again deeply in dialectics, let us take another look at the way the Buddha sometimes *gives* his teaching. He was, in fact, asked a question whose essentials were much the same though the details were different. It was the night of the Buddha's Parinibbāna, and the Wanderer Subhadda went to him and asked: 'Master Gotama, there are these monks and divines with their congregations, teachers of congregations, famous philosophers whom many regard as saints . . . have they all direct acquaintance of what they claim? or none of them? or have some and some not?' The Buddha's reply was this: 'Enough, Subhadda. Let that be. I shall teach you the Dhamma.' And he went on to expound the Eightfold Path. Now the Noble Eightfold Path is one of the four Noble Truths. The Noble Truth of Suffering, the Noble Truth of the Origin of Suffering (which is need)[1] the Noble Truth of the Cessation of Suffering (which is cessation of need), and the Noble Truth of the Way leading to cessation of suffering (which is the Eightfold Path). These four Truths— termed 'truth' (*sacca*) because they do not deceive, are founded on actual experience and nothing else, and cannot disappoint— are called the 'teaching peculiar to Buddhas' (*Buddhānaṁ sammukkamsikā desanā*), since it is precisely this teaching by which a Buddha is recognizable and distinguished.

'*Religion*' tends to rely upon faith alone, and '*philosophy*' on understanding alone. But the Buddha, in his teaching of the Truths, stresses the even balancing of *five* faculties. They are

---

[1] *Taṇhā*, usually translated as 'craving' or 'desire'. (*Editor*).

those of faith, energy, mindfulness, concentration and under-standing. While mindfulness can never be overdone, the others, if onesidedly overdeveloped or repressed, may distort the character and outlook, and spiritual health that resides in their even balancing. Faith alone is blind credulity and gambles against disappointment. Over-exerted energy agitates and dis-tracts. Too much concentration tends to sleep and quietism, while understanding unsupported by the others degenerates into craftiness and cunning. When all are being properly managed, faith functions as confidence in the ability of the others to resist opposition and to reach their fulfilment in liberation from suffering.

All the five are perfectly familiar because they are present to some extent, however small, in everyone. No one can act at all without at least faith that his act will bring the desired result. Everyone has the energy to show life. Without mindful-ness nothing at all could ever be remembered or recognized. Every time we hold a thought for the shortest space of time we concentrate. And no one could ever place their faith at all, however strong or weak, without making some judgement, how-ever bad, where to place it. Such are these five faculties at their bare unescapable minimum. And these same faculties, the Buddha says, 'end in the Deathless', which is the end of greed and hate and delusion, the end of suffering. They are with us always.

The Eightfold Path has eight factors: right view, intention; right speech, action and livelihood; and right effort, mindfulness and concentration. The five faculties are, to repeat: faith, energy, mindfulness, concentration and understanding. What have the ones to do with the others? Faith (which is faith in the other four faculties) undertakes the three path factors that constitute virtue, namely right speech, action and livelihood; for these are first undertaken (like any other action) in the faith that they will lead to the development of the rest and to the ending of suffering. Energy is right effort. Mindfulness is right mindfulness. Concentration is right concentration. Under-standing is right understanding and right intention. In this way the five faculties correspond to the Eightfold Path. They are the Path's raw material. In this way too the Eightfold Path is clearly *not* faith alone, and so is hardly adequately or rightly described as an 'observance' (observance of ritual), that is, as a 'religion' in this sense. It is equally clearly *not* understanding alone, and so is hardly adequately or rightly described as purely rationalistic in the sense of limited to logic (suffering is not a logical category, nor is liberation), that is, a 'philosophy'. Again, while it certainly has its ethical and philosophical aspects—the first in the Path in right intention, speech, action and livelihood—the second in mundane right view—and is certainly systematic, not chaotic or incoherent, yet it is hardly adequately or right to be pigeon-holed as *an* ethico-philosophical *system*. The Buddha said 'I teach only suffering and the liberation from suffering', and he said 'As the ocean has only one tast, that of salt, so my teaching has only one taste, that of liberation'. That seems hardly *a* mere *system*.

But *is* Buddhism a religion or philosophy? Would the reader not like to deal with this for himself?

2. DOES *SADDHĀ* MEAN FAITH?

PART I

Sheer ignorance; gullibility, credulity, belief, faith, trust, confidence, certainty; knowledge; set out like that, the words seem to form a sort of spectrum with faith—most disputed of all the shades—somewhere in the middle.

Perhaps it is that very middle aspect of *faith* which makes it so liable to distortions in opposite directions; for not only is it in the middle in that sense, and not only is it an essential mediating relation between 'subject' and 'object', but also it stands in between lack of knowledge and the need to know. So some see it only as pure limpid spontaneity of Truth and the noblest Human Faculty, for which no price is too high to pay, while others deride it as a wretched, even worthless, substitute for knowledge. Many try a hand at defining it, arriving at oddly diverse conclusions.

Bewildered from time to time in this way by his betters,

some ordinary man (whose knowledge is limited and who wants to believe something) may ask 'But what does the word "faith" *mean*? What are we talking *about*?' At once the extremists chip in again: 'Faith is the Noblest Attribute of Man', 'Faith is a drug for fools', 'It must be cherished for ever', 'It wants chucking out good and proper', they cry. Then the ordinary man, looking for a compromise, mostly uses his native faith in order, ostrich-like, to hide his head in a dune of euphemisms, saying perhaps something about 'Needing confidence'; but 'You can't always trust your own ears' he mutters incredulously to himself.

Others less procrustean maybe say (driving wedges between words) 'To believe only in possibilities is not faith' (Sir Thomas Browne after Tertullian) or (making specious definitions of the faculty itself) 'Belief, like any other moving body, follows the path of least resistance' (Samuel Butler) or (attempting to define its object) 'The essential characteristic of a materialist doctrine is "belief in something not dependent on our knowledge of it" ' (W. W. Carington, quoting Prof. J. B. S. Haldane, in *Mind, Matter and Meaning*) or else (painting word-pictures) 'I've caught belief like a disease, I've fallen into belief like I fell in love' (Graham Greene), and so on. Fanned by these doldrum gusts, the ordinary man drifts this way and that: he doubts here, puts his faith there, and sometimes he is right and often wrong.

Now a dispassionate glance into matters of the heart is notoriously difficult; but, if the effort is made, it *can* be perceived that exclamations about 'Noblest Attributes' and 'Wretched substitutes' are just evocative haranguings—ways of trying to push people into thinking as one does oneself, or as one thinks they ought to think, as the case may be, perhaps with the best of motives. They appear as an aspect of human behaviour telling quite a lot about the speaker's personal attitude, but precious little about faith considered as a component of experience: whether it is, for example, good or bad in itself or unavoidable. Tending covertly as they do to the extremes of rationalism or irrationalism, none of them (not even the subtle lunges) examines experience or even attempts an inquiry into why the ordinary man does not just gullibly do as he is told. Why does he not? Is it because, when pushed too far, his common sense tells him that he can't?

Let us look a little closer. Let us consider for a moment the question of action (of doing, or even saying or thinking, something). An ordinary man, now, sees the past as decided ('What's done can't be undone') but the future as semi-foreseeable though undecided ('You can never be sure how it will turn out'). So when he acts purposively, intending to do what he does (which always happens now), he seems to do so guided by what he remembers of the past and by some measure of faith—or expectation—that his present acts will have some not too inappropriate result in the rather uncertain future. Still he can never be quite sure: doubts haunt him constantly.

That indeed is the pattern of the ordinary human situation: a state of being committed in a changing scene, of (moral) certainty about a definite-seeming past, of present knowledge of acts by restricted free choice which there is no escaping, and of guessing at a more or less indefinite future potentiality, which one hopes (with a grain of justification) to influence because one believes that things will go on happening roughly as they have done. That too is the pattern which makes life valuable and tolerable for the gambler. And who never gambles at all in his heart?

On that basis, if such a very rough sketch is provisionally accepted, faith (or call it what you will—give a dog a bad name and hang it, but a rose by any other name is just as sweet) as a chancy expectation of results is, it seems, inevitably present in some form in every act done: there would be no doing anything without it. While one has *knowledge* of *what* one is doing now, even if it is only that one is sitting still and doubting, *faith* alone can cope with the unknown future (as it is apprehended) and decide *why* one does what one does. Such humdrum faith as that neither needs any special advertising as 'noble' nor can it be 'chucked out', it is simply a commonplace necessity.

So it is that parents send children to school in the faith that what is taught there will help the children to make a living.

Those same children, when adults, delegate some of their influence by vote to governments in the faith that society will thus cater better for their needs. Through faith in the order of Nature those same adults, when old, sense death edging nearer: an impending ambivalent catastrophe that as surely blots out from their certainty all form of the future as it seems an inescapable plunge into it.

Faith is left a free hand here though men have a general intellectual certainty that their physical death will take place (regardless of any considerations of immortality). Other people's bodies are seen to die, but, it is pointed out by Freud, the Unconscious, while accepting that, absolutely rejects its own mortality. Though material bodies only too publicly die and disintegrate, at the same time no materialist theory is capable of *proving* (in any sense of that word) that physical death is the end, or physical birth the beginning, of conscious activity. Hence the ambivalence of the catastrophe. Hence too the fact that faith is forced willy-nilly to exercise a free hand here.

Now that faith normally manifests itself as one of three particular types of belief (must absolutely take on one of them so long as there is ignorance and action): either (1) a dogma asserting that something of them will survive the catastrophe, or (2) a dogma asserting that nothing of them at all will survive, or (3) radical agnosticism denying that any knowledge beforehand is possible. Depending on which of the types of belief people assume (and one of the three apparently *must* be assumed) their behaviour will vary. Any act whatsoever, then, involves (where there is ignorance) one of these three assumptions indirectly or directly: to be born is to die, and to live as the ordinary man does is to act; to be in space-time is to be unsure of a future one is sure to encounter.

The reservation 'Where there is ignorance' has been made; for ignorance, as we shall see, has an organic relation with faith (which is what the ignorant have to rely on in the acts they are obliged to perform). Will anyone deny that the ordinary man is constantly bothered by immediate ignorance—about the weather tomorrow, the contents of an examination paper, what the person he is talking to is thinking, the price of goods next week, whether his memory can be trusted or not, what will happen to him, . . . —or that he is ever without some measure of it, let alone ignorance of what is going on beyond his horizons and may burst into his world? Then since he cannot avoid doing things ('But what are we going to *do*, if something happens?') he has to take risks, to supplement by faith his lack of certain knowledge—to act *as if* the weather *will be* such and such tomorrow—, and this kind we may call First-degree ignorance, which goes with simple faith. 'Take what you will, but pay the price' says Emerson.

But the ordinary man is also subject to desires and needs and fear and pain. Because he attaches importance to the results of his acts, the lack of certainty inherent in faith is often odious to him, for all that he may like a gamble now and then. Whenever facts do not prohibit his doing so, his desires prompt him to treat the faith, by which he acts, *as if it were* knowledge ('It's a dead cert!') and he may well quite honestly forget that he does not know. His defence against fear and pain is Forgetting (a mode of ignorance, which, at its deepest, takes the form of death). But if he cannot quite forget, if his forgetting mechanism fails him, he may dope himself with self-deception, refusing both to question his faith and to test its object. This we may call Second-degree Ignorance, which loses sight not only of the limits of knowledge but of truth as well. With that, his faith has become bad faith. 'If bad faith is possible at all' says a modern writer 'it is because it is an immediate and constant threat to every human project, it is because consciousness hides within its very being a permanent risk of bad faith.' Bad faith, however, is not a lie, since 'the essence of a lie implies that the liar is completely aware of the truth which he dissembles. . . . One no longer lies when one deceives oneself.' Bad faith, in short, both refuses to face all one knows and vetoes any investigation into whether the faith is well placed or not. 'O take the cash and let the credit go' says Omar Khayyam's translator (and if the cash runs out, they'll sure let us live on tick!).

At any time an ordinary man may become fed up with the consequences of misplacing his own faith or by seeing the silly things other people sometimes do out of faith. Blaming the faith instead of the misplacing of it, he may decide to throw it overboard altogether—away with all bath-water and babies too—and become a Cynic or a Rationalist. But has he not merely deceived himself once more in fancying it can be jettisoned like that; for he still has ignorance and still has to act? Even despair is no more than a mode of bad faith: faith that the situation is irremediable with refusal to seek an escape. The self-gulling goes on, and so does the risk of disappointment, anger and frustration. If he is healthy and young and lucky, perhaps he can forget about it and begin all over again. Forgetting is a very *useful* kind of ignorance: it sort of wipes the bad sums off our slates.

What is the answer, then? Must one either leave the baby unbathed or bottle the bath-water? Surely not? Surely the first thing to be done is to reduce ignorance to the 'First Degree', to become aware that one *is* ignorant and *how* one is ignorant, facing up to it courageously and remembering it, regardless of hopes and fears. That is enough for the Goal, isn't it? What more *can* be done? After all faith has been shown to be a practical necessity for the ordinary man. Without it indeed all profitable and unprofitable action alike and all possibility of remedying suffering must be paralysed. And how richly it ennobles! It is the source of all inspiration. The rapturous leap of faith at Great Moments exhilarates, uplifts and transfigures. Faith attends all good things. Faith that the very ground will receive one's foot prevents the vertiginous sensation of falling into a chasm every time one steps forward. Faith is Life, and it must be good in itself; how can it be otherwise? If the right dogma can be found, is not that the answer, the realistic answer? Why cry for the moon? . . .

True, faith is a practical necessity for the ordinary man. That is indeed what we have been trying to show. But how can the Right Dogma ever be found, and can it be absolutely trusted without a grain of bad faith as we have described it? And is faith then to be the *goal*, in which case is ignorance to remain with us for ever more? Examination of what both the theists and the atheist materialists have offered as dogma from the dawn of history down to the present day—a long time and a wide choice—is far from encouraging: consoling, doubtless but utterly inconclusive. The rather arid alternative seems to be Radical Agnosticism, which is what is usually meant by the phrase 'no faith'; no faith, that is, in the heaven the theists offer only after death, or in the substance of matter here and now which the materialists admit can inherently never be known at all and doesn't matter after death any way.

Why bother, though? Perhaps the world is not such a bad place after all. They say there is plenty of good in it if you look, so forget about the unpleasant side of it. Agnosticism tomorrow, then, and dogma today; 'Gather ye roses while ye may'; luck may be on our side.

Dogma or agnosticism . . . But before we choose, before we risk our faith going bad on us, let us take one more look . . .

*(*Editor's Note*): *The following paragraph* (*in handwriting*) *was found among the late author's papers, together with this essay and carrying the note 'above at the end of Pt I'. Since the insertion of it would have necessitated adjustments in the given manuscript, it was deemed preferable to reproduce this paragraph separately. Its fitting place would be before the second-last paragraph of the above text.*

Then if neither dogma nor agnosticism will do, why not be satisfied with some form of the critical humanism of the eighteenth to nineteenth century Europe? Criticism has been incalculably productive, and we owe to it all the material advances we enjoy today. It is Criticism that has allowed science a free hand to question and experiment. Granted that Criticism (as Inquiry) merits all that praise and far more. But that is as a means. If Criticism is to be made the goal, the *summum bonum*, against what can it be tested? A fundamental weakness always remains in the position of the critic that if he discloses his own standpoint, that standpoint is open to criticism from some other; that is why it is rarely that the academic scholar, who employs the so-called 'higher criticism' can afford to state his own position in positive terms. When the English Prime Minister Disraeli was asked what his religion was, it is said that he replied,

'My religion is that of all wise men.'—'But what is that, Mr Disraeli?'—'Wise men never say.' Criticism requires that the critic be uncommitted, that he is, or pretends he is, outside what he criticizes. The professional critic's very being depends on dialectics, the food that keeps him alive is other people's standpoints. As a means this may be invaluable: as an end it can never amount to more than an ordered form of agnosticism.

PART II

To 'Gather ye rosebuds while ye may' would be fine if there were 'roses, roses all the way'; but will our simple faith really stretch that far? Hardly.

Soon after the Buddha had attained enlightenment he surveyed the world with the new vision he had achieved. He did not see only roses. He uttered this exclamation:

'This world is racked by exposure to the contact (of pain). Even what the world calls self is in fact ill; for no matter upon what it bases its conceit (of self), the fact is ever other than these (which the conceit conceives). To be is to become: but the world has committed itself to being, delights only in being; yet wherein it delights brings fear, and what it fears is pain. Now this Life Divine is lived to abandon pain' (*Udāna* III, 10). He was not alone in this estimation of the world: 'Here, bhikkhus, some clansman goes forth out of faith (*saddhā*) from the home life into homelessness (considering) "I am a victim of birth, ageing and death. . . . I am exposed to pain. Surely an end to this whole aggregate mass of suffering is described?" ' (*Majjhima* 29).

Now in this situation how does the Buddha show the function of faith? 'One who has faith (*saddhā*) succeeds, Mahānāma, not one who has no faith' (*Anguttara, Ekādasaka* 12).

Here the question at once intrudes: Is the translation of *saddhā* by 'faith' justified? Let us try it out and see; for the contexts in which it appears will be the test. We shall be strictly consistent in our renderings.

The Buddha speaks of five faculties, or human potentialities, through whose means an ignorant ordinary man may emerge from ignorance to right understanding, and so from suffering to its cessation; they are faith (*saddhā*), energy, mindfulness, concentration, and understanding (as 'mother wit' to start with). If they can be maintained in being against opposition, they are called Powers (*Saṁyutta* XLVIII, 43). Managed by reasoned attention (*yoniso manasikāra*, awareness of the organic structure of experience) and carefully balanced, they build each other up. Maintained in being and cultivated, they merge into the Deathless (*Saṁyutta* XLVIII, 57).

The Buddha speaks of faith as one of the 'Seven Noble Treasures' (*Anguttara Sattaka* 4), one of the 'Seven True Ideas' (*Dīgha* 33), one of the 'Five Factors of Endeavour' (*Majjhima* 8), as an 'Idea on the side of enlightenment' (*Saṁyutta* XLVIII, 51), as a 'Fount of Great Merit' (*Anguttara Tika* 41), as one of the 'Three forms of Growth' (*Anguttara Tika* 48), which 'brings five advantages' (*Anguttara Pañcaka* 38). And then 'Where is the faith faculty to be met with? Among the four factors of stream-entry' (*Saṁyutta* XLVIII, 8). A stream-enterer (of whom more below) has absolute confidence (*pasāda*) in the Enlightened One, in the True Idea (the Dhamma), and in the Community, and he has the virtue beloved of Noble Ones' (*Saṁyutta* LV, 1), while another four factors of Stream-entry are: frequenting True Men, hearing the True Idea, reasoned attention, and the putting into practice of ideas that are in accordance with the True Idea (*Saṁyutta* LV, 5).

'What is the faith faculty? Here a noble disciple who has faith places his faith in a Tathāgata thus: This Blessed One is such since he is accomplished and fully enlightened, perfect in true knowledge and conduct, sublime, knower of worlds, incomparable leader of men to be tamed, enlightened, blessed' (*Saṁyutta* XLVIII, 9). 'If these five faculties are absolutely perfected, they make an Accomplished One (Arahant); if a little weaker, a Non-returner; if a little weaker still, a Once-returner; if a little weaker still, a Stream-enterer; if a little weaker still, One Mature in Faith or One Mature in the

True Idea' (*Saṁyutta* XLVIII, 12). 'Those who have not known, seen, found, realized, touched with understanding, may go by faith in others that (these five faculties) when maintained in being and developed merge in the Deathless; . . . but on knowing, seeing, finding, realizing and touching with understanding, there is no more doubt or uncertainty that when maintained in being and developed they merge in the Deathless' (*Saṁyutta* XLVIII, 44).

But then, does not the Buddha say in *Kālāma Sutta* 'Come, Kālāmans, (do) not (be satisfied) with hearsay-learning or with tradition or with legendary lore or with what has come down in scripture or with conjecture or with logical inference or with weighing evidence or with choice of a view after pondering it or with someone else's ability or with the thought "The monk is our teacher"'? Is not that an injunction to have nothing to do with faith, to 'throw away your books' as Marcus Aurelius says, and listen to no one at all?

If that statement of the Buddha's is taken as a general instruction to disregard instruction, it is then impossible to carry out; for then one could only carry it out by not carrying it out (a well-known logical dilemma). But that is not what is intended, as is shown by the rest of the passage:

'. . . or with the thought "The monk is our teacher". When you know in yourselves "Certain ideas are unprofitable, liable to censure, condemned by the wise, being adopted and put into effect, they lead to harm and suffering", then you should abandon them . . . When you know in yourselves "Certain ideas are profitable, not liable to censure, commended by the wise, being adopted and put into effect, they lead to welfare and happiness", then you should abide in the practice of them' (*Anguttara Tika* 65).

The ordinary man is affected by ignorance and he cannot dispense with simple faith, though in good faith he may grossly misplace it or dissipate it and be said to have 'no faith' (*asaddha*). But if he places it honestly and reasonably, he is called 'faithful' (*saddha*). In the Buddha's words 'A bhikkhu who possesses understanding founds his faith in accordance with that understanding' (*Saṁyutta* XLVIII, 45), to which words may be added also those of the venerable Sāriputta 'There are two conditions for the arising of right view: another's speech and reasoned attention' (*Majjhima* 43). From this it emerges that an ordinary man has need of a germ of 'mother wit' in order to know where to place his faith and a germ of unsquandered faith in order to believe he can develop his understanding. That is the starting position.

Faith thus begins to appear as a fusion of two elements: confidence (*pasāda*), and what the confidence is placed in. Faith as confidence is elsewhere described as a clearing of the mind, like water cleared of suspended mud by a water-clearing nut, or as a launching out (*pakkhandhana*), like a boat's launching out from the near bank to cross a flood to the further bank, or as a hand that resolutely grasps (a grain of 'mother wit' is needed to recognize the nut, to avoid launching out into a flood that has no other shore, to refrain from grasping a red-hot poker as a stick to lean on). Just as 'Seeing is the meaning of the understanding as a faculty' so also 'Decision (*adhimokkha*) is the meaning of faith as a faculty' (*Paṭisambhidā Ñāṇakathā*). When faith is aided by concentration 'The mind launches out (to its object) and acquires confidence, steadiness and decision' (*Majjhima* 122).

Choice of a bad object will debauch faith by the disappointment and frustration it entails; craving and desire can corrupt it into bad faith by the self-deception that it is not necessary to investigate and test the object, and then as well as error there is disregard of truth. In one of his great discourses on faith the Buddha says

'Bhāradvāja, there are five ideas which ripen in two ways (namely expectedly and unexpectedly) here and now. What are the five? They are faith, preference, hearsay-learning, weighing evidence, and choice of a view after pondering it [compare the *Kālāma Sutta* quoted above]. Now (in the case of faith) something may have faith well placed in it (*susada-*

hita) and yet it may be hollow, empty and false; and again, something may have no faith placed in it, and yet it may be factual, true and no other than it seems. In such circumstances it is not yet proper for a wise man to make the conclusion without reserve "Only this is true, anything else is wrong" . . . If a man has faith, then in such circumstances as these he preserves truth when he says "My faith is thus"; but then too he still does not, on that account alone, make the conclusion without reserve "Only this is true, anything else is wrong": he preserves truth in that way too' (*Majjhima* 95).

The other four cases are similarly treated, after which it is shown how 'preserving of truth' can be developed successively into 'discovery of truth' (path of Stream-entry) and 'arrival at truth' (fruit of the path of Stream-entry). The element of confidence has then become 'absolute' because its object has been sufficiently tested by actual experience for the principal claims to be found justified. Another discourse concludes by showing how the value of rightly placed faith serves—as the means rather than the end—in the progress from ignorance to liberation:

'Bhikkhus, I say that true knowledge and deliverance have a condition, are not without a condition. What is their condition? The seven Factors of Enlightenment (Mindfulness, interest in the True Idea,[1] energy, happiness, tranquillity, concentration, and onlooking equanimity) . . . What is the condition for these? The four foundations of mindfulness (contemplation of the body, of feelings, of cognizance, and of ideas) . . . What is the condition for these? The three kinds of good conduct (of body, speech and mind) . . . What is the condition for these? Mindfulness and full awareness . . . What is the condition for these? Reasoned attention . . . What is the condition for that? Faith . . . What is the condition for that? Hearing the True Idea (the true object of faith, the

---

[1] *Dhammavicaya*, usually translated as 'investigation of the Truth (*Dhamma*)'. (*Editor*).

saddhamma) . . . What is the condition for that? Frequenting the company of True Men (*sappurisa*)' (*Anguttara Dasaka* 62).

This shows plainly the need for a reliable guide. How is he to be found? One should be an inquirer (*vīmaṁsaka*) and make the Tathāgata the object of research and tests in order to judge whether confidence in him is rightly placed. The Buddha says:

> 'Now, bhikkhus, if others should ask a bhikkhu (who is an inquirer) "What are the evidences and certainties owing to which the venerable one says 'The Blessed One is fully enlightened, the True Idea is well proclaimed, the community has entered upon the good way'?", then, answering rightly, he would answer thus "Here, friends, I approached that Blessed One for the sake of hearing the True Idea (*Dhamma*). The teacher showed me the True Idea at each successively higher (level), at each superior (stage), with the dark and bright counterparts. According as he did so, by arriving at a direct knowledge here of a certain idea (namely, one of the four paths) among the ideas (taught) in the True Idea, I reached my goal: then I had confidence (*pasādiṁ*) in the teacher thus: 'The Blessed One is fully enlightened, the True Idea is well proclaimed, the community has entered on the good way' ". When anyone's faith in a Tathāgata is planted and rooted and established with these evidences, these phrases and these syllables, then his faith is called supported by evidence, rooted in vision, sound, and invincible by Monk or Divine or Māra or Divinity or anyone in the world' (*Majjhima* 47).

Faith as the indispensable means, but not the goal, transparent in itself, is debased or ennobled by the mode of its employment and by its goal. As understanding grows, it approximates to knowledge, while the risk of its degenerating into bad faith diminishes with the diminishing of craving.

Yes, but there are still two problems. First: was it not argued earlier that faith involves not knowing the future, and so, if faith becomes knowledge, does that not imply that the future can all be known and is therefore predetermined? Second: with craving unabated would not knowledge of everything be unbearable, would it not be Hell itself? How does craving diminish?

The key to these two locks on the gate of liberation lies in the Contemplation of Impermanence. Let us take the second problem first. It is part of the constraint imposed by ignorance and craving together that an ordinary man is led to speculate on time and permanence, and to ask such questions as 'What was I? . . . What shall I be? . . . What am I? . . .' (*Majjhima* 2): unanswerable questions to which philosophers go on furnishing many an unquestionable answer, disproving each other as they do so. But progress towards liberation from ignorance transforms and transfigures the world. One who is liberated asks no more questions (*akathankathi*). The Buddha tells his listeners:

'Bhikkhus, material form (and likewise feeling, perception, determinations and consciousness) are impermanent, changing and altering. Whoever decides about, and places his faith in, these ideas in this way is called Mature in Faith. He has alighted upon the certainty of rightness. He has alighted upon the plane of true men and left behind the plane of ordinary men. He can no more perform action capable of causing his rebirth in the animal world or in the realm of ghosts; and he cannot complete his time in this life without realizing the fruition of Stream-entry' (*Saṁyutta* XXV, 10).

Such faith decides in advance that nothing arisen can reveal any permanence at all, however brief, and since all subsequent evidence supports the decision, if that evidence is not forgotten, craving is progressively stultified in the impossibility of finding any arisen thing worth craving for and is progressively displaced by the joy of liberation.

The first problem, though, that of time, is properly a matter for insight (*vipassanā*) and can only be dealt with here by hints and pointers because of lack of space. As has already been said, the ignorant man questions, but one who is liberated does

c   33 not. The Buddha tells his listeners: 'Let not a man trace back a past Or wonder what the future holds ... Instead with insight let him see Each idea[1] presently arisen' (*Majjhima* 131). He includes the Contemplation of Impermanence under the Four Foundations of Mindfulness thus: 'He trains thus: "I shall breathe in . . . breathe out contemplating impermanence" ' (*Majjhima* 10).

Now it is in the very nature of ignorance to perceive the bare conditions for consciousness in terms of things and persons and hypostases and to project upon these percepts a varying degree of permanence, a misperception which it is the task of true vision and mindfulness to correct. During the period of transition while understanding that 'to be is to be otherwise' is still immature and helped out by faith in the impermanence of everything that is, the faith must be tested and the outcome of the tests remembered. This needs concentration and energy.

'When one gives attention to impermanence, the faith faculty is outstanding'; and in the cases of attention to pain and not-self the faculties of concentration and understanding are outstanding respectively. These are called the 'Three Gate-ways to liberation', which 'lead to the outlet from the world' (*Paṭisambhidā Vimokkhakathā*). When the Stream-entry Path is reached, a new, supramundane, faculty, the I-shall-come-to-know-the-unknown faculty (*anaññātaññassāmī't'indriya*) appears, to be subsequently followed by the new and supramundane final-knowledge and final-knower faculties (*aññindriya, aññatāvindriya*). These are gained in this life with the attainment of Arahantship.

Meanwhile, however, 'The characteristic of impermanence does not become apparent (as universal) because, when the constant rise and fall of determinations[2] [i.e. 'things'] is not given attention, it is concealed by continuity' (*Visuddhimagga* Ch. XXI). In fact the Buddha said:

' "There is no matter (or feeling, perception, determinations,[2]

---

[1] *dhamma;* 'thing' or phenomenon, material or mental. (*Editor*).

[2] *sankhāra;* usually translated as 'formations' or, in the case of the five Aggregates, 'mental formations'. (*Editor*).

34

or consciousness) whatever that is permanent . . . not inseparable from the idea of change,[1] . . . ." Taking a small piece of
cowdung in his hand, the Blessed One said ". . . If there were
even that much . . . that were permanent, . . . not inseparable
from the idea of change,[1] . . . . the living of the Life Divine[2]
could not be described as for the exhaustion of suffering. It is
because there is not . . . that it is so described" ' (*Saṁyutta*
XXII, 96).

Now that statement can be taken to imply that if time were
an absolutely independent objective reality, there would be no
liberation.

Permanence–impermanence on the one hand, and time on
the other, are but two modes of the same view. The appearance
of the three new supramundane faculties signals profound
changes in the apprehension of permanence–impermanence,
that is, of time, and consequently in actual experience itself.

To question the objectivity of time is not new even to
Western philosophy. While the objective reality of time and
space still remains one of the assumptions made by Scientists
for which they have no proof, Immanuel Kant argued irre-
futably the pure subjectivity of both. But almost a millennium
and a half before him Bhadantācariya Buddhaghosa wrote—
'What is called "time" is conceived in terms of such and such
dhammas. . . . But that (time) should be understood as only a
mere conceptual description, since it is non-existent as to any
individual essence of its own' (*Atthasālinī*; space is analogously
treated elsewhere). A century or two later it was observed
'Nibbāna (extinction) is not like other *dhammas*; in fact because
of its extreme profundity it cannot be made the object of
consciousness by one who has not yet reached it. That is why
it has to be reached by change-of-lineage cognizance (*gotrabhu*),
which has profundity surpassing the three periods of time'
(*Mūla-Ṭīkā*). When the seen, heard, sensed, and cognized (see
Udāna I, 10), are misperceived to *be* (this that *I* see, . . . that
I think about, *is* that *man*, so-and-so, that *thing* of *mine*),

[1] *viparināma-dhamma*; usually translated as 'subject to change'. (*Editor*).
[2] *brahmaeariya*; usually translated as 'Holy Life', 'Life of Purity'. (*Editor*).

to have temporal endurance and reity, it is because the three periods of time, these three modes by which we subjectively process our raw world in perceiving it, have been projected outwards by ignorance on the raw world and misapprehended along with that as objectively real. That is how we in our ignorance come to perceive things and persons and action.

These fragments are merely pointers. The contemplation of impermanence, which, when fully and unreservedly developed, necessitates the contemplations of suffering (pain) and not-self, involves the whole field of insight, which there is no space to deal with here. However, the inquiry has already led us right away from the apparent 'either-or' choice between faith-in-dogma-as-the-goal and agnosticism. By establishing a structural interdependence between faith and ignorance it has opened up a new line; and in the pursuit of that line it has uncovered an unexpected association between faith and the temporal mirage of permanence–impermanence. And so it has been possible to sketch a practical outline of the way to end here and now this whole aggregate mass of suffering. The adventure is waiting to be tested.

> 'Fruitful as the act of giving is, . . . yet it is still more fruitful to go with confident heart for refuge to the Buddha, the Dhamma, and the Sangha, and undertake the five precepts of virtue . . . Fruitful as that is, . . . yet it is still more fruitful to maintain loving kindness in being in the heart for only as long as the milking of a cow . . . Fruitful as that is, . . . yet it is still more fruitful to maintain perception of impermanence in being for only as long as the snapping of a finger' (*Anguttara Navaka* 20).

But does *saddhā* really mean 'faith'? Let the reader judge for himself.

3. CESSATION OF BECOMING
(WITH A NOTE ON *FAITH*)

Why do normal people normally react with panic and horror to the idea of cessation of becoming or cessation of consciousness? There are at least two reasons. There is first the failure to see both sides of life, the negative destructive as well as the positive constructive, which are as it were the obverse and reverse of each piece of experience; a refusal to face the ambivalence of experience, and a putting on of blinkers to shut out, as far as one can, what is disturbing. It is by this that life is made to look nice, and appears tolerable. The process is largely automatic and subconscious, so it is mostly never enquired into. With the blinkers on one does not see what is unwelcome and one quickly forgets the unwelcome that intrudes.

And here I want to distinguish two kinds of suffering: (1) 'enjoyable suffering and pain' (the arduousness of exhausting sports, self-mortification, 'being ill', masochism and sadism, etc., etc.), which are not properly suffering because they are enjoyed and welcomed; (2) 'horror' or 'nausea'—all those things (whatever they may be and they vary with different people) that produce horror, nausea and vertigo because they are absurd and menace the core and pattern of our personal existence. Everyone knows that borderline across which he 'cannot go' even in thought and it is that, not the former, that people automatically shut out and cannot face. Yet one knows at times—in the middle of the night perhaps when one is sleepless, or on encountering some revolting experience—that this horror haunts every form of experience, always and ever—and hastily one readjusts the blinkers that had slipped. Put the beautiful before you and the horror behind you. Yes, but then I shall not dare to turn round.

The world is a bad place. Is it? But it seems that this haunting—and this self-delusion by wearing blinkers—is not an attribute of the world. The haunting is in consciousness itself, in its very nature. Just as, when I set up any object in the sunlight, a shadow is cast because it is the nature of sunlight to cast shadows, so anything that comes into the light of consciousness casts a shadow of the unknown, and it is in the unknown that the horror resides, in the dark of knowledge where the patterns can no longer be traced, where chaos resides, and whence utterly hostile systems may emerge and devour and digest us.

Again this insecurity resides in consciousness because it cheats. It lives between the past and the future like a reflection between two opposing mirrors. I put my head between the opposing mirrors and I see the reflection of the reflection of the reflection . . . which suggests recession to infinity, but I cannot see that infinity because (even if the glasses were clear enough) my head and its reflections are in the way. But then if I slightly displace one mirror so that my head is no more in the way then the series of reflections passes out of the field of the mirrors at some stage of the reflections which it must now do, unless the mirrors are made of infinite size. So I am forced by this set of experiences to infer an infinity which the very circumstances deny the possibility of my experiencing. That is one essential aspect of consciousness—it cheats.

Another example is the moon. I see as an experience an existent crescent or an existent half-moon or full moon and there are perceptions of existents that are repeated (which existents are in fact each over and done with as soon as experienced). Consciousness groups together these repeated experiences and forms a concept that 'transcends' all these possible existents, and which concept or 'transcendence' it presents as 'the moon'. But 'the moon' can never be experienced and even when visualized it is only as one of its aspects. It is a fake. This concept 'the moon' is then projected upon the objective world where it appears to lurk behind existence as Kant's '*Ding an sich*' or, say, Eddington's 'reality' that the physicists are trying to discover behind what they investigate. Suppose a man gets lost in the desert and he wanders all night, when the sun comes up he may see lots of tracks in the sand all pointing the way he is going. He thinks 'Marvellous! I am on the high road. Lots of people have gone this way already. I am alright.' So he follows them. They are in fact his own tracks made in the night by his walking in circles (which people actually do). If he does not stop to consider and goes on following them, he will get nowhere. He will die. If he put aside his assumption and looked about him, it is possible he might find the way of escape.

This is what I mean by the failure to see both sides of life— to see things and ourselves as they and we really are, in their relationship. This is what Māra (if we like personification) tries his utmost to keep us from seeing, for it is by this that we can slip out of his clutches. Māra is Death—but he is also Life, for 'all that is subject to arising is subject to cessation', 'all that is born and lives dies'. Byron said somewhere:

Sorrow is knowledge: they who know the most
Must mourn the deepest o'er the fatal Truth.
The Tree of Knowledge is not that of life.

But it is Māra that makes us mourn because he makes his living by that, just as a rubber-estate owner makes his living by the trees that he cultivates and bleeds, and cuts down when they are old.

But there is another, equally fundamental, reason that makes people shy at the notion—their notion—of cessation. This is a very deep-rooted double misconception: (1) there is the idea that by 'cessation', by 'extinction', something 'good' and 'valuable' and 'lasting' will be 'lost for ever', and (?) there is an uncritical assumption that consciousness will somehow continue to survive—will be 'there'—to be aware of this as an 'everlasting privation'. 'Does all this' they say 'only end in extinction? But a state of nothingness is horrible!' and there the whole double misconception lies like a pair of Siamese Twins in a bed. But there is, in the last analysis, no 'entirely good' and 'lasting' individual thing or state discoverable anywhere. Whatever appears good melts away in the end. But the subconscious cheating of the mind seizes on the good, and rejects, and forgets, that it melts away. By a 'sleight of mind' that is one of consciousness's essential functions, the fancy is presented that it is possible to skim the good off the world, like cream off a bowl of milk, and live in that cream in 'eternal bliss'. But, alas, like the cream, the bowl of heavenly bliss is not permanent. Such is the 'good' that is supposed to be 'lost'. And then there is the instinctive feeling, the uncritical automatic reaction that takes cessation somehow to mean a survival of conscious awareness of that loss, in spite of the fact that the proposition was in the first place 'cessation of consciousness'. This is the verbal-mental sub-conscious cheating that has only to be examined fearlessly to see it as a mere self-contradiction. If consciousness ceases and with it its objects, there is no question of conscious awareness of privation. If there is awareness of loss and privation, con-sciousness has not ceased, and it is not such cessation that is being talked about. This misconception (often honestly enough believed in owing to uncritical acceptance) is often used to deride the Buddhists without seeing that it hurts only him who uses it. And not only the Buddhists, for Śankara in his com-mentary to the Bṛhadāraṇyaka Upaniṣad says: 'The Buddhists themselves do not deny the existence of gods and heavens (or hells)—they are not atheists—but only that the gods are omni-potent or ever-lasting—they change and die, let one down, make one let oneself down, because they cannot help it, because consciousness and its objects with its disease of impermanence, are there too.'

Consciousness without object is impossible—not conceivable —and objects without consciousness, when talked about, are only a verbal abstraction; one cannot talk or think about objects that have *no* relation to consciousness. The two are inseparable and it is only a verbal abstraction to talk about them separately (legitimate of course in a limited sphere).

But it is in the consideration of this cessation as the goal that the real comfort and safety are to be found. There is no cheating here, and no anxiety to exclude haunting opposites. All else, however 'good' it seems, is only temporary, because there is consciousness there to know and to change. So there is no permanent safety from attack or harm, and there is no perma-nent safety from one's being led to do harm; even if that harm is merely changing.

The matter of faith. It is commonly felt and often stated that 'faith' is a weakness, a mere substitute for knowledge, a 'blind

40

belief in dogma' and 'unnecessary'. But the point overlooked is that there is an element of faith in every conscious act. It is another of the 'false' aspects inherent in all consciousness—the presenting of objects in such wise that the perception of them necessitates inference about what is hidden, what they hide. This is in fact an aspect of faith. Without this faith nothing can be done at all—faith that things will repeat themselves and happen as one expects. But the case is most clearly seen in the case of death. Death is an obvious fact. Described in terms of life, it is meaningless, like a blank featureless wall, or a black chasm to vision, that nevertheless by its very existence, by its basis in experience, necessitates inference about it. The three main inferences are: that life of some sort continues after death; or that it does not; or plain agnosticism. Whichever I adopt is a matter of pure faith (I leave out 'evidence' for and against other alternatives here). But I cannot avoid adopting one of the three.

On the other hand, faith about, say, 'phoenixes rising from their own ashes' is simply this same universal attribute of consciousness applied to a fantasy, an assumption (the phoenix) that has no basis in experience; what is unnecessary here is not the faith but the assumption. Now many 'faiths' place faith in baseless assumptions. And when people discover this, they not only reject the assumption (rightly), but, because they fail to discriminate, they deceive themselves into thinking that they can do without the faith too. All that has happened to them, though, is that they have transferred their faculty of faith to the basis of experience and have simultaneously forgotten that they are using it. Now to forget that one has a sharp knife in one's hand is dangerous.[1]

4. CONSCIOUSNESS AND BEING

What follows will have to be stated in terms of ordinary speech, though that necessarily involves the word 'is' and logical con-

[1] Here the manuscript ends. This undated fragment which, in the manuscript, follows immediately after the preceding essay, may have stimulated the author to treat the subject more fully in the essay 'Does Saddhā mean Faith?', included in this publication. (*Editor*).

structions, because speech is hardly possible without them; nevertheless they have to be regarded here as a makeshift, and the whole of what follows tends to undermine the ultimate value of speech, retaining it, however, as a necessity for communication in conditions where separateness and individuality predominate.

The word 'consciousness', it seems to me, can only refer to what one might define provisionally as 'the knowing that cannot know itself without intermediary and that cannot function in experience (of which it is an indispensable component) except negatively'.

To the question 'What *is* consciousness', then, on a low level a provisional answer might be 'it is the pure subjective' or 'it *is* the bare knowing of what it *is not* that constitutes (orders) experience and allows it being'. It must be added that, when consciousness *is*, it seems to be individualized by what it knows. But on another ('higher') level the 'is' in the question has still to be questioned, and so the low-level (and logical) answer is only a conventional makeshift, a conventional view, nothing more. And this qualification applies not only to logically inductive and deductive statements necessitating use of the word 'is', but also to descriptive statements that appear in 'logical' form, using that term, or any equivalent.

When I ask myself 'What does the verbal expression "universal consciousness" refer to?', I confess to be unable to find an answer, because, in spite of its 'attractive' form, I cannot distinguish it from 'non-consciousness' (see below), and so I seem to have no alternative but to regard the phrase as one of those abstract expressions that appear on the surface to mean something, but when more closely examined, do not. (This, I know, may seem shocking; but I am more interested here in finding the facts than in avoiding shockingness.)

The more I examine and observe experience (what else can one do? build castles?), the more I find that I can only say of consciousness (and in this I find a notable confirmation in the Pali Suttas) that it seems only describable (knowable) 'in terms of what it arises dependent upon' (i.e. seeing-cum-seen, . . . mind-knowing-cum-mind-known or 'mind-cum-ideas'), that is, negatively as to itself. And so, instead of being said to *appear*, it should rather be called 'that negativeness or "decompression of being" which makes the appearance of life, movement, behaviour, etc., and their opposites possible in "things" and "persons" '. But while life, etc., cannot *be* or *not be* without the co-operation of the 'negative presence' of consciousness, which 'gives room' for them (and itself) to 'come to *be*' in this way (gaining its own peculiar form of negative being, perhaps from them)—the only possible way of *being*—they are, by ignorance, simultaneously individualized in actual experience. Unindividualized experience cannot, I think, be called experience at all. Thus there *appears* the positive illusion also of 'individual consciousness': 'illusion' because its individuality is borrowed from the individualness of (1) its percepts, and (2) the body seen as its perceiving instrument. Unindividualized perception cannot, any more, I think, be called perception at all. The supposed individuality of consciousness (without which it is properly inconceivable) is derived from that of its concomitants. This illusory individualization of consciousness—this mirage—manifests itself in the sense both of 'my consciousness' and of 'consciousness that is not mine' (as e.g. in the sensation of 'being seen' when one fancies or actually finds one is caught, say, peeping through a key hole, and from which the abstract notion of 'universal consciousness' develops) but the example shows that the experience of 'being seen' does not necessarily mean that *another's consciousness is seeing one*—one may have been 'mistaken' in one's fancy owing to a guilty sense though the experience was just as real at the time, before one 'found no one was there'. To repeat what has already been said: the supposed 'my consciousness' seems only 'distinguishable' from the supposed 'consciousness that is not mine' on the basis of the particular non-consciousness (i.e. 'material' body, etc.) through which its negativity is manifested and with which it is always and inevitably associated in some way. It is impossible, I think, to over-emphasize the importance of this fact. So, of the concept, 'universal consciousness' I at present think that the word 'universal' misleads (perhaps some hidden desire for power to 'catch all consciousness in the net of one's understanding' and so escape the horrors of the unknown seduces one to catch at this seemingly attractive term).

Again it may be asked: What knows universal consciousness? Would not individual consciousness, if the 'universal' is accepted, be held inadequate to judge it, and how can it know itself, or what are the means by which it can know itself and distinguish itself from 'non-consciousness' and 'individual consciousness'? I can find no answer to that and so I conclude that, if I ask it, that is simply because I must have started out with an unjustified assumption about the nature of consciousness (which, platitudinous as it may seem to say it, is horribly difficult to understand and handle in view of its negativity: when one talks about 'consciousness' normally, one finds on examination that one has not been talking about it at all but about the 'positive' things like pleasure and pain, action, perception, etc., etc., that always accompany and screen it). Is the question then really necessary? Consciousness, of course, cannot be denied as a necessary constituent of experience, but the trouble starts when we begin to ask what consciousness (or its nature) *is*: We have assumed the individuality of consciousness, apparently unjustifiably, because of the observed individuality of the objective part of experience through which we say it is manifested; and the assumption of its 'individuality' logically leads to the further assumption of some 'universal' form. Why?

Now, as I said earlier, when I begin to ask what something *is* (*is*, say, consciousness individual or universal or both or neither?), we have taken *being* for granted and failed to examine the nature of a part of my question. In one sense consciousness seems correctly describable as functioning (that is in its 'true negativity') by putting everything in question: What *is* this? What *am* I? What *is* life? What *is* consciousness? What *is* being? . . . Now here the emphasis must be removed from 'what' and 'this' and placed squarely on 'is'. Suppose I suggest: for 'is' read 'belief-attitude' (as a mode of craving combined with ignorance), or in other words: 'it is the nature of consciousness to *make be* (with the aid of desire-for-being and of ignorance-of-how-anything-comes-to-be) and the nature of being to depend on consciousness'. The multiplicity and the contradictoriness of the answers normally given to these questions ought to be sufficient evidence for something of the sort, or at least for the suspicion that all the methods of answering them in the way normally done are radically wrong in some way. In fact the contradictory answers in all their variety, as usually given, each bolstered up by logic, betray, it seems to me, just that form of ignorance-craving combination which make perception/non-perception, change/immortality, time/eternity, life/death, action/inaction, choice/fatality, unity/variety, individuality/universality, seem not only possible but real—though then it seems necessary or 'right' (here we have craving) to determine what among these *is* (here we have ignorance) real and what *is not*, and the trouble begins again: I begin asserting: 'I *am* this, I *am not* that', 'this *is* that', 'A *is* B', 'consciousness *is* life', 'truth *is* beauty', 'life *is* good', 'killing *is* right', 'the end *is* the justification of the means', 'I *am*', 'God *is*', etc., etc., all of which others may deny. Then perhaps we get angry and come to blows. How many more people in history have been killed for the sake of opinions about what *is* and what is *not* than have been killed for the sake of facts? Viewpoints, interpretations and opinions about the raw material of experience differ, less or more, from individual person to individual person. The more consistent and logically strengthened any moral or religious or philosophical system becomes the more possible it becomes for it to be contradicted by an opposing system, and then bare craving has to arbitrarily choose and bash the opponent on the head if it can. That is why Buddhism (specially Nāgārjuna, but also Theravāda) favours a dialectic that pulls down all such positivistic-negativistic systems (the positive is always haunted by the negative, and so there is really no true *via negativa* or *via positiva* in any absolute sense). It pulls them down using their own premises.

Of whatever I can say that it *is*, by that very fact I imply that it *is not*: It *is* this, *is not* that: it then is in virtue of what it is not, being so constituted by the consciousness that determines it thus. But the consciousness on which its being depends is negative, whose negativity appears in objective things as their temporality and change, the change in their being. But while the *being* of whatever is objective to it appears as positive, even though it may change, its own being appears as a negation of itself and a denial, flight or movement, the temporalizing of the temporalized objective world.

Now, perhaps, you will understand why it is really impossible for a Buddhist to answer the question 'Does Buddhism teach the extinction of consciousness—*is* nibbāna the extinction of consciousness?' On the basis of what has been said above could it be answered yes or no without examining each term of the question?

There is, of course, another, different, approach to the analysis of (not the answer to) that question: Why should consciousness (however conceived) seem preferable to cessation-of-consciousness (however conceived)? Consciousness of deprivation, of an 'abyss of nothingness', is not cessation of consciousness. Would not any *preference* (absolute one-sided choice) for one over the other show craving in the aim if that were set up as the ultimate aim? The desire-to-end-craving, as I see it, is a provisional measure adopted while craving is still present in order to use craving to terminate itself, while the aim is absence-of-craving and consequently ending of suffering; use of the word *is* (which implies presence of ignorance) in *this* way is also use of present ignorance to terminate itself, while the aim is (to me in this state) liberation from ignorance.

Second, suppose a state of consciousness without suffering: then would it not have to be entirely without change since the slightest change in the state must imply a degree of suffering intruding; but can a state of consciousness absolutely without change be distinguished at all from absence of consciousness? I do not see how it can. However a mixture of longing for the incompatible (craving), and fear of or disinclination to face the facts of the association and complexity which are inseparable from conscious experience (ignorance), can make it seem as possible and realizable as the catching of the red in a rainbow with a butterfly net. So out we go with our butterfly nets chasing colours . . . and get wet instead. Craving and ignorance persist in heaven though suffering may be suspended there for a time.

That is how I see Emerson's 'take what you will but pay the

price'. I take it to mean 'pay death as the price of life' or 'pay suffering as the price of consciousness': one may get it on tick, but if one does not pay up when the bill comes in the bailiffs distrain. But that does not mean that I think one should counter with undiminished craving and ignorance and use them to denounce life and consciousness, etc. I say one should take them as they *are* and develop understanding of them. That, as I see it, and only that, along with the sharing of it, is the true source of joy—not joy of life haunted by fear of loss-of-consciousness, and so on. This you know, so I am not saying anything new.

If I ask myself 'Is it possible for me to end consciousness?', I have to reply to myself that I see no possibility at present (though what might happen *if* I succeeded in ending craving and ignorance, of which I see no prospect at present, is, of course, hard to say!). If the possibility were available now, I at present see no sound reason why I should not avail myself of it. Pure speculation! Yes, but at least it prevents me coming down one-sidedly in favour of consciousness or in favour of non-consciousness in the crude mode. I do *not* regard death (my life's end or murder or suicide) as the ending of consciousness: to presume that conscious-continuity (negativity) ends because a particular continuity of its material objective world including its body ends seems to me a pure assumption whose opposite is just as valid, with possibly better logical arguments in favour of it if the evidence is observed without bias. However, for the likes of me what happens to me at death cannot be known, consequently I am at liberty to assume (since I cannot avoid assuming something about it) what seems most reasonable. Death seems above all to be forgetting: I do not know; but since I have to believe something about it whether I like it or not, I do not believe that consciousness ends with death. Memory may well do so. I don't, however, know that this is what I *want* not to believe.

It is, I think, rather important to bear in mind one thing in regard to what has been said above. It is that, with this view, there are two scales of value (not so much divorced as crossing at right-angles) which must be carefully discriminated between.

The physical world of consciousness-being-action in which we *live* and *are*, biassed by ignorance and propelled by craving, is governed by perception of being and the practical values based on that. But any positive metaphysical system, whether based only logically or emotionally on it, which is founded on that, is haunted by the shadows that it cannot avoid casting and that it cannot itself see (like the Sun). It acts in virtue of cause and effect and its thought is logical by its dependence on the word 'is'. As far as we live *in* this world we have to live its mode and by its values, or we risk falling into wells through star-gazing. But *none* of its laws are made *absolute* (without divorcing idea from experience). The Void, of which it cannot be said that it is or is not, nor that it has consciousness or has none, while it denies absoluteness to any experiential value— alike to being and to consciousness—cannot be identified. And that is the doctrine of not-self (*anattā*), as I see it in one aspect at present. This voidness cannot be 'is-ed' and so introduced into the worldly scheme; except as the denial of absoluteness of all particular values. It has no more effect on ordinary life than the theory of relativity. But just as that theory completely alters calculation of enormous speeds, so, as I see it, this void-element completely alters calculations of extraordinary situations: of death—either as killing or as suicide or as the partner of old age.

II. KNOWLEDGE AND CONDUCT[1]

PROF. O. H. DE A. WIJESEKERA

---

1. BUDDHIST ETHICS

It will be realized by careful students of Buddhism, particularly in its earliest form as preserved in the *Digha Nikāya, Majjhima Nikāya, Sutta Nipāta*, etc., that most of the dialogues are entirely devoted to ethical discussions. This will be found to be especially the case with the *Majjhima Nikāya*, as well as the *Mahāvagga* of the *Sutta Nipāta*, while a good many of the Suttas in the *Dīgha Nikāya* are also ethical in character. Thus it will be seen that an exhaustive examination of all the data is necessary for a complete study of this important subject, and this has to be said in spite of the useful treatise *The Ethics of Buddhism* by Dr Tachibana of Tokyo, for, as it was pointed out in the introduction to the Colombo edition of that work, he has only classified the moral categories of Buddhism without entering upon any discussion of the main problems of ethics in relation to the Buddhist view. It is hoped that the present discussion will, at least, to some extent, indicate the lines along which such a study must be conducted, and lead students of the subject to a critical appreciation of its main problems.

It is universally recognized that Buddhism can claim to be the most ethical of religio-philosophical systems of the world. No less an authority than Professor Radhakrishnan himself

---

[1] Paper read at a Symposium on 'Buddhism's Contribution to Art, Letters and Philosophy', arranged in November 1956, by the Working Committee for the 2500th Buddha Jayanthi, Government of India, in collaboration with the UNESCO, to commemorate the 2500th anniversary of the Parinirvana of the Buddha.—Reprinted from *The Maha Bodhi*, December 1956.

calls it 'Ethical Idealism' and says that the Buddha gave an 'ethical twist' to the thought of his time. 'We find in the early teaching of Buddhism', he remarks, 'three marked characteristics, an ethical earnestness, an absence of any theological tendency and an aversion to metaphysical speculation'.[1] Even Albert Schweitzer, a leading Western philosopher and one of the most astute critics of Indian thought has not grudged the Buddha the honour of being 'the creator of the ethic of inner perfection'. He writes: 'In this sphere he gave expression to truths of everlasting value and advanced the ethics not of India alone but of humanity. He was one of the greatest ethical men of genius ever bestowed upon the world.'[2] Professor T. W. Rhys Davids who spent a life-time in the study of Buddhism has admirably brought out in his *American Lectures* the importance of the study of Buddhist ethics in modern life and thought:

'The point I stand here to submit to your consideration is that the study of ethics and especially the study of ethical theory in the West has hitherto resulted in a deplorable failure through irreconcilable logomachies and the barrenness of speculation cut off from actual fact. The only true method of ethical inquiry is surely the historical method . . . and I cannot be wrong in maintaining that the study of Buddhism should be considered a necessary part of any ethical course and should not be dismissed in a page or two but receive its due proportion in the historical perspective of ethical evolution.'[3]

Oswald Spengler who perhaps ranks as the greatest philosophical student of world culture believes that Buddhism, which for him expresses 'the basic feeling of Indian civilization', 'rejects all speculation about God and the cosmic problems; only self and the conduct of actual life are important to it'.[4] Such statements as these emphasizing the ethical importance

---

[1] *Indian Philosophy*, Vol. 1, p. 358.
[2] *Indian Thought and its Development*, p. 117.
[3] *Buddhism*, pp. 185, 186.   [4] *Decline of the West*, Part I, p. 356.

of the Buddha's teaching can be quoted from numerous other authorities. But to any unbiassed and careful student of religion or philosophy it would be needless to stress this importance too much, for, as we shall attempt to show in this paper, Early Buddhism—by which term we generally refer to the doctrines as found in the dialogues of the major Nikāyas—presents a unique synthesis of ethics and philosophy, of morality and knowledge, of action and thought.

To estimate correctly the greatness and the universality of the Buddha's ethics one has to obtain a mental picture of the moral ferment and the spiritual unrest that prevailed in India just before the appearance of the Buddha. Traditional religion as professed by the theologians and the metaphysicians of the Upanishads was being undermined by the constant and vehement attacks of materialists and sceptics. Therefore, before we turn to the actual ethical system of Early Buddhism it is essential to discuss as briefly as possible the development of the moral consciousness during the time of the pre-Buddhistic Upanishads as well as the attitude to the moral problem of the various heretical philosophical schools such as those promulgated by the numerous 'titthiyas' and 'ājīvakas'.

There were some Upanishadic thinkers who had discovered and formulated the main principles of moral behaviour in conformity with their respective views of life. Earlier, Brahmanism had established a rigid and dreadfully static morality by its insistence on the universality of the ritual act (karma=yajña). Hence the actual morality inculcated did not go beyond what was practically necessary in the conduct and successful performance of the sacrifice. Thus evolved a conception of 'dharma', originally 'ritualistic duty', and its ethical correlates such as 'śraddhā' the faith needed in bestowing gifts (dakṣinā) and alms (dāna) to the priesthood who were the mediators between man and his gods. Such was the moral code of the ritualistic religion. The earliest Upanishads cary out these very moral tendencies and thus it cannot be said that they had completely transcended the ethical externalism of the Brahmanic religion. When Sākalya in the Bṛhadāraṅyaka Upanishad (3.9) asked Yajñavalkya: 'And on what is sacrifice based?' 'On gifts to the

51

priests,' replied Yajñavalkya. 'And on what are the gifts to the priests based?' 'On faith (*śraddhā*), for when one has faith one gives gifts to the priests. Verily, on faith are gifts to the priests based.' Similarly, *Chāndogya Upanishad* (2.23) enumerates three branches of duty: 'Sacrifice, study of the Vedas, alms-giving,—that is the first; austerity, indeed, is the second; a student of sacred knowledge (*brahmacārin*) dwelling in the house of a teacher is the third.' Though Upanishadic ethics start with such compromises to ritualism, an attempt is progressively made to conceive a higher kind of morality. For example, the Upanishadic thinkers attribute the highest power to truth (*satya*) in contrast to untruth (*anṛta*). Speakers of falsehood were put to the test by the ordeal of the heated axe. Says the *Chāndogya Upanishad* (6.16): 'Speaking untruth he covers himself with untruth; he seizes hold of the heated axe and is burned. Speaking truth he covers himself with truth; he seizes hold of the heated axe and is not burned.' It is important to observe here that what is true is held to be in conformity with the natural order of things, the cosmic law (*ṛta*), and that what was untrue was what went against that order (*anṛta*). It is to the credit of Indian culture that at a very early period in its history from the cosmological conception of world-order(*ṛta*) they had derived a notion of an ethical order in man. Thus the gradual development of a practical code of ethics is seen in these Upanishads. Quarrelsomeness, tale-bearing (*piśunā*), slander (*upavāda*) are regarded as evil traits tending to make people small (*alpāh*) of character. The three-fold offspring of Prajāpati, gods, men, and asuras are respectively taught by him (*Bṛh. Up.* 5.2) that to restrain (*damyata*), to give (*datta*), and to be compassionate (*dayadhvam*) are the three greatest virtues. There was also a certain conception of social ethics as is implied in the declaration of Aśvapati Kaikeya:

> Within my realm there is no thief,
> no miser, nor a drinking man,
> none altarless, none ignorant,
> no man unchaste, no wife unchaste.

> —*Ch. Up.* 5.11

It is important to students of Buddhist ethics to find the *Chāndogya Upanishad* (8.4,5) condemning to rebirth in the form of small creatures those who commit theft, drink liquor, invade the teacher's bed, kill brahmins, as well as those who consort with them. 'Brahmacarya' which generally means 'the chaste life of a student of sacred knowledge' is extolled and its goal is set forth as the Brahma-world. In the very next paragraph this life of abstinent religious duty (*brahmacarya*) is said to include all other forms of moral behaviour such as sacrifice, silent asceticism, fasting, and hermit life in the forest.

There are many passages in the Upanishads establishing as the highest moral ideal or goal of the spiritual life the Brahma-world which is identified with immortality (*amṛtam*). It is also necessary to point out that the *raison d'être* of ethics in the Upanishads is derived from metaphysics: 'Verily, O Gargi, at the command of that Imperishable (*akṣarasya praśāsane*) men praise those who give, the gods are desirous of a sacrificer, and the fathers (are desirous) of the Manes-sacrifice' (*Bṛh. Up.* 3.8). Further, according to the Upanishads the criterion of moral judgement is merely *conventional*, being nothing other than the practice of elderly and learned brahmins:

'Now if you should have doubt concerning an act, or doubt concerning conduct, if there should be these brāhmaṇas, competent to judge, apt, devoted, not harsh, lovers of virtue (*dharma*)—as they may behave themselves in such a case, so should you behave yourself in such a case' (*Tait. Up.* I, II).

In the last phase of the development of Upanishadic thought morality dwindles into insignificance. This results from the static conception of spiritual life as is inevitable from the identity of the human soul *as it is* with the highest ideal, Brahman, sometimes referred to as the highest Self (*Ātman*). This metaphysical abstraction naturally removes all urgency and necessity for any ethic, for, if man *as he is*, is already one with his ideal, what would be the need for spiritual effort, why worry about a moral life at all! 'Whoso were to know me (*Ātman*)', teaches the *Kauśītaki Upanishad* (3.2), 'not by any action of his can the

53

world be injured, not by murdering his mother or his father, not by stealing or by killing the embryo . . . '. This over-emphasis of the *Ātman*-knowledge and the consequent disregard of the moral life discloses the inner weakness of the absolutist pantheism of the Upanishads. Two of the most critical Hindu students of Upanishadic thought, Ranade and Belvalkar, regard this as the worst trait of the philosophy of absolutism:

'Here, indeed, is touched what may be called the danger line of Upanishadic ethics. To say that the *ātman* dies not is legitimate. To say that weapons cannot cut him nor fire burn him is also a legitimate varying of the phrase. But to argue that, therefore, the murderer is no murderer, and there is nobody really responsible for his action is to carry this *"śāśvatā"* or *"akriyā"* doctrine to a point which, if seriously preached, would be subversive of all established social institutions and religious sacraments.'[1]

These considerations not only indicate to us that the absolutism of the Upanishads inevitably ended in a kind of amoralism but also that there could be a dangerous side to religious and spiritual conservatism. It was as a reaction against such dogmatism in philosophy and ethics that there arose several heterodox philosophies which not only denied the authority of the conservative ethics of the Upanishads but even went to the extent of declaring moral scepticism, moral nihilism and moral anarchism. It is significant that our earliest sources for the study of these doctrines are the Buddhist Nikāyas themselves. There was a strong school of philosophical opinion which encouraged a downright ethical nihilism (*natthikavāda*).

'There is no such thing as alms, sacrifice or oblation; good and bad actions bear no fruit or consequence; there is no (distinction between) this world and the next; there is no (moral obligation towards) father or mother; there are no beings of spontaneous generation, and there are no recluses and brahmins in this world of virtuous conduct who with

[1] *History of Indian Philosophy*, II, p. 399.

insight (*abhiññā*) have realized and proclaimed (the true nature of) this world and the next.'

This moral nihilism was based on a crass materialism in philosophy:

'Man as he is is constituted out of the four elements; when he dies earth combines with earth, water with water, heat with heat and air with air; the sense functions are merged in the ether and all that is left of him are his greyish bones after the cremation; the value of the alms-giving is merely in the imagination of the giver and to affirm the moral consequences of the act is a hollow assertion; both the foolish and the wise are annihilated and completely cut off at death.'[1]

This was the doctrine that Ajita Kesakambali, among others, is reported to have professed. Then there were others who denied moral causation (*ahetuvādins*). Their main thesis was as follows:

'There is no cause or reason for the depravity of beings; they become depraved without cause or reason; they become pure without cause or reason; there is no such thing as self-agency or the agency of another or human effort; there is no such thing as power or energy or human strength or human endeavour; all animals, all creatures, all beings and all living things are without initiative, without power and strength of their own; they just evolve by fate, necessity and fortuitous concatenation of events; and it is according to their peculiar nature as belonging to one of the six classes that they experience ease or pain, and it is only at the end of the appointed period—after one has passed through the 8,400,000 periods of wandering in *saṃsāra*—that there shall be an end of pain; thus there is no such thing as that one should experience the result of *kamma* and thereby put an end to it either through virtuous conduct or precept, asceticism or "*brahmacarya*"; consequently there is neither spiritual growth nor decline, neither depravation nor exaltation, inasmuch as in

---

[1] *Majjhima Nikāya* I, 515.

saṃsāra pain and pleasure are determined and circumscribed. As automatically as a ball of thread thrown up rolls along unreeling itself, so do both the foolish and the wise reach their salvation at the termination of their appointed course in *saṃsāra*.'[1]

The foremost leader of this school was Makkhali Gosāla, and from the importance attached to the refutation of his theories in the early Buddhist books we may infer that he had a large following. He roundly denied all *initiative* and *choice* in man, being rigidly deterministic. The only redeeming feature of this philosophy was its belief in some form of moral ideal, however wrongly the process of its accomplishment was conceived. Therefore, the Buddhist books disparagingly call this 'the purity through *saṃsāra*' (*saṃsāra suddhi*), because the theory postulated that purity occurred just by saṃsāric evolution over which man had no control. This was further condemned as '*akiriyāvāda*' or 'theory of non-action'. Another teacher, Pūrana Kassapa, held the opinion that the act had no moral consequences, that merit (*puñña*) did not result from good action and demerit (*pāpa*) from bad action; 'giving, generosity, restraint, self-control, and truth-speaking did not conduce to merit'.[2] This doctrine, too, is condemned as '*akiriyāvāda*' or a denial of the efficacy of the act. Another school professed a fatalistic pluralism and the most prominent teacher of this doctrine was Pakudha Kaccāyana:

'The following seven things are neither made nor commanded to be created; they are barren (and so nothing is produced out of them), steadfast as a mountain-peak, as a pillar firmly fixed. They move not, neither do they vary, they trench not one upon the other, nor avail aught as to ease or pain or both. And what are the seven? The four elements—earth, water, fire, air—and pleasure and pain and the soul as the seventh. So there is neither slayer nor causer of slaying, hearer or speaker, knower or explainer. When one with a sharp sword cleaves a head in twain, no one thereby deprives

---

[1] *Dīgha Nikāya* I, 54.   [2] *Dīgha Nikāya*, p. 52.

anyone of life; a sword has merely penetrated into the space between seven elementary substances.'[1]

As this doctrine is obviously based on the Upanishadic concept of the indestructibility and the unchangeability of the '*ātman*' it has been called '*sassatavāda*' or eternalism. In ethics it also leads to an '*akiriyāvāda*' or amoralism like the previous philosophies. Then there was the ethical scepticism of the agnostic philosopher, Sañjaya Belaṭṭiputta, who refused to pass final judgement on any such metaphysical problem as the existence of a future world or on any ethical question. When questioned about the moral consequences of good and bad acts he would resort to the four-membered formula of prevarication and refuse to set down a definite opinion.[2] The doctrines of these rival teachers not only led to clashes with the dogmatism and orthodoxy of the Upanishadic moralists but also resulted in interminable conflicts among themselves, thus creating that state of moral ferment to which we referred earlier and which characterized Indian religion just before the advent of the Buddha. It was a critical epoch in the history of Indian religion and the Buddha with His principle of the golden mean (*majjhimāpaṭipadā*) brought sanity and a sense of poise to a society harassed by ideological disturbances and shaken about by heated metaphysical wranglings and ethical disputations. Apart from these doctrines which led to a moral upheaval there was the Jaina system of ethics with its rigid formalism and externalism frequently criticized in the Buddhist books. Nigaṇṭha Nāthaputta emphasized the external act in preference to the mental act.[3] In addition to all these ethical doctrines the *Dīgha* and *Majjhima Nikāyas* make constant reference to the inevitable moral upshot of philosophical materialism in general, referred to as the perverted philosophy (*viparītadassana*) that denied all morality; it is branded as the heresy *par excellence* (*micchādiṭṭhi*), the evil doctrine (*pāpakaṃ diṭṭhigataṃ*), and moral nihilism (*natthikavāda*).[4] This view which is

---

[1] *Majjhima Nikāya* I, 517.   [2] *Dīgha Nikāya* I, 58.
[3] *Majjhima Nikāya* I, 372 ff.
[4] *Ibid.*, I, 130, 287, 401; *Dīgha Nikāya* II, 316.

prominently attributed to a prince known as Pāyāsi-rājañña asserted the following three propositions: (1) there is no world beyond; (2) there are no beings reborn otherwise than from parents; (3) there is no result or consequence of good or bad acts.[1] As opposed to this *micchādiṭṭhi* early Buddhism sets forth *sammādiṭṭhi* or the correct view of life on which it bases its ethics. Let us now turn to an examination of that fundamental philosophical basis of Buddhist morality.

According to Early Buddhism man's appearance in this world is clearly not due to a mere concatenation of physical factors. Many statements in the dialogues make it clear that a non-physical factor is necessary for successful conception.[2] Such concatenation is due to *upadhisakhāras* generated by previous saṃsāric experiences[3] and it is precisely in this context that it is affirmed that the reborn individual is neither the same nor another (*na ca so na ca añño*).[4] It may be observed that in the latter portion of this statement (*na ca añño*) moral responsibility is definitely asserted. Life thus come into being is said to be characterized by several marks (*lakkhaṇa*) such as impermanence, unsatisfactoriness, liability to disease and corruption, extraneousness, subjection to dissolution, voidness, and insubstantiality.[5] These characteristics are sometimes brought under the three headings of *anicca*, *dukkha* and *anattā*, or *anicca*, *dukkha* and *vipariṇāmadhamma*.[6] Thus is set forth the Noble Truth of the Unsatisfactoriness (*dukkha-sacca*) of saṃsāric existence (*bhava*), which is sometimes analysed as threefold *dukkhatā* (*dukkha-dukkha*, *saṅkharā-dukkha* and *vipariṇāma-dukkha*).[7] Such unsatisfactoriness is due to the continuous change or *becoming* that is *saṃsāra*.[8] This very dynamic nature of saṃsāric life with its self-generated potentialities tends to a continuation of individuality (*nāma-rūpa*) or personality (*attabhāva*). Thus is it asserted in Early Buddhism that there is a life beyond (*atthi paro loko*),[9] which is proved by

---

[1] *Dīgha Nikāya* II, 316, 317.
[2] *Majjhima Nikāya* I, 265; *Dīgha Nikāya* II, 63.
[3] *Sutta Nipāta*, v. 728.
[4] Cp. *Saṃyutta Nikāya* II, 20.
[5] *Majjhima Nikāya* I, 435.
[6] *Ibid.*, I, 232.
[7] *Dīgha Nikāya* III, 216.
[8] *Sutta Nipāta*, v. 742.
[9] *Majjhima Nikāya* I, 403.

the super-normal experience of the Perfect Ones (arahants) who are perceivers of the world beyond (*paralokaviduno*) by virtue of their having acquired the faculties of recollecting past births (*pubbenivāsānussati*) and observing the passing away and rebirth of beings (*sattānaṃ cutupapatti-ñāṇa*),[1] the latter being also termed the super-normal vision (*dibba-cakkhu*). Buddha Himself exercised this power on several occasions when requested to explain the bourne (*gati*) of his departed disciples.[2] The Early Buddhist conviction of this fact of saṃsāric continuity is, therefore, beyond doubt and it is no wonder that those who refused to admit a life beyond were dubbed *micchādiṭṭhikas*. It is clear then on what foundation the ethical system of Early Buddhism rests. Once this saṃsāric continuity with all its attendant *dukkha* is granted, the ideal of man's perfection turns out to be the release (*nissaraṇa*) therefrom. This is the Goal of Buddhist ethics which consequently is conceived as the cessation of becoming (*bhava-nirodha*) or the ending of *dukkha*, generally called *Nibbāna*. Thus we discover that the *raison d'être* of Buddhist ethics is the fundamental fact of saṃsāric *dukkha*. Hence the essential basis of the Buddhist moral life (*brahmacariya*) lies not in some metaphysical hypothesis conceived by *a priori* reasoning but, as Buddha pointed out to Mālunkyaputta, on the conviction that 'verily there is birth, there is decay, there is death, etc.', of which the destruction is declared to be possible in this very life.[3] Thus the mere speculation on metaphysical problems, usually referred to as ten, is condemned as unprofitable. Similarly Buddha tells Udāyi that such ultimate questions as those that concern the beginning (*pubbanta*) and the end (*aparanta*) of things, being solvable only by developing the higher faculties (*vijjā, abhiññā*) but not by the exercise of mere reason, it becomes imperative for man to accomplish the ethical process which alone could lead to the acquirement of such faculties.[4] Therefore, the importance of the ethical process for the realization of *Nibbāna* is unquestionable, and, as Dhammadinnā points out to Visākha, the moral life finds its apex, goal and consummation in *Nibbāna*.[5]

[1] *Dīgha Nikāya* I, 82.   [2] See *Dīgha Nikāya*, Suttas 16, 18, 19.
[3] *Majjhima Nikāya* I, 431.   [4] *Ibid.*, II, 31, 32, 38.   [5] *Ibid.*, I, 304.

The foregoing discussion of the fundamental basis of the Buddhist ethic, its *raison d'être* and its goal, will help the student of Buddhism and the student of ethics to appreciate the important bearing that the Buddhist view of morality has to the burning questions of ethics such as the problem of evil, and the problem of ethical relativity. To an unbiassed student of Buddhism it appears that Early Buddhism offers definite solutions to these problems and as such it has a claim to serious consideration in this respect.

Our brief presentation of the philosophical basis of Buddhist ethics will have stressed the extreme urgency of the problem of evil for Early Buddhism as well as its all-embracing and profound nature as indicated by its saṃsāric context. The concept of evil as discussed by Western thinkers, pertaining as it does to merely this visible life, covers only a minute aspect of the problem but it can be seen that fundamentally there is no difference between the two issues for as Early Buddhism viewed it, '*dukkha-dukkhatā*' which is defined as man's conflict with his environment, is only one aspect of the general unsatisfactoriness of saṃsāric becoming (*bhava-dukkha*). Thus it is to be expected that a thinking person (*viññū puriso*) cannot but be impressed by the obtrusiveness of evil or *dukkha* around him. But this was exactly the point on which Professor Joad condemned Buddhism in his book *Matter, Life and Value* (p. 369), published in 1929 in which he complained that 'for Buddhism as for Job man is born to trouble as sparks fly upward' and declared: 'I differ, therefore, from the dominant philosophy of the East in not despising the ordinary life of struggle and enjoyment of effort and reward.' It is ironically significant, however, that after the lapse of only thirteen years he was compelled to radically alter his opinion, for in his later book, *God and Evil* (1942), he was forced to admit: 'I conclude that attempts which are made . . . to show that evil is not a real and fundamental principle belonging to the nature of things are unsuccessful.' Such coincidence as this between Early Buddhism and Western philosophy on the problem of evil will necessarily remain partial in so far as such philosophers confine their observations merely to the experience of the individual in this visible existence. But,

as we have attempted to show above, what is specially characteristic of the Buddhist *Weltanschauung* (world-view) is the
undeniable fact that this short span of a few score of years on
earth is not the whole of one's empirical existence but only a
temporary manifestation of a saṃsāric process that extends for
innumerable 'lives' in the past and may also extend for an
indefinable period in the future.

Now, since this deeper significance of the general unsatisfactoriness of saṃsāric life and also the possibility of release
therefrom has to be accepted on the validity of the experiences
of the Perfect Ones, Early Buddhism recommends *saddhā* or
the reliance on the experience of such arahants who have
realized the higher vision and on their statements, after
adequate investigation as to their worth.[1] Hence *saddhā* is held
up to be the basis of the ethical process which ultimately leads
to the realization of the highest truth (*paramasacca*) and
therewith the goal.[2] Thus in practical ethics *saddhā* comes to
be regarded as one of the five good things to be cultivated
(*paricaritabbaṃ*), although the definite warning is given that
mere faith in the teacher is not sufficient for complete ethical
progress.[3] The faith (*śraddhā*) of Vedic morality to which we
have previously referred is considered to be mere blind faith
(*amūlikā saddhā*), and is consequently condemned by the
Buddha in a talk with the brahmin Bhāradvāja.[4] It is on account of this that *saddhā* in Early Buddhism is said to be two-
fold, the faith that may be empty, void and false in its fruition,
and the faith that is bound to lead to genuine consequences.[5]
We cannot escape the conclusion that the *saddhā* encouraged
in Early Buddhism is only the result of an inference from the
realization of arahants as to the possibility of one's own
realization of the goal. Hence the only kind of faith that is
advocated, if it could be called faith at all, is what is designated
'logical faith' (*ākāravatī saddhā*).[6] The conversion of laymen to
the belief that it was necessary to lead the higher moral life
under the Buddha or His disciples was always prompted by

---

[1] *Majjhima Nikāya* I, 173.   [2] *Ibid.*, II, 171.   [3] *Ibid.*, II, 94.
[4] *Ibid.*, II, 170.   [5] *Ibid.*, No. 95.   [6] *Ibid.*, I, 401.

this kind of *saddhā*—a fact attested to at numerous places in the Canon.

The layman who thus takes up the spiritual life through his reliance on (*uddissa*) such a teacher is said to have started his career (*paṭipanno*) along the Path (*magga, paṭipadā*) to *Nibbāna*. This Path is said to consist of three stages or parts usually called the three *sampadās* or the three *khandhas*. The first of these stages is *sīla* or ethical conduct, and practical morals have a meaning for the disciple only till such time as he arrives at the next stage of the Path, namely, concentration (*samādhi*). But the goal is not reached even then, and a still higher stage of development must be gone through and this is technically known as *paññā* (wisdom). What is generally believed to be the Eightfold Path in Buddhism is included within these three stages as the learned Dhammadinnā explained to Visākha.[1] How far, then, practical morality is of significance to one aspiring for the Buddhist goal becomes clear when it is considered that *sīla* forms only the initial stage of such process. In fact, Early Buddhism administers a warning to the aspirant to master morality but not allow morality to get the better of him, and it is clearly laid down that even virtuous conduct has to be transcended at one stage. It need not, therefore, appear paradoxical when it is asserted in the same context that the disciple should try to put a final end to meritorious forms of good conduct.[2] Thus for Buddhism morality is not an end in itself. It is considering these features of the Path which, it is obvious, transcend Ethical Perfectionism, as is understood by Western moralists, and also the metaphysical perfection implied in the Upanishads, that it is claimed that the Exalted One is the originator and proclaimer of a unique Way.

It is to be observed that in the spiritual evolution as indicated in this Path the question of Happiness as the ideal of morality finds a perfect solution. It is said that in the stage of concentration when the aspirant reaches the fourth *jhāna* both happiness and its opposite cease to concern him for he becomes indifferent to both pleasurable and painful feeling (*vedanā*). Up to that moment the aspirant is to experience inner happiness.

[1] *Majjhima Nikāya* I, 301.   [2] *Ibid.*, II, 27.

This inner form of happiness is clearly differentiated from worldly happiness which is called 'low, vulgar, and ignoble' inasmuch as such happiness depends on the senses. It is expressly stated that this latter form of material happiness is to be shunned[1] and hence to classify Buddhism as any form of Hedonism, as Dr Pratt has done in his *Pilgrimage of Buddhism* (p. 20), is quite unjustifiable. Over and above this sensuous happiness which has an erotic basis (*kāma*) as well as the inner jhānic happiness which is non-erotic (*nekkhamma*) is placed *Nibbāna*, as even this jhānic happiness is not final (*analaṃ*), for it is only in the ultimate state of spiritual attainment (*saññāvedayitanirodha*) that happiness assumes its most perfect form. This state which is the *summum bonum* of Buddhism can be styled Happiness only in an exceptional sense. Yet, Buddha persists in calling it happiness in the face of the criticism of heretics, for, as He once explained to Ānanda, He did not regard a state as happy just because of pleasurable feeling, and also because he considered that there could be levels of 'happiness' relative to the stage of spiritual evolution. Thus, if in the ideal state of *Nibbāna* the aspirant transcends the subtlest forms of happiness and is not tinged by them, it would not be quite apposite to identify the Early Buddhist ideal in ethics with that of Eudaemonism. But this does not deny the fact that for Buddhism just as for modern psychology and biology man, as well as other living beings, by nature seeks for pleasure and avoids pain (*sukhakāmo dukkhapaṭikkūlo*).

It can now be seen that there is a sense in which we may assert that the ethical process of Buddhism is intended to release man from the miseries of saṃsāric existence (*dukkha*) and take him to the ultimate Happiness or the Good (*attha*) that is *Nibbāna*. In this Buddhism does not go against the basic psychology of man's nature, but endeavours to bring about its refinement and sublimation until it totally transcends the level at which it is found in saṃsāric existence. Thus Nibbānic Happiness must be considered as the ideal for every living being. Hence is derived also the *criterion* of moral judgement according to the ethical philosophy of Early Buddhism which we have

[1] *Majjhima Nikāya* III, 230, 233.

attempted to outline above. This criterion of Buddhist ethics is emphasized in several places and seeks to determine whether a particular act would obstruct or not oneself or others in the attempt to win this release (*nissaraṇa*) from *Dukkha* or saṃsāric Evil. In his admonition to Rāhula, Buddha makes it perfectly clear that 'whatever act tends to the obstruction or harm (*vyābādha*) of oneself and others (on the Path) is to be considered bad (*akusalaṃ*) as its upshot is pain and its result Evil'.[1] It is significant that the word '*vyābādha*' means both *harm* to the individual concerned and *obstruction* to spiritual progress. Therefore, subjectively an act (*kamma*) becomes good (*kusala*) or bad (*akusala*) according as it promotes or hinders spiritual progress, and objectively it is considered to be meritorious (*puñña*) or demeritorious (*apuñña*) according as it is beneficial (*hita*) or harmful (*ahita*) to the similar progress of others. Sir Edward Arnold in his *Light of Asia* has beautifully summed up this idea:

Kill not—for pity's sake—and lest ye slay
The meanest thing upon its upward way.

To inflict pain, for instance, either on oneself of others is to cause distraction of mind by inciting evil and harmful emotions which cannot be but an obstacle on the 'upward way'.

Thus the ethical content of an act is psychological and its source is volitional. Accordingly, Early Buddhism considers as ethical only those acts which are volitional (*sañcetanika*).[2] Thus the *Anguttara Nikāya* (III, 415) attributes to the Buddha the statement that the real act (*kamma*) is an act of volition (*cetanā*). This is natural inasmuch as the intensity of the act depends on the extent to which it is committed deliberately (*sañcicca*).[3] For instance, it is pointed out that an infant who is not conscious even of his own body cannot commit any sin. In technical language this would mean that all acts are not ethically significant but only those that are voluntary, that is to say, willed by the agent. This being the fundamental sense

---

[1] *Majjhima Nikāya* I, 415.　　　　[2] *Ibid.*, III, 207, cp. I, 377.
[3] *Ibid.*, I, 523, II., 103.

in which an act is conceived in Buddhist ethics what we *do* and *say* have only an *indirect* ethical significance, whereas what we *think* or *will* is *directly* ethical. In a conversation with the Jain Dīghatapassi Buddha emphasizes the greater ethical importance of the mental or volitional act (*mano-kamma*) as compared with the verbal (*vacī-kamma*) or the physical act (*kāya-kamma*).[1] Hence the Buddha's emphasis on the elimination of the cardinal evils of attachment (*rāga, lobha*), ill-will (*dosa*) and infatuation (*moha*) for they *directly* affect the nature of our volitions, while other evil acts such as meat-eating and drinking of liquor, etc., affect the mind only indirectly. Therefore, while the distinction between absolute and relative moral values seems meaningless and unnecessary according to the Buddha, there appears to be some sense in which we may divide voluntary acts or ethically significant acts into *direct* and *indirect* according as they affect the main ethical purpose of leading to the release from saṃsāric existence. It thus becomes clear that for the Buddha moral judgements are not to be based on some *a priori* conceptions of objectively real values like goodness, truth and beauty, as is usually held by idealistic philosophers, nor are they to be regarded as *subjective* or *relative* from all points of view as asserted by most scientific and materialistic thinkers. According to Mr Bertrand Russell it would seem that ethics are a mere matter of taste. 'If two men differ about values', he says summing up his ethical doctrine, 'there is not a disagreement as to any kind of truth but a difference of taste.'[2] Similarly, Professor Edward Westermarck for whom all ethical judgements have an emotional basis is the leading exponent of a theory of Ethical Relativity, which, however, adds that moral phenomena are not made meaningless just because they happen to fall within the subjective sphere of experience. For him, nevertheless, ethics remain still *relative*, because moral judgements depend on economic, social and psychological (emotional) circumstances.[3] According to the Buddha, however, moral judgements assume a permanent

---

[1] *Majjhima Nikāya*, I, 373.   [2] *Religion and Science*, p. 237.
[3] *The Origin and Development of Moral Ideas*, pp. 4, 18, 19; *Ethical Relativity*, p. 220.

value in so far as they are based on the *point of view of the end*
which, as we have stressed above, is the release from saṃsāric
Evil. But we may add that there is a sense in which moral
values are *relative* even for the Buddha, and this derives only
from the existence of levels of spiritual experience corresponding to the respective stages of the Path to which we have
already referred.

The above discussion should make it clear that the ethics of
the Buddha is prompted by one *motive*, viz., the desire for release
and relies on no external *sanctions* such as God, Church or
State, but is pre-eminently *autonomous* in character.[1] In fact,
the desire for release and the psychological observation that
attachment, hate and infatuation directly affect the nature of
our volitions, sum up the *motives* and *sanctions* of Buddhist
morality. In this discussion, however, we have taken for granted
the most important fact of the freedom of the human will. We
regarded man as intrinsically a morally free agent who had
within him the power to choose between alternative courses of
action. Is this justifiable according to the Buddha's doctrine?
Certainly, yes. There is, in fact, no more important conviction
in the whole of Buddha's philosophy than the idea that within
this individuality (*nāma-rūpa*) there is the *potentiality* of release
if only man wills that way.[2] Therefore, in spite of the fact that
there is in a sense *determinism* to the extent that empirical
existence is admittedly conditioned and thus is obviously subject to the vicissitudes of birth, decay and death, there is in
man the power (*balaṃ, viriyaṃ*)[3] to overcome all this by the
strength of will (*chando*).[4] Human life is regarded by the Buddha
as in every way the best suited for this effort and birth among
the animals, etc., is consequently deprecated, for it is only in
man that the *power to will* exists in such a high degree with
infinite capacity to develop higher by self-discipline and
meditation. Early Buddhism does not deny the importance of
environmental factors in the moulding of man's conduct but,
on the other hand, it does not in the least subscribe to any

[1] See my Introduction to Tachibana's *Ethics of Buddhism* (Colombo,
Bauddha Sāhitya Sabhā, 1961).
[2] *Samyutta Nikāya* I, 62. [3] *Majjhima Nikāya* I, 407. [4] *Ibid.*, I, 313.

theory that man's conduct is merely a set of reactions to external stimuli or unconscious tendencies, or that it is determined by social and economic factors alone, for it would be admitted even by the most adverse critics of the Buddha that no one raised Man and his noblest gift, the human Reason or Will, to such dignity as that greatest of ethical teachers born in the philosophically rife atmosphere of India twenty-five centuries ago.

2. THE BUDDHIST CONCEPTION OF TRUTH

PROF. K. N. JAYATILLEKE, PH.D. (LONDON)

Buddhism is the first missionary religion in the history of humanity with a universal message of salvation for all mankind. The Buddha after His Englightenment sent out sixty-one disciples in different directions asking them to preach the doctrine for the weal and welfare of mankind. He is said in one of the earliest texts to have been 'born for the good and happiness of humanity' (*manussaloke hitasukhatāya jāto*; *Sn.* 683). Addressed as 'the King of kings' (*rājābhirāja*; *Sn.* 553), He says, 'I am a King, the supreme King of Righteousness, with righteousness do I extend my kingdom, a kingdom which cannot be destroyed' (*Sn.* 554).

The era in which the Buddha was born marks a turning point in history for everywhere in the world from Greece to China we notice a new awakening and a quest for truth. A historian says:

'This sixth century BC was, indeed, one of the most remarkable in all history. Everywhere . . . men's minds were displaying a new boldness . . . It is as if the race had reached a stage of adolescence—after a childhood of 20,000 years.[1] To the east of India, in China, appeared the great religious teachers, Lao Tze and Confucius, the founders of Taoism and Confucianism, respectively. To the west there was Zarathrustra in Persia, the founder of Zoroastrianism, Prophet Isaiah in Israel and Pythagoras in Greece.'

A student of religion observes:

'It was in these days, rather than in those which made Bethlehem of Judea famous, that the principle of "peace on

[1] H. G. Wells, *A Short History of the World* (London, Penguin Books, 1945), p. 90.

earth, goodwill to men" first began to sweep across the world like a cleansing wind.'[1]

Buddhist legends say that at this time the world over people were looking forward to the birth of a Supremely Enlightened One, an event which happens very rarely (*kadāci karahaci*) in history. With an air of expectancy the Prophet Isaiah says: 'For unto us a child is born, unto us a son is given . . . and his name shall be called Wonderful Councellor, The Mighty God, The Everlasting Father, The Prince of Peace.' It is a strange coincidence that almost contemporaneous with this prophecy[2] was born the Buddha to whom all these titles have been given within a few centuries of His birth, for He has been called the *Acchariya-puggala*—the Wonderful Person, *Satthā devamanus-sānam*—the Councellor of gods and men, *Brahmātibrahmā* (also *Devātideva*)—the God among gods, *Ādi-Pitā*—the eternal Father and *Sāntirāja*—the Prince of Peace.

In India men prayed and longed for the Truth:

> From the unreal lead me to the real!
> From darkness lead me to light!
> From death lead me to immortality!
> —*Bṛhadāranyaka Upaniṣad* 1.3.28
> (c. 700 BC)

There appeared many sages who claimed to have discovered as many paths to immortality and some of these are described in the Upaniṣads, the scriptures of the Ajivikas and Jains. Then appeared the Buddha who announced in no unmistaken terms:

> Open to them are the doors of Immortality;
> Those who have ears, let them send forth faith.
> —*M.* I, 169 (c. 528 BC)

---

[1] Ed. Robert O. Ballou, *The Pocket World Bible* (London, 1948), p. 3.

[2] '. . . Gautama Buddha, who taught his disciples at Benares in India about the same time that Isaiah was prophesying among the Jews in Babylon . . .', H. G. Wells, *op. cit.*, p. 90.

The Truth of *Nirvāna* that Buddha discovered is called in the Canon 'the Truth' (*sacca*) and the fundamental doctrines that He proclaimed are summed up in the 'Four Noble Truths' (*cattāri ariyasaccāni*). We do not propose in this article to describe or explain any of these 'truths' but shall concern ourselves with the more prosaic task of examining what is meant by the term 'truth'. This is a purely philosophical investigation and the reader may wonder what such academic philosophy has to do with the religion of the Buddha.

Here it is necessary to draw attention to another unique feature of the religion of the Buddha, namely, that it is the only religion of any religious teacher, which is the outcome of a consistent philosophy, which claims to tell us about the ultimate facts of existence and reality. The religion of the Buddha is a way of life resulting from the acceptance of a view of life, which is said to be factual (*yathābhūtam*). His philosophy is not without an epistemology or an account of the nature of knowledge. A detailed examination of this epistemology or theory of knowledge is outside the scope of this brief essay[1] and we shall, therefore, take up this problem of what is meant by the term 'truth' as explained and understood in the Canonical texts.

We use the term 'truth' to characterize statements or more exactly to characterize what is expressed by statements, namely, propositions. To take an example we say, for instance, that the statement 'there is an artificial lake in Kandy' expresses a truth. Not all true statements have a relevance for religion. The above statement about the Kandy lake has no bearing on religion. But the statement that 'life is impermanent and insecure' has a relevance for religion, for the religious quest (*brahmacariyesanā*) or the noble quest (*ariyapariyesanā*) is the quest for security and permanence.

The Four Noble Truths state the following propositions: (i) life within the Cosmos, being infected with impermanence and insecurity, is subject to unhappiness, however 'happy' we may be in a relative sense even for very long periods of time; (ii) this unhappiness is caused by the operation of the unsatisfied

---

[1] See the author's *Early Buddhist Theory of Knowledge* (London, George Allen & Unwin), p. 550.

desires for sensuous gratification, for selfish pursuits and for destruction, which continually seek satisfaction; (iii) the cessation of these desires, which cannot be brought about by violent means (suicide) but only by self-development coincides with the realization of supreme happiness; (iv) the total development of the moral, intuitive and spiritual-intellectual aspects of one's personality culminates in this final realization and enlightenment.

These propositions which are claimed to be true are also said to be useful (*atthasaṃhitaṃ*) in the sense that they are relevant to our weal and welfare and a knowledge of these helps us to attain the goal of all human (and divine) spiritual development. At the same time there are propositions which do not serve such a purpose and are useless in the above sense. Propositions also may be agreeable and pleasant to hear as well as the reverse. If we tabulate the possibilities in terms of propositions, which may be true or false, useful or useless, pleasant or unpleasant, we get the following possibilities:

1. True	..	.. useful	..	.. pleasant
2. True	..	.. useful	..	.. unpleasant
3. True	..	.. useless	..	.. pleasant
4. True	..	.. useless	..	.. unpleasant
5. False	..	.. useful	..	.. pleasant
6. False	..	.. useful	..	.. unpleasant
7. False	..	.. useless	..	.. pleasant
8. False	..	.. useless	..	.. unpleasant

In the *Abhayarājakumāra Sutta*, it is said that the Buddha asserts propositions of the types one and two and that He does not assert propositions of the types three, four, seven and eight. The possibilities five and six are omitted, probably because it was considered that they did not, in fact, exist. The passage reads:

'The Tathāgata does not assert a statement which He knows to be untrue, false, useless, disagreeable and unpleasant to others (8). He does not assert a statement which He knows to be true, factual, useless, disagreeable and unpleasant to others (4). He would assert at the proper time a statement which He knows to be true, factual, useful, disagreeable and unpleasant to others (2). He would not assert a statement which He knows to be untrue, false, useless, agreeable and pleasant to others (7). He would not assert a statement which He knows to be true, factual, useless, agreeable and pleasant to others (3). He would assert at the proper time a statement which He knows to be true, factual, useful, agreeable and pleasant to others (1).' (*M.* I, 395.)

So the Buddha makes assertions which are true and useful and either pleasant or unpleasant. In the *Suttanipāta* it is said that 'one should say only what is pleasant' (*Sn.* 452). This is, no doubt, the general rule, though exceptionally one may say what is unpleasant as well for the good of an individual, just as out of love for a child one has to cause a certain amount of pain in order to remove something that has got stuck in its throat (*M.* I, 394, 5). Even the truth, it should be noted, should be stated only 'at the proper time'.

We normally make unpleasant statements when we are motivated by anger, jealousy, envy, malice or hatred and we try to rationalize what we do by imagining that our utterances are being made from the best of motives for the good of others. This is the reason why we should be extremely suspicious when we make such unpleasant statements.

What is the defining characteristic of truth? The words commonly used in the Pāli to denote 'truth' mean 'what has taken place' (*bhūtaṃ*), 'what is like that' (*tacchaṃ*) and 'what is not otherwise' (*anaññathā*). It is the object of knowledge. 'One knows what is in accordance with fact' (*yathābhūtaṃ pājānāti D.* I, 83). These usages suggest the acceptance of what is called in philosophy the correspondence theory of truth. According to the theory, truth is 'what accords with fact' and falsity 'what discords with fact'. True and false beliefs, conceptions, and statements are defined in this manner in the *Apaṇṇaka Sutta*:

'When, in fact, there is a next world, the belief occurs to me that there is a next world, that would be a true belief. When, in fact, there is a next world, if one thinks that there is a next world, that would be a true conception. When, in fact, there is a next world, one asserts the statement that there is a next world, that would be a true statement' (*M*. I, 403).

Similarly for falsity: 'When, in fact, there is a next world, the belief occurs to me that there is no next world, that would be a false belief . . .' (*M*. I, 402).

While truth is thus defined in terms of correspondence with fact, consistency or coherence is also considered a criterion of truth. The Canonical texts are quite aware of the principle of contradiction. In one place it is stated that 'if p (a certain statement) is true, not-p is false and if not-p is true, p is false' (*S*. IV, 298, 9). But we also find in the texts statements of the following sort:

(i) S is both P and not-P, e.g. the universe is both finite and infinite;
(ii) S is neither P nor not-P, e.g. the universe is neither finite nor infinite.

These statements appear to be self-contradictory to people who are acquainted only with Aristotelian logic. How can a universe be both finite and infinite when according to the law of contradiction it cannot be both finite and infinite? And how can a universe be neither finite nor infinite, when according to the law of excluded middle it must be either finite or infinite? Western scholars completely misunderstood the nature of these assertions and what they misunderstood they attributed to the idiocy of the Indians. The Belgian scholar, De la Vallée Poussin, makes the following observations about this logic: 'Indians do not make a clear distinction between facts and ideas, between ideas and words; they have never clearly recognized the principle of contradiction. Buddhist dialectic has a four-branched dilemma: *Nirvāna* is existence or non-existence or both existence and non-existence or neither existence nor non-existence. We are helpless.'[1]

[1] *The Way to Nirvana*, Cambridge University Press, 1917, p. III.

Today with the discovery of many-valued logics and the consequent realization that Aristotelian logic is only one of many possible systems, the significance of this Buddhist logic of four alternatives (*catuṣkoṭi*) could be better understood. Briefly, this is a two-valued logic of four alternatives unlike Aristotelian logic, which is a two-valued logic of two alternatives. It is two-valued since it asserts that all propositions are either true (*saccaṃ*) or false (*musā*). Also according to this logic we say that something either is the case or is not the case; there is no other possibility. But in actual conversation in certain situations we use statements of the form 'both is and is not' (i.e. 'he is both bald and not bald') or 'neither is nor is not'. The Buddhist logic uses these statements descriptive of these classes of situations. A discussion of the precise nature of this system of logic would lead us into discussions of a technical nature, but an example would make it clear as to what is meant by the third and four possibilities which are logically impossible according to the Aristotelian scheme. If we talk about the extent of the universe we find, for instance, that we can think of four and only four possible mutually exclusive alternatives, viz.

(i) The universe is finite in all respects, i.e. it is finite and spherical (*parivaṭumo*).
(ii) The universe is infinite in all dimensions.
(iii) The universe is finite in some dimensions and infinite in other dimensions; this is what is meant by saying that 'the universe is both finite and infinite'.
(iv) If the universe was unreal or space was subjective, then we cannot predicate spatial attributes like 'finite' or 'infinite' of the universe. In such a situation we may say, 'the universe is neither finite nor infinite'.

We see from the above that the alternatives three and four are not self-contradictory as Western scholars supposed some time back in their ignorance of the true nature of logical systems. According to this four-fold (*catuṣ-koṭi*) Buddhist system of logic the above four alternative views about the extent of the universe are clearly seen as four possible alternatives. (It may also be seen that only one and not more than one alternative may be true.) According to the Aristotelian system, on the other hand, we can only make the statements 'the universe is finite' and 'the universe is not finite'. By the latter statement it is not clear whether we are stating that the universe is not finite in all dimensions or in one or some dimensions only (views ii and iii). The fourth alternative cannot even be stated since according to the law of excluded middle the above two are the only alternatives possible and one of them must necessarily be true. The Buddhist four-fold logic makes it possible to state the four alternative theses clearly as mutually exclusive and together exhaustive possibilities. It is no more true or false than the Aristotelian and its merits should be judged by its adequacy for the purpose for which it is used.

The propositions of a specific or general character which can be thus stated in the form of the four alternatives belong to the class of statements which concern the events in the space-time-cause world. Statements about Nirvana or the Super-cosmic which is a reality that is non-spatio-temporal and unconditioned (*na paṭiccasamuppannaṃ*) fall outside the scope of logical discourse (*atakkāvacara*).

That consistency is held to be a criterion of truth is clear from the fact that the Buddha very often appeals to this principle in arguing with his opponents. He uses dialectical arguments in Socratic fashion to show that some of the theories held by his opponents were false. He starts with one of the assumptions of his opponents and proceeds step by step until at a certain stage in the discussion he is able to show that 'his (opponent's) later statement is not compatible with the former nor the former with the later' (*na kho te sandhīyati purimena vā pacchi-maṃ pacchimena vā purimaṃ*; *M.* I, 232). It is assumed that a theory is false unless it was consistent. In the *Suttanipāta*, referring to diverse mutually contradictory theories the question is asked: 'Claiming to be experts, why do they put forward diverse theories—is truth many and at variance?' (*Sn.* 885). The answer given is: 'Truth, verily, is not multiple and at variance' (*Sn.* 886). In this context the statement is made that 'truth is one without a second' (*ekaṃ hi saccaṃ na dutīyam atthi, Sn.* 884). The presence of logical coherence and compatibility in all the statements of a theory and the absence of contradiction is clearly recognized as a criterion of truth.

Now although consistency is accepted as a criterion of truth, it need not necessarily be the case that a consistent theory is true. A true theory must be consistent but consistency alone is no infallible or sufficient criterion of truth. Consistency, no doubt, lends plausibility to the truth of a theory but we must not forget that it is also possible for a person to lie consistently and thereby present an appearance of truth. A religious philosophy like that of Spinoza's, which is founded on *a priori* reasoning may appear to be true if it is consistent but it would nevertheless be false if it does not correspond with fact. There could be mutually inconsistent theories each of which was internally consistent.

It is a remarkable fact that the Canonical texts recognize this fact. The *Sandaka Sutta* refers to religions, based on pure reasoning and speculation, as being unsatisfactory (*anassāsikaṃ*) and not necessarily true, even when the reasoning is sound. The Buddha says that one should not accept a view on the basis of pure reasoning (*mā takka-hetu*) for there could be either mistakes in logic (*sutakkitam pi hoti duttakkitam pi hoti*; *M.* I, 520) or even otherwise the findings of such reasoning may or may not be true of external reality (*tathā pi hoti aññathā pi hoti, ibid.*). This is, in fact, a very modern view.

But it is important to note that there is another sense of consistency recognized in the Canonical texts. This is the consistency between the behaviour of a person and his statements. In this sense it is claimed that the Buddha 'practised what He preached and preached what He practised' (*yathāvādi tathākāri, yathākāri tathāvādi*; *It.* 122). One does not normally speak of this kind of consistency as *logical* consistency; but when Toynbee says that 'the Buddha was an illogical evangelist',[1] and speaks of His 'sublime inconsistency' (*op. cit.*, p. 64) or 'sublimely illogical practice' (*op. cit.*, p. 73) he is using 'illogical'

[1] A. Toynbee, *An Historian's Approach to Religion* (London, O.U.P. 1956), p. 77.

in this novel sense. Toynbee's conclusions are based on a faulty understanding of the Canonical texts and as we have shown elsewhere some of his criticisms have already been forestalled and met in the Pali Canon itself.[1]

There is also a reference to 'partial truths' (*paccekasacca*) in the Canon. Some religious teachers, it is said, comprehend part of the nature of man and his destiny in the universe and mistakenly assume that this is the whole truth. For instance, according to the description given of the origin of a theistic religious philosophy in the *Brahmajāla Sutta* a person from the world of Brahmā (one believed to be a Personal Creator God) is born on earth, lives a homeless life, practises meditation and sees the heavenly world from which he came but does not see beyond. He concludes that Heaven and earth and all in it was created by the person who is adored as 'God, the Mighty God, the Omnipotent, the All-seeing, the Ruler, the Lord of all, the Maker, the Creator, the Most High, the Ordainer and Almighty Father of beings that are and are to be' (*D.* I, 18). This is cited as a typical case where the partial and limited experience of a mystic forms the basis of a generalization applied to all reality. The conclusions are said to be wrong but the limited value and validity of the experience is not denied. The diversity of religious theories is attributed to the universalization of limited experiences valid in their own sphere. The parable of the blind men and the elephant is narrated to illustrate this fact. A number of men born blind are assembled by the king who instructs that they be made to touch an elephant. They touch various parts of the elephant such as the forehead, ears, tusks, etc. They are then asked to describe the elephant and each reports mistaking the part for the whole that the elephant was like that portion of the elephant, which was felt by them (*Udāna*, 68).

So truth is what corresponded with fact and was consistent although whatever is consistent is not necessarily true; for a pack of lies could very well be consistent. Partial truths had a partly factual basis.

[1] Vide K. N. Jayatilleke, 'A Recent Criticism of Buddhism' in *Univ. of Ceylon Review*, Vol. 15, Nos. 3 and 4, pp. 136 ff.

The Buddhist conception of truth has also been called pragmatic. Poussin says[1]: '*Nous avons défini l'ancienne dogmatique comme une doctrine essentiellement "pragmatique"* . . .' (We have defined the ancient teaching as a doctrine essentially 'pragmatic'). But it is necessary to clarify the sense in which it is pragmatic. It is not pragmatic in the narrow utilitarian sense of the word for although in the classification of different types of propositions no mention is made of propositions which are both false and useful, true propositions could be either useful or useless in the Buddhist sense of the term as being 'conducive to one's spiritual welfare' or not.

Man should give ear to true propositions which are useful in this sense and not fritter away his energies in trying to solve metaphysical questions, pertaining to the origin and extent of the universe, for instance, which have no bearing on the moral and spiritual life. The parable of the arrow illustrates this well when it says that a man struck with a poisoned arrow should be concerned with removing the arrow and getting well rather than be interested in purely theoretical questions (about the nature of the arrow, who shot it, etc.), which have no practical utility. In the Siṃsapa forest the Buddha takes a handful of leaves and says that what He has taught is as little as the leaves in His hand and that what He knew but did not teach is like the leaves in the forest (*S*. V, 437). He did not teach these things because 'they were not useful, not related to the fundamentals of religion and not conducive to revulsion, dispassion, cessation, peace, higher knowledge, realization and Nirvana' (*M*. I, 431). The parable of the raft has the same motive and is intended to indicate the utilitarian character of the truths of Buddhism in a spiritual sense. The Buddha says: 'I preach you a Dhamma comparable to a raft for the sake of crossing over and not for the sake of clinging to it . . .' (*M*. I, 134). A person intending to cross a river and get to the other bank, where it is safe and secure, makes a raft and with its help safely reaches the other bank but however useful the raft may have been, he would throw it aside and go his way without carrying it on his shoulders; so it is said that 'those who realize the Dhamma to be like

[1] *Bouddhisme*, 3rd edn (Paris, 1925), p. 129.

a raft should discard the Dhamma as well, not to speak of what is not Dhamma' (*M*. I, 135). The value of the Dhamma lies in its utility and it ceases to be useful though it does not cease to be true when one has achieved one's purpose with its help by attaining salvation.

While moral and spiritual truths are useful (*atthasaṃhitaṃ*) and truth is not defined in terms of utility, it seems to have been held that the claim of a belief to be true was to be tested in the light of personally verifiable consequences. Thus the truth of rebirth is to be verified by developing the memory of pre-existence (*pubbenivāsānussati*). Verifiability in the light of experience, sensory and extra-sensory, is considered a characteristic of truth but what is thus claimed to be true is considered to be true only by virtue of its 'correspondence with fact' (*yathābhūtaṃ*). Thus verifiability is a test of truth but does not itself constitute truth.

Many of the important truths of Buddhism are considered to lie between two extreme points of view. Extreme realism which says that 'everything exists' (*sabbaṃ atthīti*) is one extreme and extreme nihilism which asserts that 'nothing exists' (*sabbaṃ natthī ti*) is the other extreme—the truth lies in the middle (*S*. II, 76). The dogma of personal immortality (*sassatadiṭṭhi*) is one extreme and the dogma of annihilationism (*ucchedadiṭṭhi*) is the other (*S*. III, 98). Similar antinomies are the Materialist conception that the body and the soul are not different and the Dualist conception that they are different (*S*. II, 60), the Determinist thesis that everything is conditioned by past factors (*sabbam pubbekatahetu*) and the Indeterminist thesis that nothing is due to causes and conditions (*sabbam ahetu appaccaya*; *A*, I, 173). The view that we are entirely personally responsible for our unhappiness and the opposite view that we are not at all responsible for our unhappiness (*S*. II, 20), extreme hedonism (*kāmasukhallikānuyogo*) and extreme asceticism (*attakilamathānuyogo*) (*S*. IV, 330). In all these instances it is said that the Buddha 'without falling into these two extremes preaches the Dhamma in the middle'. Thus the mean between two extreme views is held to be true. The 'middle way' (*majjhimā paṭipadā*) which is a mean both in

79

the matter of belief as well as of conduct is said to 'make for knowledge . . . and bring about intuition and realization' (*M.* I, 15). That these truths lie in the middle, seems to be a contingent fact to be discovered empirically.

A distinction that gained currency in the scholastic period but which has its origin in the Canon itself is the contrast between conventional truth (*sammuti-sacca*) and absolute truth (*paramattha-sacca*). It is said that 'just as much as the word "chariot" is used when the parts are put together in order, there is the conventional use (*sammuti*) of the term "being" when the psycho-physical constituents are present' (*S.* I, 135). The statement 'there is a being' is true in reference to a person only in the conventional sense for there is no entity or substance (soul) in reality corresponding to the word 'being'. Therefore, it would be false or meaningless to say 'there is a being' in an absolute sense. The reality of the empirical individual is not denied. The Buddha is quite emphatic on this point. In the *Poṭṭhapāda Sutta* where the question is discussed He approves of His interlocutor's statement: 'I did exist in the past, not that I did not; I will exist in the future, not that I will not, and I do exist in the present, not that I do not' (*D.* I, 200). Only it does not make sense to speak of a substantial soul or entity in the absolute sense since such a soul or entity is not verifiable. We can compare this distinction with the contrast that is sometimes made by scientists between the conventional commonsense point of view and the scientific point of view. As a scientist says, 'the kitchen sink, like all the objects surrounding us, is a convenient abstraction'.[1]

[1] Sherman K. Stein, *Mathematics* (San Francisco and London, W. H. Freeman & Co., 1963).

3. THE BUDDHIST CONTRIBUTION TO PHILOSOPHIC THOUGHT

PROF. E. A. BURTT

Sage Professor of Philosophy, Cornell University

Ten or fifteen years from now, if I am still in the land of the living, I shall hope to write something more substantial on this topic. To do so would require that one achieve a broad perspective on the history of thought, in the West and in the East, and that he adequately assess the long run significance of Buddhism with its various schools when viewed in such a perspective. What I offer in this paper is my best present surmise as to the main conclusions that more sustained and mature reflection would approve.

In developing this anticipatory surmise I shall sketch four ideas, each of which seems to me highly likely to play an important part in such an assessment. With one partial exception, I believe that these ideas were present in Gautama's own philosophy. And, so far as I can tell, they were original with Him, in the form in which I shall describe them and in their significant challenge to philosophy. I do not wholly agree with all of them; what I mean in emphasizing them is that philosophers, especially in the West, need to ponder them with utmost seriousness; no philosophy which has failed to understand them and to meet their challenge can hope to stand.

PART I

The first of these ideas is that philosophy, in its investigations, its analyses, and its explanations, must start from where we are rather than from somewhere else. Now, when expressed in such a general form, this idea is far from unique with Buddhism; much Chinese thinking, especially in the Confucian tradition, assumes this principle, and what the West calls 'empirical' philosophy has consciously accepted it. One of the questions confidently asked by empiricists through the centuries is: Where else can we start than from experience?

But human experience is so defective and untidy, in so many

F

ways, that keen thinkers in every age have been sorely tempted to start with something else—something neater, simpler, more rational, more perfect—and to conceive experience as the product of this something else. Different schools of thinkers succumb to this temptation in different ways; let us briefly review a few of them.

Religious thinkers wish to begin (and also to end) with God, or Brahman. Convinced as they are that He alone is eternally real and that all else in existence depends on Him, this seems to them the only reasonable conclusion to draw. It is presumptuous, they will admit, for man in his finitude to assume that he can see things from the standpoint of the Ultimate, yet, since an explanation from that standpoint would alone be true, one must make the best attempt that he can. Thinkers who incline toward materialism wish to start with the atoms—the simple units which are the building blocks of the physical universe—together with the modes of their combination. These, they are sure, last for ever, while all the experienced compounds that arise from them sooner or later pass away. Thinkers who find their haven in the realm of logic and mathematics wish to start with the abstract entities and the fully rational laws there revealed. They do not see how the world of experience can be analysed or explained in any other way than in terms of this logical structure.

Nonetheless, is there any reason to suppose that experience must submit to any of these demands? It is what it is, and if we wish to understand we must avoid imposing any dubious requirements upon it, however reasonable those requirements might seem to be.

It is at just this point that the Buddha's interpretation of the principle: Let us start from where we are, is peculiarly challenging. Chinese acceptance of the axiom never quite worked free from limitations due to the Chinese cultural heritage; it was frankly or subtly pervaded by the conviction that experience as we now confront it is a lapse from the Golden Age of Yao and Shun and needs to recover that lost ideal. Western philosophies of experience have been haunted by provincial and transitory notions of what sort of process experience is. Hume—

the most influential empirical thinker of the past—thought it must be a temporal sequence of 'impressions' and 'ideas', as he conceived those mental phenomena. More recent empiricists have reduced experience to 'sense data' in their relational patterns, boldly assuming all that is involved in this complex and questionable concept.

As I interpret Him, Gautama realized quite clearly that 'starting where we are' cannot be a purely passive principle like that of Western empiricism but must express an active interpretation of experience; He realized also that if it is to give effective guidance it must be freed so far as possible from any limitations of time or place. Experience must be conceived in universal human terms—in terms of factors that are basic in the daily living of people everywhere and always. What this meant concretely in His mind was twofold. On the one hand, we must approach experience as an unqualifiedly dynamic affair incapable of being understood in relation to any static goal or any fixed structural forms. On the other hand, we must approach it as a process in which men and women are groping toward the conditions of stable and secure well-being, away from the confused mixture of suffering, numbness, frustration, and transitory happiness in which they now exist. He was confident that sound axioms of analysis and of explanation would grow out of the confrontation of experience in these terms, and in no other way.

I am sure that the challenge of this idea has by no means been fully appreciated, either by the philosophies of the East or by those of the West. So far as the West is concerned, the notion of starting where we are has been so deeply affected by the assumptions of empirical science that attempts to conceive experience in any richer and more inclusive way have faced almost insuperable handicaps. So far as India is concerned, it has been impossible for most of her philosophic minds to escape from domination by the fixed conviction that since Brahman is the only unqualified reality, experience must somehow be explained or construed in relation to it. Many among them will admit that this quest cannot hope to succeed—all our categories of interpretation apply within the phenomenal

83

world but not to the relation between that world and the transcendent reality. They will also admit that even if it could succeed, the explanation reached would have meaning only to the saints who have realized union with Brahman; but they need no explanation—they have left behind the state in which searching for a logical system to encase the world is an insistent demand. It is not a bold conclusion then that the Buddha's position will continue to exert a profound challenge until both Western and Eastern philosophies have taken its claims more soberly into account than they thus far have.

PART II

The second of these four ideas is the one usually referred to as Buddha's agnosticism[1] with respect to metaphysical problems— His deep conviction that one should avoid attachment to any particular solution of these issues, and that when we need to refer to what lies beyond present experience it should be in terms of its contrast with what experience discloses rather than in terms of supposedly common factors.

The very provocative challenge of this idea is brought out most sharply when one considers it in relation to the points of view in Western thought that have most nearly filled a similar role—namely, the agnosticism of the last seventy-five years, the skepticisms of earlier philosophy, and the doctrine that in view of the limits of rational knowledge some form of faith is ultimately valid.

Late nineteenth-century agnosticism, as represented by T. H. Huxley, was a consequence of assuming the exhaustive competence of empirical science so far as knowledge is concerned. The only knowledge man can attain (so it was firmly believed) is the knowledge that is verifiable by science, hence in the case of metaphysical and theological questions that by their very nature lie beyond such verification, the only justifiable position is to hold that we cannot know which answer to

---

[1] The term 'agnosticism', implying ignorance on the Buddha's part, is not of course acceptable to Buddhists. But the Buddha did, for reasons indicated by the author, maintain an attitude which could (wrongly) be construed as agnosticism. (*Editor*).

them is the true one. The positivism of our century rests on the same foundations, but adopts the more extreme contention that these questions are not merely unanswerable but are even sense-less. A question whose scientific verification is impossible is no genuine question; it is just a series of words. As for the skep-tics of ancient and of early modern times, they did not restrict their drastic criticism to trans-empirical matters; the more redoubtable among them, at least, believed it possible to under-mine any conclusions drawn by reason. And in their case there seems to have been no positive insight to which this devastating criticism was expected to lead. With those who have been eager to limit rational knowledge so as to leave room for religious faith, there is the necessity of facing a difficult dilemma. Either the faith is entirely discontinuous with the operations of reason, in which case the acceptance of one form of faith rather than another would seem to be a purely blind commitment; or else it is continuous with them, in which case the positive relation between faith and knowledge needs to be clearly defined. Religious thinkers in the West have found it very hard to form-ulate a persuasive position with regard to this dilemma.

The Buddha's agnosticism, I believe, is different from any of these viewpoints and avoids the specific difficulties that each of them confronts.

I find no adequate support for the conclusion that Gautama condemned speculative thinking as such. His agnosticism was the expression of three fundamental convictions. First, there was the conviction implied by the major idea above described, that beliefs about questions lying beyond experience are irrele-vant to the real problems of life, and if our minds worry about them attention is inevitably distracted from the issues on which we crucially need a solution. We need to understand ourselves, in our aspiration to end suffering, and to find the dependable conditions of well-being; it will take all the intellectual energy we possess to carry out successfully this task. He was sure, therefore, that He must discourage those whose keenness of mind tempts them into metaphysical speculation from wasting their precious powers in this fashion.

Second, there was the conviction, constantly confirmed by

observation, that those who become attached to this or that metaphysical doctrine tend to make dogmatic claims for it and to engage in argumentative wrangling with those who hold a different position. Now, on the one hand, it seemed to Him clear that this unhappy outcome is unavoidable, once one devotes himself to answering these questions; thinkers will be enticed by different theories about them, and since they are trans-empirical there is no way of establishing objectively one proposed solution as against others. On the other hand, it was clear that this outcome, far from leading toward release from self-centred craving, reveals an unfortunate form of bondage to it. Such a situation shows that metaphysical doctrines are intrinsically incapable of being asserted in serenity and compassion, and if this is the case they should not be asserted at all. Only the truth that can be spoken in love—the truth that ends discord rather than fosters it—is really truth.

Third, there was the final conviction that even when these difficulties are avoided any attempt to refer in positive terms to that which transcends our present experience is bound to be misleading, and to show effects which will obstruct our quest for liberation. A person who is fully thinking to start from where we are, and is also ready to centre his intellectual powers on the real problem of life, finds that at one point he will need to speak of that which lies beyond experience, and to relate it in the most clarifying fashion he can to experience as we now find ourselves immersed in it. He will need a term by which to refer to the goal toward which spiritual growth is leading; he must answer questions as to what it is that will have been achieved when the process of liberation is complete. But even at this point serious difficulties arise if such questions are answered in positive terms. Shall he say that peace will have been achieved, or joy, or love? To say this would be true, not false. However, to say it would be misleading, and perhaps seriously so. Anyone to whom it is said will inevitably interpret the meaning of these words in the light of his experience to date. But if he is still in bondage to blind and selfish craving the meaning he will give them is infected throughout by that bondage. He will think of peace as the hoped-for quiescence achieved when his longings

have been satisfied; he will imagine joy as the pleasurable con-
comitant of such a state; love will mean his devoted attachment
to this or that person whose help he needs in the quest for these
satisfactions. The radically different qualities that these words
would denote to one who has achieved liberation are completely
beyond him. But what would happen if, under these circumstances, he were encouraged to dwell hopefully on these words, and
to indulge freely in the images they suggest to his mind? He
would try more zealously than ever to satisfy his immature
desires and thus to realize these goals as he now pictures them,
instead of being inspired to strive toward the superior state
that can be achieved only when such desires are laid aside. For
this reason the true goal must be described in negative terms—
it is *Nirvana*. Not *Nirvana* in the sense of utter extinction, but
Nirvana as the state in which the blind, demanding turmoil
that has enslaved the person seeking liberation has been rooted
out.

On Buddha's carefully considered presuppositions, there is
no escape from a thorough-going agnosticism in this form.
Perhaps the philosophic world will find that He was right.

PART III

The third of these ideas grows directly out of this agnosticism.
I shall put it in the form of a paradoxical question. Is the only
sound philosophy a form of no-philosophy? So far as I can tell,
nothing quite comparable to this idea has appeared in the West.
The ancient skeptics, who exemplified something verbally
similar, did not share the further insight that is essential to
this idea in its Buddhist guise; nor does Ludwig Wittgenstein,
who in his famous *Tractatus* holds that all one can really do in
relation to other philosophers is to wait till they say something
and then show that they have actually said nothing.[1] And, so
far as I can tell also, this idea was not definitely adopted by
Gautama Himself. In Him we meet an approach to it in the
silence that He sometimes maintained in the presence of metaphysical questionings—at least when the meaning of that silence
is considered in relation to His readiness to deal with all inquirers

[1] *Tractatus Logico-Philosophicus* (London, 1922), pp. 187f.

on their own ground. This readiness betokened a remarkable capacity to probe their perplexities in full awareness of individual differences and thus in a way most likely to be helpfully clarifying to each person. The idea comes before us full grown and articulate only in the *Mādhyamika* Philosophy of Nāgārjuna and his great successors.

Granted the basic Buddhist assumptions, what is the real task of philosophy? It cannot be, of course, what most philosophers have supposed, namely, to reach solutions to speculative questions. In general terms, the answer is that its function is to contribute, in the way systematic intellectual analysis can, to the guidance of seekers for ultimate liberation. But how should it do this with specific reference to the great issues that philosophers perennially raise? As I interpret the *Mādhyamika* thinkers, they are confident that they understand the reason for His way of dealing with metaphysical questions and are revealing it more fully than He did. Their crucial conviction here is a very simple one. It is that the quest for a positive answer to puzzles about the nature of reality is not an expression of the aspiration toward spiritual perfection; however subtle the disguise may be, it is an exhibition of compulsive demands that need to be overcome, not satisfied. These demands are characteristic of intellectually keen minds; they represent the kind of obstruction to the full achievement of liberation to which such minds are peculiarly apt to succumb.

What then should be done about these speculative cravings? Essentially, to discourage those who are seduced by them from expecting their satisfaction, and to entice them to seek instead the kind of spiritual insight that needs no rational articulation and is, indeed, capable of none. This, of course, cannot be accomplished by a hostile attack on their transcendental searchings, so natural to persons of great logical power, nor by a refutation of their major conclusions which rests on some alternative set of theoretical assumptions. Such attacks would only provoke them to a more ardent attachment to the obstructive notions that symbolize and express their enslavement. What this programme calls for is, rather, that one compassionately place himself within the framework in which their self-deceptive

88

thinking moves, and show, by a fuller logical unfolding of their premises than because of their bondage they could achieve, that there are inherent contradictions in all the explanatory categories that they confidently employ. To carry out such a task of internal criticism requires that the thinker pursuing it on the one hand, show himself as competent in systematic philosophical analysis as those whom he is criticizing, and that, on the other hand, he have attained a deeper level of spiritual insight, so that his radical criticisms may express the loving understanding without which their constructive promise would be lost. And it means also, that, in intent, at least, he is setting up no alternative philosophical system in place of the refuted systems of others. Were he to do this he would himself have fallen prey to the temptations that have misled those whose doctrines and hopes he has swept away.

I can think of no more searching challenge to philosophers of the West than is contained in this idea, and thinkers of the East also need to square themselves more profoundly with it than most of them as yet have done.

PART IV

The fourth of these ideas is one which underlies each of the other three, and hence may be stated quite briefly. This is the idea that theoretical inquiry is not independent of practical action, as keen thinkers are prone to suppose, but is itself one factor in human action—the factor in virtue of which any action can be consciously guided instead of expressing a purely blind urge.

Now the West has produced pragmatic philosophies which have stressed this principle, and Eastern thought has been influenced by it to a very large extent. But I believe that in His way of conceiving it Gautama caught a rather distinctive insight, which not too many even among His own followers have fully shared. The pragmatism of John Dewey, a generation ago in the West, expressed a clear insistence that theory is one aspect of practice, whose role is to give it intelligent guidance, but in Dewey this insight reflected the limitations of his time and place. Especially was it confined by the orientation of Western

89

empirical science and by the social reforms that in Dewey's mind constitute the only sound goals of practical action. In the East this kind of limitation has, of course, been absent. Nonetheless, most non-Buddhist modes of thought, and not a few Buddhist ones, have been captive to traditional Eastern notions as to what sort of thing practical action must be and how intellectual inquiry is related to it.

It seems to me that Gautama's insight here included two features, one of which was expressed in clearer and more radical form than His predecessors had given it, and the other was probably original with Him. As for the former, I am thinking of the thoroughly dynamic conception of experience and, therefore, of human action that has already been mentioned. One consequence of this conception was that intellectual searching itself is interpreted in terms of this dynamic framework; far from being the halting expression within finite experience of a changeless transcendent consciousness, it exhibits the interaction of the same combining and separating forces that other modes of action reveal. As for the latter feature, I believe Gautama must have apprehended a principle whose implications for a theory of truth are, at least, equally radical. Certainly His own compassionate action, in relation to inquirers who came to Him, was constantly guided by this principle. It grows out of the recognition that whatever one says to another person, whether one is aware of it or not, has practical effects in the experience and action of that person. In particular, it either has the effect of eliciting his constructive capacities and fostering his growth toward spiritual freedom, or the contrary effect of confusing his emotions, dulling his aspiration, and stimulating his attachment to deceptive beliefs. Now so far as a speaker has gained liberation himself, he will be alertly aware of these effects, and his dominant motive will be so to speak, in everyone's presence, as to express a compassionate concern for the listener's dynamic growth toward unfettered well-being. All his philosophic thinking and every item in its verbal expression will be guided by this concern; it will be a part of the discovering, exploring, creative action which his whole experience in relation to every living creature will exemplify.

This idea is the most searching and challenging of the four I have sketched. Its drastic implication for philosophy may be succinctly stated in the principle that truth must be a dynamic and loving truth if it is to be truth at all.

In conclusion, I do not feel sure at present what qualifications in the case of each of these ideas are needed if they are to enter into the enduring deposit of man's philosophic reflection. But I do feel sure that such qualifications will only be accurately formulated when thinkers, both Eastern and Western, have pondered these ideas with the deepest sensitivity and the most adventurous vision of which they are capable.

III. BUDDHISM AND SCIENCE

PROF. K. N. JAYATILLEKE

BUDDHISM AND THE SCIENTIFIC REVOLUTION

It is an historical fact that the scientific revolution which took its rise in the seventeenth century in the West was largely responsible for upsetting the earlier religious conception of the universe. Not only did science controvert the specific dogmas of Western religion, but it seemed to have undermined the foundations as well as the fundamental concepts implicit in the religious outlook on things.

The new cosmology of Copernicus, Galileo, and their successors altered the geocentric picture of the universe although it was pronounced to be 'contrary to the Holy Scriptures'. The new biology (the theory of evolution) upset the doctrines of the special creation and the fall of man. And the new psychology seemed to show that man's mind like his physical body worked on a pattern of causal law and that however deep one plumbed into its depths there was not discoverable in it an unchanging soul which governed its activities entire.

But much more serious was the effect of the scientific outlook on the general religious attitude which involved a belief in a Personal God, in purpose and in the objectivity of moral values. Science made its discoveries and progressed quite comfortably on the assumption of universal causation without the necessity for teleological explanations or divine intervention. It dealt with an amoral universe indifferent to the aspirations of men. As among men, moral values like economic values were subjective since they were dependent on the needs and desires of men, and an ethical humanism was the best that could be hoped for.

Even such an ethics need not be universal for, as anthropologists discovered, different societies seem to have followed different moral codes which suited them and ethical relativism was the scientific truth about the nature of moral values.

Of course there are those who still cling to the dogmas in the face of science or believe in them in a non-literal sense. But the position remains very much the same although people are no longer optimistic (after two world wars and in the throes of a third) about the ability of science to usher in a brave new world of peace and plenty. It has also been granted that mechanistic explanations of the universe need not necessarily rule out teleological ones. Science too has given up the crude materialism of the eighteenth century and scientists no longer attempt to explain the universe on machine models, while some scientists have denied that strict determinism holds in the sphere of the atom. But all this is still a far cry from religion.

What place would Buddhism occupy in such a context? Are its dogmas and attitudes no better or no worse than those of any other religion? Some Western writers on religion seem to have assumed that this was so, but if one reads through the Buddhist texts, one begins to wonder whether the scientific revolution would have at all affected religion adversely if it had taken place in the context of Early Buddhism.

I say this because I find that Early Buddhism emphasizes the importance of the scientific outlook in dealing with the problems of morality and religion. Its specific 'dogmas' are said to be capable of verification. And its general account of the nature of man and the universe is one that accords with the findings of science rather than being at variance with them.

To take this last point first, we find for instance that the Early Buddhist conception of the cosmos is in essence similar to the modern conception of the universe. In the Pali texts that have come down to us we are literally told that hundreds and thousands of suns and moons, earths, and higher worlds, constitute the minor world system, that a hundred thousand times this is the middling world system, and a hundred thousand times the middling world system is the major world system. In modern terminology it would seem as if a minor world

93

system (*cūlanikā-loka-dhātu*) is a galaxy of which we observe about a hundred million through our best telescopes. The Buddhist conception of time is equally immense.

There is, of course, no theory of biological evolution as such mentioned in the Buddhist texts, but man and society as well as worlds are pictured as changing and evolving in accordance with causal laws.

Then in psychology we find Early Buddhism regarding man as a psycho-physical unit whose 'psyche' is not a changeless soul but a dynamic continuum composed of a conscious mind as well as an unconscious in which are stored the residua of emotionally charged memories going back to childhood as well as into past lives. Such a mind is said to be impelled to act under the influence of three types of desires—the desire for sense-gratification (*kāma-taṇhā*), the desire for self-preservation (*bhava-taṇhā*) and the desire for destruction (*vibhava-taṇhā*). Except for the belief in rebirth, this conception of the mind sounds very modern, and one cannot also fail to observe the parallel between the threefold desires of Buddhism and the Freudian conceptions of the eros, libido, and thanatos.

I have brought out these similarities not with the intention of showing that Buddhism teaches modern science but that the scientific revolution does not have the same adverse effect on Buddhism as it had on another religious tradition.

Now let us turn to the content of Buddhism as a theory about the nature and destiny of man. First of all it holds that the honest and impartial search for truth even in matters moral and religious is no bar to one's spiritual progress. On more than one occasion the Buddha has admonished honest seekers after the truth in the following words:

'You have raised a doubt in a situation in which you ought to suspend your judgement. Do not accept anything because it is rumoured so, because it is the traditional belief, because the majority hold to it, because it is found in the scriptures, because it is the product of metaphysical argument and speculation, or after a superficial investigation of facts, or because it conforms with one's inclinations, because it is authoritative or because of the prestige value of your teacher.'

Critical investigation and personal verification was to be the guide to true morality and religion. 'If anyone were to speak ill of me, my doctrine and my order', says the Buddha,

'do not bear any ill-will towards him, be upset or perturbed at heart, for if you were to be so it will only cause you harm. If on the other hand anyone were to speak well of me, my doctrine and my order, do not be overjoyed, thrilled or elated at heart, for if so it will only be an obstacle in your way of forming a correct judgement as to whether the qualities praised in us are real and actually found in us.'

A scientific outlook was thus considered necessary not only for discovering the truly moral and religious life but even for the continual self-examination which such a life demands.

The field of moral and religious phenomena is, again, not a realm of mystery but one in which the law of cause and effect holds. The principle of causal determination, namely, that A is the cause of B if 'whenever an event A an event B occurs, and B does not occur unless A has occurred' is laid down by the Buddha in these very terms, and he further states that 'he speaks only of causes and of things which arise from causes'. Thus all phenomena, including moral and spiritual experience (with the sole exception of Nirvāna which is not a conditioned phenomenon) are said to be conditioned by causal laws. Such laws are classified according to their sphere of operation as physical laws (*utuniyāma*) biological laws (*bījaniyāma*) psychological laws (*cittaniyāma*) and moral and spiritual laws (*dhammaniyāma*).

Now there are three laws which are said to govern the life and destiny of the individual. They are the law of continuity which makes for the persistence of individuality (*bhava*), the law of moral retribution (*karma*) whereby morally good acts tend to result in pleasant consequences for the individual and morally evil acts in unpleasant consequences, and finally, the

95

law of causal genesis (*paṭiccasamuppāda*) which is intended to explain the above two laws.

The law of continuity, popularly known as rebirth, ensures the persistence of the dynamic unconscious of the individual with the death of the physical body. If this unconscious is not attuned to higher worlds by the moral and spiritual development of the individual, it is said generally to persist in the spirit-sphere (*petti-visaya*) as a discarnate spirit, and subsequently get reborn as a human being. Critics of Buddhism often suggest that this theory of rebirth is dogmatically accepted or taken for granted in Buddhism, but a careful study of the texts, would show that this is not the case.

Buddhism arose at a time when there was intense speculation on the problem of survival. There were also several schools of materialism all of which denied survival altogether and there were the sceptics who merely doubted the possibility of survival. Even experiments such as the weighing of the body immediately before and after death were performed in order to discover any evidence of survival. One of the materialist theories mentioned and dismissed by the Buddha was that consciousness was a by-product of the material elements being mixed up in certain proportions to form the organic body 'in the same way in which the red colour is produced by suitable mixtures of betel, are-canut and lime' (none of which is red). Several such materialist theories as well as a number of one-life-after-death-theories, some of which held that the soul was conscious after death, others that it was unconscious (but existing), and yet others that it was super-conscious after death, are examined and disposed of by the Buddha. The theory of rebirth is offered as one capable of being verified by developing the faculty of seeing our former births, a potentiality which is said to be within the reach of all of us.

Rebirth is therefore not a dogma to be accepted on faith but a hypothesis capable of being scientifically verified. The available evidence for rebirth today is roughly of two sorts. There is the spontaneous evidence of numerous people from both East and West who have claimed to remember their past lives, in some cases of which the memories have been confirmed by further investigation (e.g. The case of Shanti Devi, *Illustrated Weekly of India*, December 15, 1935; The case of Nellie Horster, *Milwaukee Sentinel*, September 25, 1892). There is also the more reliable and more abundant evidence of psychiatrists and psychologists who have discovered that under hypnotic trance the subject's memories can be traced back not only to childhood but to prior earth lives as well, in some cases of which the facts have been verified (e.g. A. de Rochas, *Les Vies Successives*, Bibliothèque Charcomac, Paris; Ralph Shirley, *The Problem of Rebirth*, Rider & Co., London; Professor Théodore Flournoy, *Des Indes à la planète Mars*; Professor Charles E. Cory, 'A Divided Self', in *Journal of Abnormal Psychology*, Vol. XIV, 1919).

The law of moral retribution or karma as taught in Buddhism has also been criticized on the grounds that it amounts to fatalism. This again is due to ignorance of the Buddhist teaching. Causation in Buddhism is carefully distinguished by the Buddha, on the one hand from Strict Determinism and on the other from Indeterminism. The Buddha argues that if everything was determined, then there would be no free will and no moral or spiritual life would be possible and we would be slaves of the past: and if on the other hand everything was indetermined (*adhicca-samuppanna*) or fortuitous, then again the moral and spiritual life would not be possible, for the cultivation of moral and spiritual values would not result in moral and spiritual growth. It is because the world is so constituted that everything is not strictly determined or completely indetermined that the religious life is possible and desirable, according to the Buddha.

In order to explain rebirth and karma, some of the Upanishadic thinkers who accepted these doctrines had recourse to the concept of *ātman* or a changeless soul. The individual continued to be the same because he had a permanent soul which was the agent of all the actions of the individual as well as the experiencer of their fruits. The Buddha was quick to see that such metaphysical entities explained nothing and that it was meaningless to assert or deny an unverifiable entity. He therefore rejected the concept of soul while maintaining the doctrine

G

of the observable continuity of the individuality, and explained the above two laws of continuity and moral retribution in terms of all the verifiable phenomenal factors which determine the continued genesis and growth of the individual. This is too elaborate to be set out in detail. In brief, it describes how the individual is conditioned by his psychological past (going back to past lives which set the general tone of his character) and the genetical constitution of his body derived from his parents, and continues to act in and react with his environment accumulating the experiences of this life in his evolving consciousness (*samvattanika-viññāṇa*) which continues after the death of the body if the threefold desires in it be still active.

Personal and direct knowledge of the operation of these three laws constitutes the 'threefold knowledge' (*tissovijjā*) which the Buddha and his disciples claimed to have. The awareness of the fact that and the way in which one is being conditioned is said to result in one ceasing to be conditioned, a state which corresponds to the attainment of the unconditioned and supreme felicity of Nirvana. This is salvation in Buddhism, which is literally salvation from the bondage of finite conditioned existence.

Strictly, Nirvāna is said to be beyond description or conception, the reason given being that it is a state so radically different from the type of existent things which we can conceive of that no meaningful description or definition of it can be given in conceptual terms. It is said that to say that one 'exists' in Nirvana is wrong, for existence is a concept that applies to phenomenal things and has reference to space and time, for Nirvāna is 'timeless, in that one cannot speak of it as being in the past, present or future', is not located in space and is not causally conditioned, unlike all phenomenal things: but it is also said to be equally wrong to say that one 'does not exist' in Nirvāna since this implies a state of oblivion and annihilation. Nevertheless both positive as well as negative descriptions are given though they are not to be taken as exact definitions, as Nirvāna is 'beyond the scope of logic'.

Negatively it is the absence of all unhappiness, and all phenomenal existence is said to be infected with unhappiness;

we are unhappy either because we experience mental or physical pain and have forebodings for the future, or because the pleasant experiences that we have are insecure and never lasting. This is to take a realistic view of life even in the face of the fact that as the Buddha says 'human beings enjoy on the whole more pleasant experiences than unpleasant ones', and therefore it would not be correct to call it pessimism since it has nothing to do with wishful thinking. Positively Nirvana is described as a state of 'supreme felicity' (*paramam-sukham*).

The way of salvation is described as an eightfold path in which the first step is that of right understanding and living in accordance with the true philosophy of life, and as a result having right aspirations, right speech, right actions, right mode of living, and right mindfulness, culminating in the growth of religious joy and the spiritual and intuitive awareness of right meditation or contemplation. The full fruit of right contemplation, however, can be reaped by those giving up the active social life for the contemplative life. This meditative life is characterized by the stages of personal mystical consciousness (*rūpā-jhāna*) and impersonal mystical consciousness (*arūpa-jhāna*) culminating in the attainment of Nirvāna. With the growth of his mind and spirit there are said to emerge certain faculties latent in him such as telepathy and clairvoyance and the ability to see his past lives. These cognitive faculties, as explained earlier, make it possible for the individual to realize the conditioned state in which he is, and thereby to attain the Unconditioned. Considering the requirements of the path, the Way to Nirvana is therefore described as the culmination of a person's moral development (*sīla*), intuitional or spiritual development (*samādhi*) as well as his intellectual or cognitive development (*paññā*). The Buddha was once asked 'whether he hoped to save one-third of the world, one half of the world or the whole world by offering this Way of Salvation', to which he replied that he does not claim to save one-third of humanity, but that just as a skilful doorkeeper guarding the only entrance to the palace knows that all those who seek the haven of this palace must enter by this door, even so all those in the past who were saved, who in the present are being saved

99

and who in the future will be saved, have entered, are entering and will enter by this door.

Such is the teaching of Early Buddhism, whish is offered as a self-consistent scientific hypothesis touching the matters of religion and morality which each person can verify for himself. In fact, not being based on revelation, the fact that it has been verified by him and hundreds of his disciples and is capable of being verified by every earnest seeker is put forward as the criterion of its truth by the Buddha. The empirical and pragmatic test of science is for the Buddha the test of true religion. The faith that he requires is the trust that is required to put to the test a certain philosophy of life by devoting one's entire being to living it every moment of one's life. And its worth is to be realized by its fruits thereof, by each person for himself. Like the scientists working in other fields, the Buddhas or the Perfect Ones have merely discovered these truths which are there for all time and have preached them for the good of the world. Each one has to seek and work out his own salvation; no one can save another and the Perfect Ones do merely point the way.

It would be seen that such a religion is in accord with the temper and the findings of science, so that Buddhism is not likely to be at variance with science so long as scientists confine themselves to their methodology and their respective fields without making a dogma of materialism.

As for purpose, the Buddhist view is that the world as such has no purpose to accomplish though individuals in it may choose their own ends and thus make their lives purposeful; the end recommended by Buddhism being Nirvāna. The Buddha would argue that if the world had a purpose to be attained in a final consummation, then either salvation would be assured for all or some would be foredoomed and damned for eternity; but according to the Buddha there is no necessity or inevitability in progress; no one is destined to attain Nirvāna unless he wished to. But as for moral values Buddhism upholds their objectivity, for according to the Law of karma, a drunkard, for instance, unless he repents (i.e. changes his ways) tends to be reborn as a moron whatever the opinions or wishes of the drunkard or the members of his society may be.

IV. THE POWER OF MINDFULNESS

THE VEN. NYĀNAPONIKA MAHĀTHERA

Is mindfulness actually a power in its own right as claimed by the title of this essay? Seen from the view-point of the ordinary purposes of life it does not seem so. From that angle, mindfulness, or attention, has a rather modest place among many, and seemingly more important, mental faculties that serve the purposes of variegated wish-fulfilment. There, mindfulness means just 'to watch one's step' so that one may not stumble or miss a chance in the pursuit of one's aims. Only in the case of specific tasks and skills is mindfulness sometimes cultivated more deliberately, but here too it is still regarded as a subservient function, and its wider scope and possibilities are not recognized.

Even if one turns to the Buddha's doctrine, taking only a surface view of the various classifications and lists of mental factors in which mindfulness appears, one may be inclined to regard this faculty just 'as one among many', and may get the impression that here too it has a rather subordinate place and is easily surpassed in significance by other faculties.

Mindfulness, in fact, has, if we may personify it, a rather unassuming character. Compared with it mental factors like devotion, energy, imagination or intelligence are certainly 'more colourful personalities', making an immediate and strong impact on people and situations. Their conquests are sometimes rapid and vast, though often insecure. Mindfulness, on the other hand, is of an unobtrusive nature. Its virtues shine inwardly, and in ordinary life most of its merits are passed on to other mental faculties, which generally receive all the credit. One must know it well and cultivate its acquaintance before one can appreciate the value and the silent penetrative influence of mindfulness. Mindfulness walks slowly and deliberately, and its daily task is of a rather humdrum nature. Yet, where it places its feet it cannot easily be dislodged, and it acquires and bestows true mastery of the ground it covers.

Mental faculties of such a nature are, like actual personalities of a similar type, often overlooked or underrated. In the case of mindfulness it required a genius like the Buddha to discover the 'hidden talent' in the modest garb and to develop the vast inherent power of that potent seed. It is, indeed, the mark of a genius to perceive, and to harness, the power of the seemingly small. Here, truly, it happens that 'what is little becomes much'. A revaluation of values takes place. The standards of greatness and smallness change. Through the master mind of the Buddha, mindfulness is finally revealed as the Archimedean point from where the vast revolving mass of the world's suffering is levered out of its two-fold anchorage in Ignorance and Craving.

The Buddha spoke of the power of Mindfulness in a very emphatic way:

'Mindfulness, I declare, is all-helpful.'

(Samy. Nik. 46, 55)

'All things can be mastered by Mindfulness.'

(Angutt.Nik., Aṭṭhaka Nip., 83)

And further, that solemn and weighty utterance opening and concluding the *Satipaṭṭhāna Sutta*, the Discourse on the Foundations of Mindfulness:

'This is the only way, monks, for the purification of beings, for the overcoming of sorrow and lamentation, for the destruction of pain and grief, for reaching the right path, for the attainment of Nibbāna, namely the four Foundations of Mindfulness.'

BARE ATTENTION

If, in ordinary life, mindfulness, or attention, is directed to any object, it is rarely sustained long enough for the purpose of factual observation. Generally it is followed immediately by emotional reaction, discriminative thought, reflection, purposeful action, etc. Also in life and thought governed by the Dhamma, mindfulness (*sati*) is mostly linked with Clear Comprehension (*sampajañña*) of the right purpose, of reality, etc. But for tapping the actual and potential *power* of mindfulness it is necessary to understand and deliberately cultivate it in its basic, unalloyed form, which we shall call 'Bare Attention'.

By Bare Attention we understand the clear and single-minded awareness of what actually happens *to* us and *in* us, at the successive moments of perception. It is called 'bare' because it attends to the bare facts of a perception without reacting to them by deed, speech, or mental comment. Ordinarily, that purely receptive state of mind is, as we have remarked, just a brief phase of the thought process of which one is often scarcely aware. But in the methodical development of mindfulness, aiming at the unfolding of its latent powers, Bare Attention is sustained for as a long a time as one's strength of concentration permits. Bare Attention is the key to the meditative practice of *Satipaṭṭhāna*, opening the door to mind's mastery and final liberation.

Bare Attention is developed in two ways: (1) as a methodical meditative-practice with selected objects; (2) applied, as far as practicable, to the normal events of the day, together with a general attitude of Mindfulness and Clear Comprehension. The details of the practice have been described elsewhere, and need not be repeated here.[1]

The purpose of these pages is, in the first instance, to meet any doubts as to the efficacy of this method, i.e. as to the actual power of mindfulness. Particularly in an age like ours, with its superstitious worship of ceaseless external activity, there will be those who ask: 'How can such a passive attitude of mind as that of Bare Attention possibly lead to the great results claimed for it?' In reply, one may be inclined to suggest to the questioner not to rely on the words of others, but to put those assertions of the Buddha to the test of personal experience. But those who do not yet know the Buddha's teaching well enough to accept it as a reliable guide, may hesitate to take up, without good

[1] See Nyanaponika, *The Heart of Buddhist Meditation* (London, Rider & Co., 1962).

reasons, a practice that, just on account of its radical simplicity, may appear strange to them. In the following, a number of such 'good reasons' are therefore proffered for the reader's scrutiny. They are also meant as an introduction into the general spirit of Satipaṭṭhāna and as pointers to its wide and significant perspectives. Furthermore it is hoped that he who has taken up the methodical training will recognize in the following observations certain features of his own practice and be stimulated in their deliberate cultivation.

FOUR SOURCES OF POWER IN BARE ATTENTION

We shall now deal with four aspects of Bare Attention, which are the mainsprings of the Power of Mindfulness. They are not the only sources of its strength but they are the principal ones to which the efficacy of this method of mental development is due. These four are:

1. the functions of 'tidying-up' and 'naming', exercised by Bare Attention;
2. its non-violent, non-coercive procedure;
3. the capacity of stopping and slowing-down;
4. the directness of vision bestowed by Bare Attention.

1. THE FUNCTIONS OF 'TIDYING' AND 'NAMING'

TIDYING UP THE MENTAL HOUSEHOLD

If anyone whose mind is not harmonized and controlled through methodical meditative training, should take a close look at his own every-day thoughts and activities he will meet with a rather disconcerting sight. Apart from the few main channels of his purposeful thoughts and activities, he will everywhere be faced with a tangled mass of perceptions, thoughts, feelings, casual bodily movements, etc., showing a disorderliness and confusion which he would certainly not tolerate, e.g. in his living-room. Yet this is the state of affairs that he takes for granted within a considerable portion of his waking life and normal mental activity. Let us now look at the details of that rather untidy picture.

First we meet a vast number of casual sense-impressions, sights, sounds, etc., that pass constantly through our mind. Most of them remain vague and fragmentary, and some are even based on faulty perceptions, misjudgements, etc. Carrying these inherent weaknesses they often form the untested basis for judgements and decisions on a higher level of consciousness. True, all these casual impressions need not and cannot be objects of focussed attention. A stone on our road that happens to meet our glance, will have a claim on our attention only if it obstructs our progress or is of interest to us for any other reason. Yet, if we neglect too much these casual impressions, we may stumble over many an actual, or figurative, stone, and overlook many a gem lying on our road.

Next, there are those more significant and definite perceptions, thoughts, feelings, volitions, etc., which have a closer connection with our purposeful life. Here too we shall find that a very high proportion of them is in a state of utter confusion. Hundreds of cross currents flash through the mind, and everywhere there are 'bits and ends' of unfinished thoughts, stifled emotions, passing moods, etc. Many of them meet a premature death owing to their innate feeble nature, our lack of concentration, or through being suppressed by new and stronger impressions. If we observe our own mind, we shall notice how easily diverted our thoughts are, and how often they behave like undisciplined disputants constantly interrupting each other and refusing to listen to the other side's arguments. Again, many lines of thought remain rudimentary or are left untranslated into will and action, because courage is lacking to accept the practical, moral or intellectual consequences of these thoughts. If we continue to examine closer the reliability of our average perceptions, thoughts or judgements we shall have to admit that many of them are just the products of habit, led by prejudices of intellect and emotion, by our pet preferences or aversions, by laziness and selfishness, by faulty or superficial observations, and so on.

Such a look into long-neglected quarters of the mind will come as a wholesome shock to the observer. It will convince him of the urgent need for methodical mental culture extending not only to a thin surface-layer of the mind, but also to those vast twilight regions of consciousness to which we have now paid a brief visit. The observer will then become aware of the fact that a reliable standard of the inner strength and lucidity of consciousness in its totality cannot be derived from the relatively small sector of the mind that stands in the intense light of purposeful will and thought; nor can it be judged by a few optimal results of mental activity achieved in brief, intermittent periods. The decisive factor in determining the quality of individual consciousness is whether that dim awareness characteristic of our every-day mind and the uncontrolled portion of every-day activity tends to increase or decrease.

It is the daily little negligence in thoughts, words and deeds going on for many years of our life (and as the Buddha teaches, for many existences), that is chiefly responsible for creating and tolerating that untidiness and confusion in our minds which we have described. The old Buddhist Teachers said: 'Negligence produces a lot of dirt and dust, even a whole heap of refuse. It is as if in a house only a very little dirt collects in a day or two; but if this goes on for many years, it will grow into a vast heap of refuse.'[1]

It is the dark, untidy corners of the mind where our most dangerous enemies dwell. From there they attack us unawares, and much too often they succeed in defeating us. That twilight world peopled by frustrated desires and suppressed resentments, by vacillations and whims and many other shadowy figures, forms a background from which upsurging passions—greed and lust, hatred and anger—may derive powerful support. Besides, the obscure and obscuring nature of that twilight region is the very element and mother-soil of the third and strongest of the Roots of Evil (*akusala-mūla*), i.e. Ignorance or Delusion.

Attempts at eliminating the mind's main defilements—greed, hate and delusion—must fail as long as these defilements find refuge and support in these uncontrolled dim regions of the

[1] Comy. to *Sutta-Nipāta* v. 334.

mind; as long as the close and complex tissue of those half-articulate thoughts and emotions forms the basic texture of mind into which just a few golden strands of noble and lucid thought are woven. But how to deal with that unwieldy, tangled mass? Man usually tries to ignore it, and to rely on the counteracting energies of his surface mind. But the only safe remedy is just to face it—with mindfulness. Nothing more difficult is needed than to acquire the habit of noticing these rudimentary thoughts as often as possible, i.e. to direct Bare Attention to them. The working principle here is the simple fact that two thoughts cannot exist at the same time: if the clear light of mindfulness is present, there is no room for mental twilight. When sustained mindfulness has secured a firm foothold, it will be a matter of comparatively secondary importance in which ways the mind will then deal with those rudimentary thoughts, moods and emotions. It may just dismiss them and replace them by purposeful thoughts; or it may allow them, and even compel them, to complete what they have to say. In the latter case, they will often reveal how poor and weak they actually are; and it will then not be difficult to dispose of them, once they are forced into the open. This procedure of Bare Attention is very simple and effective; the difficulty here is only the persistence in applying it.

Observing a complex thing means identifying its component parts, singling out the separate strands forming that intricate tissue. If this is applied to the complex currents of mental and practical life, automatically a strong regulating influence will be noticeable. As if ashamed in the presence of the calmly observing eye, the course of thoughts will proceed in a less disorderly and wayward manner; it will not so easily be diverted and will resemble more and more a well-regulated river.

During decades of the present life and throughout millenniums of traversing the Round of Existence, there has been steadily growing within man a closely fitted system of instinctive and reflex actions (beneficial and harmful ones), of prejudices of intellect and emotions—in brief, of bodily and mental habits that are no longer questioned as to their rightful position and useful function in human life. Here again it is the application of Bare Attention that loosens the hard soil of these often very ancient layers of the human mind, thus preparing the ground for sowing the seed of methodical mental training. Bare attention identifies and pursues the single threads of that closely interwoven tissue of our habits. It sorts out carefully the subsequent justifications of passionate impulses and the pretended motives of our prejudices; it fearlessly questions old habits often grown meaningless, and by uncovering their roots it helps in abolishing all that is seen to be harmful. In brief, Bare Attention lays open the minute crevices in the seemingly impenetrable structure of unquestioned mental processes. Then the sword of Wisdom wielded by the strong arm of constant meditative practice will be able to penetrate these crevices, and finally to break up that structure where it is required. If the inner connections between the single parts of a seemingly compact whole become intelligible, then it ceases to be inaccessible.

If the facts and details of its conditioned nature become known, there is a chance of effecting fundamental changes in it. In that way, not only those hitherto unquestioned habits of the mind, its twilight regions and its normal processes as well, but even those seemingly solid, indisputable facts of the world of matter—all of them will become 'questionable' and lose much of their self-assurance. Many people are so impressed and intimidated by that bland self-assurance of assumed 'solid facts' that they are reluctant to take up any spiritual training, doubting whether it can effect anything worthwhile at all. The results of applying Bare Attention to the task of tidying and regulating the mind will therefore greatly encourage those who are still hesitant to enter a spiritual path.

In conclusion, we wish to point out that the tidying or regulating function of Bare Attention is of fundamental importance for that 'purification of beings', mentioned by the Buddha as the first aim of *Satipaṭṭhāna*. It refers of course to the purification of their minds, and here the very first step is to bring an initial order into the way of functioning of the mental processes. We have seen how this is done by Bare Attention. In that sense, the Commentary to the Discourse on Mindfulness explains the words 'for the purification of beings' as follows.

'It is said: "Mental taints defile the beings; mental clarity (*citta-vodāna*) purifies them." That mental clarity comes to be by this Way of Mindfulness (*satipaṭṭhāna-magga*).'

NAMING

We have mentioned before that the tidying or regulating function of Bare Attention takes the form of sorting out and identifying the various confused strands of the mental process. That identifying function is, like any other mental activity, connected with a verbal formulation. In other words, 'identifying' proceeds by way of expressly 'naming' the respective mental processes.

There is an element of truth in the 'word-magic' of primitive men. 'Things that could be named had lost their secret power over man, the horror of the unknown. To know the name of a force, a being or an object was (to primitive man) identical with the mastery over it.'[1] That ancient belief in the magical power of 'knowing the name' appears also in many fairy tales and myths where the power of a demon is broken just by facing him courageously and pronouncing his name.

In the practice of Bare Attention, one will find a confirmation of that power of naming. Particularly, the 'demons of the twilight region' of the mind cannot bear the simple, but clarifying question about their 'names', much less the knowledge of these names, which alone is often sufficient to diminish their strength. They cannot bear the calmly observing glance of the Wanderer on the Buddha's Way of Mindfulness. That glance, however, has not the effect of driving them back into their hiding places, but it has, on the contrary, the magical power to force these demons of our passionate impulses and obscure thoughts into the open, into the daylight of consciousness. There they will feel embarrassed and obliged to justify themselves, though, at this stage of Bare Attention, they have not yet even been subjected to any closer questioning except that about their 'names', their identity. If forced into the open, while still in an incipient stage, they will be incapable of withstanding scrutiny, and will

[1] Anagarika B. Govinda: *The Psychological Attitude of Early Buddhist Philosophy*, London, Rider & Co., 1961.

just dwindle away. Thus a first victory over them may be won, even at an early stage of the practice.

The appearance in the mind of undesirable and ignoble thoughts, even if they are very fleeting and only half-articulate, is an unpleasant experience to one's self-esteem. Therefore such thoughts are often shoved aside, unattended and unopposed. Often, also, they are camouflaged by more pleasing and respectable labels which hide their true nature. Thoughts disposed of in either of these two ways, will increase the accumulated power of ignoble tendencies in the subconscious. Furthermore, the procedure adopted will weaken one's will to resist the arising and the dominance of mental defilements, and it will strengthen the tendency to evade the issue. But by applying the simple method of clearly and honestly 'naming', that is registering, any undesirable thoughts, these two harmful devices, ignoring and camouflaging, are excluded, and their detrimental consequences on the structure of subconsciousness and on our conscious mental effort, are avoided.

Calling those ignoble thoughts, or one's shortcomings such as laziness, by their right names, will arouse in one's mind a growing inner resistance and even repugnance against them, which may well succeed in keeping them in check and finally eliminating them. Even if these undesirables are not fully brought under control by such means, they will carry with them the impact, that is the recollection, of a repeated resistance against them, and this will weaken them in cases of their reappearance. If we may continue to personify them, we may say that they will no longer feel to be unopposed masters of the scene, and this diffidence of theirs will make it considerably easier to deal with them. It is the power of moral shame (*hiri-bala*) that has been mustered here as an ally, and it is methodically strengthened by these simple, yet subtle psychological means.

The naming and registering extends of course also to noble thoughts and impulses which will be encouraged and strengthened by it. Without such deliberate attention to them, they may often pass unnoticed and remain barren, while a clear awareness of them will stimulate their growth.

It is one of the most beneficial features of Right Mindfulness, and in particular of Bare Attention, that it enables us to utilize for our progress all external events and all inner processes of mind. Even the unsalutary can be made a starting point for the salutary if, through the device of 'naming' or 'registering', it becomes an object of detached knowledge.

In several passages of the *Satipaṭṭhāna Sutta* the function of 'naming' or 'bare registering' seems to be indicated through formulating the respective statements by way of direct speech. There are not less than four such instances in the Discourse:

1. 'When experiencing a pleasant feeling, he knows, "I experience a pleasant feeling"', etc.
2. 'He knows of a lustful (state of) mind, "Mind is lustful"', etc.
3. 'If (the hindrance of) sense desire is present in him, he knows, "Sense desire is present in me"', etc.
4. 'If the enlightenment factor Mindfulness is present in him, he knows, "The enlightenment factor Mindfulness is present in me"', etc.

In conclusion, it may briefly be pointed out that the *tidying-up* and the *naming* of mental processes is the indispensable preparation for fully understanding them in their true nature, which is the task of Insight (*vipassanā*). These functions, exercised by Bare Attention, will help in dispelling the illusion of compactness (*ghana-vinibbhoga*) of mental processes; they will also be helpful in tracing their specific nature or characteristics, and in noticing their momentary arising and disappearing.

2. THE NON-COERCIVE PROCEDURE

Both the world surrounding us and the world of our own mind are full of unwanted experiences and frustrations, of hostile and conflicting forces. Man knows from his own bitter experience that he is not strong enough to meet and conquer in open combat, each one of these antagonistic forces around him and within him. He knows that, in the external world, he 'cannot have everything as he wants it', and that, in the inner world of his mind, passions and impulses, whims and fancies, are often victorious over the voices of duty, reason and higher aspirations.

Man knows further that often an undesirable situation will even worsen if excessive pressure is used against it. Thus passionate desires may grow in intensity if one tries to silence them by sheer force of will. Disputes and quarrels will go on endlessly and grow fiercer, if they are fanned again and again by angry retorts or by vain attempts to crush the other man's position entirely. A disturbance during work, rest or meditation, will be felt more strongly and will have a longer-lasting impact if one reacts to it by resentment, anger, or by attempts to suppress it.

Again and again man will meet with situations in life where he cannot *force* issues. But there are ways of mastering some of the vicissitudes of life and many of the conflicts of mind, without an application of force, by non-violent means, which may often succeed where attempts of coercion, internal or external, have failed. Such a way of non-violent mastery of life and of mind is *Satipaṭṭhāna*. By the methodical application of Bare Attention, being the basic practice in the development of Right Mindfulness, all the latent powers of a non-coercive approach will gradually unfold themselves, with their beneficial results and their wide and unexpected implications. Here, in this context, however, we are mainly concerned with benefits for the mastery of mind and for progress in meditation that may result from a non-coercive procedure. But we shall also throw occasional side glances to the repercussions on every-day life. It will not be difficult for a thoughtful reader to make more detailed application to his own problems.

The antagonistic forces that appear in meditation, and are liable to upset its smooth course, are of three kinds:

1. external disturbances, as noise, etc.;
2. mental defilements (*kilesa*), including lust, anger, dissatisfaction, sloth, etc., which may arise at any time during meditation;
3. various incidental stray thoughts, surrender to daydreaming, etc.

The occurrence of these distractions is the great stumbling block for a beginner in meditation who has not yet acquired sufficient dexterity to deal with them effectively. To give thought to those disturbing factors only when they actually arise at the very time of meditation, will be quite insufficient. If caught unprepared in one's defence, one will struggle with them in a more or less haphazard and ineffective way, and with a feeling of irritation which will form an additional impediment. If disturbances of any kind and an unskilful reaction to them occur several times during one session, one will feel utterly frustrated and irritated, and may have to give up further attempts at meditating at least for the present occasion.

In fact, even meditators who are quite well informed, by books or teacher, about all details concerning the subject of meditation chosen, are often lacking in instruction how to deal skilfully with those varieties of disturbance mentioned above. The feeling of helplessness in face of them is the most formidable initial difficulty for a beginner in meditation. Many have accepted defeat at that point, abandoning prematurely any further effort at methodical meditation. As in worldly affairs so in meditation, one's way of dealing with the 'initial difficulties' will often be decisive for success or failure.

When faced by inner and outer disturbances, the inexperienced or uninstructed beginner will generally react in two ways: he will first try to shove them away lightly, and if he fails in that, he will try to suppress them by sheer force of will. But these disturbances are like insolent flies: by whisking—first lightly and then with increasing vigour and anger—one may succeed (or not) in driving them away for a while, but mostly they will return with an exasperating constancy, and the effort and vexation of 'whisking' will have produced only an additional disturbance of one's composure.

Satipaṭṭhāna through its method of Bare Attention, offers a non-violent alternative to those futile and even harmful attempts at suppression by force.

A successful non-violent procedure in mind-control has to start with the right mental attitude. There must be first the full cognizance and sober acceptance of the fact that those three

H

antagonistic forces or disturbing factors are cohabitants of the world we live in, whether we like it or not. Our disapproval of them will not alter the fact. With some of them we shall have to come to terms, and concerning others—the mental defilements—we have to learn how to deal with them effectively until they are finally conquered.

1. Since we are not the sole inhabitants of this densely populated world, there are bound to be *external disturbances* of various kinds, as noise, interruption by visitors, etc. We cannot always live in 'splendid isolation', 'from noise of men and dogs untroubled', or on 'ivory towers' high above the crowd. Right meditation is not escapism; it is not meant for providing hiding places of temporary oblivion. Realistic meditation has the purpose of training man's mind to face, to understand and to conquer this very world in which we live and which also includes numerous obstacles to the life of meditation.

2. A *Satipaṭṭhāna* Master, the Venerable U Sobhana Mahāthera (Mahāsi Sayadaw) of Burma, said: In an unliberated worldling *mental defilements* are sure to arise again and again. He has to face that fact, and he should know these defilements well, in order to apply again and again the appropriate remedy of *Satipaṭṭhāna*. Then they will grow weaker, more short-lived, and will finally disappear. To know the occurrence and nature of defilements is therefore as important for a meditator as to know the occurrence of his noble thoughts.

By facing one's own defilements one will be stirred to increase the effort to eliminate them. On the other hand, by trying to avert one's glance when they arise, out of a false shame or pride, one will never truly join issue with them, and always evade the final and decisive encounter; and by hitting blindly at them, one will only exhaust, or even hurt, onself. But by observing carefully their nature and behaviour when they arise in one's own mind, one will be able to meet them well prepared, to forestall them often, and finally to banish them fully. Therefore meet your defilements with a free and open glance! Be not ashamed, afraid or discouraged!

3. The third group of intruders disturbing the meditator's mind are the stray thoughts and day-dreams which may

consist of various memories and images of the recent or remote past, including those emerging from subconscious depths; thoughts of the future: planning, imagining, fearing, hoping; the casual sense-perceptions that may occur at the very time of meditation, often dragging after them a long trail of associated ideas. Whenever concentration and mindfulness slacken, stray thoughts or day-dreams will appear and fill the vacuum. Though they seem insignificant in themselves, they are, through their frequent occurrence, a most formidable obstacle, not only for the beginner, but in all cases when the mind is restless or distracted. Like the mental defilements, they will be entirely excluded only when, at the stage of holiness (*Arahatta*), perfect mindfulness has been obtained, keeping unfailing watch at the door of the mind. But it can certainly be achieved that, even for long continuous periods of meditation, these invaders are kept at bay.

To all these facts about the three kinds of disturbing factors full weight must be given and the facts must be fully absorbed by our mind, if they are to shape our mental attitude. Then, in these three disturbing factors, the Truth of Suffering will manifest itself to the meditator very incisively through his own personal experience: 'Not to obtain what one wants, is suffering.' Also the three other Noble Truths should be exemplified by reference to that very situation. In such a way, even when dealing with impediments, the meditator will be within the domain of *Satipaṭṭhāna*: he will be engaged in the mindful awareness of the four Noble Truths, being a part of the Contemplation of Mental Objects (*dhammānupassanā*).[1] It is a characteristic of Right Mindfulness, and one of its tasks, to relate the actual experiences of life to the truths of the Dhamma, and to use them as opportunities for its practical realization. Already here, at this preliminary stage devoted to the shaping of a correct and helpful mental attitude, we have the first successful test of our peaceful weapons: by understanding our adversaries better, we have consolidated our position which was formerly weakened by an emotional approach; and by transforming these

[1] See *The Way of Mindfulness* by Bhikkhu Soma (3rd. ed., Buddhist Publication Society, Kandy), p. 52, last para. of the Section on Breathing.

adversaries into teachers of the Four Noble Truths we have won the first advantage over them.

If mentally prepared by a realistic view of these three factors antagonistic to meditation, one will be less inclined to react at once by irritation when they actually arise. One will be emotionally in a better position to meet them with the non-violent weapons of which we shall now speak.

There are three devices of countering disturbances which should be applied in succession whenever the preceding device has failed to dispose of the disturbance. All three are applications of Bare Attention, differing in the degree or intensity of attention given to the disturbance. The guiding rule here is: to give no more mental emphasis to the disturbance than actually required by circumstances.

1. First one should notice the disturbance clearly, but lightly; that is, without emphasis and without attention to details. After that brief act of noticing, one should try to return to the original object of meditation, and one may well succeed in it if the disturbance is weak by nature, or one's preceding concentration of mind was fairly strong. If, at that stage, we are careful not to get involved in any 'conversation' or argument with the intruders, we shall, on our part, not give them a reason to stay long; and, in a good number of cases, the disturbances will depart soon, like visitors who do not receive a very warm welcome. That curt dismissal of them may often enable us to return to our original meditation, without any serious disturbance to our composure of mind.

The non-violent device is here: to apply Bare Attention to the disturbance, but with a minimum of response to it, and with a mind bent on withdrawal. This is the very way in which the Buddha himself dealt with inopportune visitors, as described in the *Mahāsuññatā-Sutta* (*Majjh.* 122): '. . . with a mind bent on seclusion . . . and withdrawn, his conversation aiming at dismissing (those visitors)'. Similar was Sāntideva's advice on how to deal with fools: if one cannot avoid them one should treat them 'with the indifferent politeness of a gentleman'.

2. If, however, the disturbance persists, one should repeat the application of Bare Attention again and again patiently

and calmly; and it may well be that the disturbance will vanish when it has spent its force. Here the attitude is: to meet the repeated occurrence of a disturbance by a reiterated 'No', by a determined refusal to be deflected from one's course. It is the attitude of patience and firmness. The capacity of watchful observation has to be aided here by the capacity to wait and to hold one's ground.

These two devices will generally be successful with incidental stray-thoughts, day-dreams, etc., which are feeble by nature, but also the other two types of disturbances, the external ones and defilements, may yield quite often.

3. But if, for some reason or other, they do *not* yield, one should now turn one's full and deliberate attention to the disturbance, accept it as an object of knowledge, and transform it thus from a *disturbance* of meditation to a legitimate *object* of meditation. One may continue with that new object until the external or internal cause for attending to it has ceased, or one may even retain it for that session of meditation, if it proves satisfactory.

If there is, for instance, disturbance by persistent noise, we should give to it our undivided attention. But we should take care to distinguish it well from any reaction of ours concerning it, e.g. by resentment, which likewise should be clearly recognized in its own nature, whenever it arises. In doing so, we shall have undertaken the Contemplation of Mind-objects (*dhammā-nupassanā*), according to the following passage of the Discourse: 'he knows the ear and sounds, and the fetter (e.g. resentment) arising through both.' If the noise is intermittent or of varying intensity, one will be easily able to discern the rise and fall (*udayabbaya*) in its process, and to add, in that way, to one's direct insight into impermanency (*aniccatā*).

The attitude towards recurrent mental defilements, as thoughts of lust, restlessness, etc., should be similar. One should face them squarely, but distinguish them from one's reaction to them, e.g. connivance, fear, resentment, irritation. In doing so, one is making use of the device of 'naming', and one will reap its benefits which have been outlined before. In the recurrent waves of passion or restlessness one will likewise learn to distinguish gradually phases of 'high' and 'low', their 'ups and downs', and may also gain other helpful knowledge about their behaviour. By that procedure, one again remains entirely within the range of *Satipaṭṭhāna*, by practising the Contemplation of the State of Mind (*cittānupassanā*) and of Mind-objects (*dhammānupassanā*; i.e. attention to the Hindrances).

This method of transforming disturbances of meditation into objects of meditation, as simple as it is ingenious, may be regarded as the culmination of non-violent procedure. It is a device very characteristic of the spirit of *Satipaṭṭhāna*, by making use of all experiences as aids on the Path. In that way, enemies are turned into friends, because all these disturbances and antagonistic forces have become our teachers; and teachers, whoever they may be, should be regarded as friends.

We cannot forgo to quote here from a noteworthy little book, which is a moving human document of fortitude and practical wisdom acquired by suffering: it is *The Little Locksmith* by Katherine Butler Hathaway:

'I am shocked by the ignorance and wastefulness with which persons who should know better throw away the things they do not like. They throw away experiences, people, marriages, situations, all sorts of things because they do not like them. If you throw away a thing, it is gone. Where you had something you have nothing. Your hands are empty, they have nothing to work on. Whereas, almost all those things which get thrown away are capable of being worked over by a little magic into just the opposite of what they were . . . But most human beings never remember at all that in almost every bad situation there is the possibility of a transformation by which the undesirable may be changed into the desirable.'

We have said before that the occurrence of the three disturbing elements cannot always be prevented. They are parts of our world, and their coming and going follows its own laws irrespective of our approval or disapproval. But by applying Bare Attention we can well prevent our being swept away or dislodged by them. By taking a firm and calm stand on the secure ground of Mindfulness, we shall repeat in a modest degree, but in an essentially identical way, the historic situation under the Bodhi Tree when Māra[1] at the head of his army in vain claimed possession of the soil on which the seat of Enlightenment rested (as he will claim every inch of the world's surface). Trusting in the power of mindfulness, we may confidently repeat the Master's aspiration before his Englightenment: *Māmaṁ ṭhānā acacayi!* 'May he (Māra) not dislodge me from this place' (*Padhāna Sutta*).

Let the intruders come and go, like any other members of that vast, unceasing procession of mental and physical events that passes along before our observant eyes, in the practice of Bare Attention.

Our advantage here is the quite obvious fact that two thought moments cannot be present at one and the same time. Attention refers, strictly speaking, not to the present but to the moment that has just passed away. Thus, as long as mindfulness holds sway, there will be no 'disturbance' or 'defiled thought'. This gives us the chance to hold onto that secure ground of an 'observer's post', to the potential 'throne of enlightenment'.

By the quietening and neutralizing influence of detached observation as applied in our three devices, the interruptions of meditation will increasingly lose the sting of irritation, and, thereby, their disturbing effect. This will prove to be an act of true *Virāga* ('dispassion') which literally means 'decolouring'. That is to say, these experiences will lose their emotional tinge that excites towards lust, aversion, etc., and they will appear as 'bare phenomena' (*suddha-dhammā*).

The non-violent procedure of Bare Attention endows the meditator with a 'light but sure touch' that is so essential for handling the sensitive, evasive, and refractory nature of our mind, as well as for dealing with various difficult situations and obstacles in life. When speaking of the even quality of energy required for attaining to the meditative absorptions, the 'Path of Purification' (*Visuddhi-magga*) illustrates it by describing a test which the ancient students of the art of surgery had to undergo as a proof of their skill. A lotus leaf was placed

[1] The personification of the forces antagonistic to Enlightenment.

in a bowl of water, and the pupil had to make an incision through the length of the leaf, without cutting it entirely or submerging it. He who applied an excess of force, either cut it into two or pressed it into the water, while the timid one did not even dare to scratch it. In fact, it is something like the gentle but firm hand of the surgeon that is required in mental training, and this skilful and well-balanced touch will be the natural outcome of the non-violent procedure in the practice of Bare Attention.

3. STOPPING AND SLOWING DOWN

For a full and unobstructed unfoldment of the mind's capacities, the influence of two complementary forces is needed: of *activating* and *restraining*. That two-fold need was recognized by the Buddha, the great knower of mind. He advised that the Faculties of Energy (*viriy'indriya*) and of tranquil Concentration (*samādh'indriya*) should be kept equally strong and well balanced.[1] Furthermore, He recommended three of the Seven Factors of Enlightenment (*bojjhāṅga*) as suitable for rousing the mind,[2] and another three for calming it.[3] In both cases, among the Spiritual Faculties and the Enlightenment Factors, it is Mindfulness (*sati*) that not only watches over their equilibrium, but actively stimulates the growth of their activating as well as their restraining power.

Mindfulness, though seemingly of a passive nature, is in fact also an activating force. It makes the mind alert, and alertness is indispensable for all purposeful activity. In the present inquiry, however, we shall be mainly concerned with the *restraining* power of mindfulness. We shall examine how it

[1] For the teaching on the Balance of the Spiritual Faculties. See *Anguttara-Nik.* VI, 55; *Visuddhi-Magga* Ch. IV—Comy. to *Satipaṭṭhāna Sutta* (in 'Way of Mindfulness', by Bhikkhu Soma, p. 134).

[2] These three are: the Enlightenment Factors of Truth-investigation, Energy and Rapture. See *Samy.-Nik.* 46, No. 53, quoted in *Vis. Magga*, Ch. IV.

[3] These three are: the Enlightenment Factors of Tranquillity, Concentration and Equanimity. See *Samy.-Nik*, 46, No. 51.

makes for disentanglement and detachment, and how it positively helps in the development of the mental qualities required for the work of Deliverance.

In practising Bare Attention, we *keep still* at the mental and spatial place of observation, amidst the loud demands of the inner and outer world. There is in it the strength of tranquillity, the capacity of deferring action and applying the brake, of *stopping* rash interference, of suspending judgement while *pausing* for observation of facts and wise reflection on them. There is also a wholesome *slowing down* in the impetuosity of thought, speech and action. Keeping still and stopping, pausing and slowing down—these will be our key words when speaking now of the restraining effect of Bare Attention.

An ancient Chinese book says: 'In making things end, and in making things start, there is nothing more glorious than *keeping still*.'

In the light of the Buddha's teaching, the true 'end of things' is Nibbāna which is called the '*stilling* of formations' (*saṇkhārānaṁ vūpasamo*), that is their final end or cessation. It is also called 'the Stopping' (*nirodha*). The 'things' or 'formations' meant here, are the conditioned and impersonal phenomena rooted in their twofold cause, craving and ignorance. The end of formations comes to be by the end of 'forming', i.e. by the end of world-creating kammic activities. It is the 'end of the world' and of suffering, which, as proclaimed by the Buddha cannot be reached by walking, by migrating or transmigrating, but is to be found only within ourselves. That 'end of the world' is heralded by each deliberate act of *keeping still, stopping* or *pausing*. 'Keeping still', in that highest sense, means: stopping the accumulation of Kamma. It means: refraining from perpetually adding to our entanglements in Saṁsāra, abstaining from our unceasing concern with evanescent things. By following the Way of Mindfulness, and training ourselves to keep still, or pause, in the attitude of Bare Attention, we refuse to take up the world's persistent challenge to our dispositions for greed or hatred. We protect ourselves against rash and delusive judgements; we refrain from blindly plunging into the labyrinths of interfering action with all its inherent dangers.

'He who abstains from interfering, is everywhere in security.'

—*Sutta-nipāta*, verse 953

'He who keeps still (or: knows where to stop) will not meet danger.'

—*Tao-Te-Ching*, Chapter 44

The Chinese saying quoted earlier, says in its second part that there is nothing more glorious in *making things start* than keeping still. Explained in the Buddhist sense, these things effectively started by keeping still, are 'the things (or qualities) making for decrease of kammic accumulation' (*apacayagāmino dhammā*), and, in dealing with them, we may follow the traditional division of mental training into Morality (or Conduct), Concentration (or Tranquillity) and Wisdom (or Insight). All three are decisively helped by the attitude of *keeping still*, as cultivated by Bare Attention.

1. *Conduct.* How can we improve our conduct, its moral quality and its skill in taking right decisions? If we earnestly desire such an improvement, it will generally be the wisest to choose the line of least resistance. We might suffer discouraging defeat if we turn too early against those short-comings which have deep roots in old habits or in powerful impulses. We shall be better advised to pay attention first to those blemishes of our actions or speech and to those errors of judgement which are caused by thoughtlessness and rashness, and there are many of them. There are numerous instances in the lives of most of us where one short moment of reflection might have prevented a false step, and thereby warded off a long chain of misery or moral guilt that started with a single moment of thoughtlessness. But how can we curb our rash reactions and replace them by moments of mindfulness and reflection? This will depend on our capacity to *stop and pause*, to apply the brakes at the right time, and that we can learn well by practising Bare Attention. In that practice we shall train ourselves 'to look and wait', to suspend, or slow down, reactions. We shall learn it 'the easy way', in situations of our own choice, within the limited field of experiences met with during the periods of meditative practice. When facing again and again the incidental sense-impres-

sions, feelings or stray thoughts which interrupt our concentration; when curbing again and again our desire to respond to them in some way or other; when succeeding again and again in keeping still in face of them—then we shall be well prepared for preserving that inner stillness also in the wider and unprotected field of everyday life. We shall have acquired a presence of mind that will enable us to pause and stop, even if we are taken by surprise, or are suddenly provoked or tempted.

Our present remarks refer to those blemishes of conduct which are liable to arise through thoughtlessness and rashness, but might more or less easily be checked through mindfulness. Dexterity in dealing with them will, however, also affect those more obstinate deviations from moral conduct which are rooted in strong passionate impulses or in deeply ingrained bad habits. The increased tranquillity of mind achieved in keeping still for Bare Attention, will restrain the impetuosity of passions, and the acquired habit of 'pausing and stopping' will act as a brake to the unquestioned repetition of bad habits.

By being able to keep still for Bare Attention, or to pause for wise reflection, very often the first temptation to lust, the first wave of anger, the first mist of delusion will disappear without causing serious entanglement. At which point the current of unwholesome thought-processes is stopped, will depend on the quality of mindfulness. If mindfulness is keen, it will succeed in calling a stop at a very early point of a series of defiled thoughts or actions, before we are carried along by them too far. Consequently, these particular defilements will not grow beyond their initial strength, less effort will be required to check them, and less kammic entanglements, or none, will follow.

Let us take the example of a pleasant visual object which has aroused our liking. At first that liking might not be very active and insistent. If, already here, the mind is able to keep still for detached observation or reflection, it will be easily possible to divest the visual perception of its still very slight admixture of lust, and to register it as 'just something seen that has caused a pleasant feeling'; or the effect of the attraction felt is sublimated into quiet aesthetic pleasure. If that earliest chance has been missed, the liking will grow into attachment and into desire to possess. If a stop is now called, the thought of desire may gradually lose its strength; it will not easily turn into an insistent craving, and no actual attempts to get possession of the object of desire will follow. But if the current of lust is still unchecked, the thought of desire (=*akusala-mano-kamma*, 'unwholesome mental kamma') may express itself by speech (=*akusala-vacī-kamma*, 'unwholesome verbal kamma'): one asks for the desired object, or even demands it with impetuous words. A refusal will cause the original current of lust to branch out into additional streams of mental defilements, either of sadness or of anger. But if even at this late stage one can stop for quiet reflection or Bare Attention and, accepting the refusal, renounce wish-fulfilment, further complications will be avoided. But if clamouring words are followed by action (=*akusala-kāya-kamma*, 'unwholesome bodily kamma'): if, driven by craving, one tries to get possession of the object of one's desire by stealth or force, then the kammic entanglement is complete, and the full impact of its consequences will be experienced by the doer. Still, if even after the completion of the evil act, the doer stops for reflection, i.e. if mindfulness takes the form of remorseful retrospection, it will not be in vain: it will preclude a hardening of character and may prevent a repetition of the same course of action.

The Exalted One said once to His son Rāhula:

'Whatever action you *intend* to perform, by body, speech or mind, you should consider that action . . . If, in considering it, you realize: "This action which I intend to perform will be harmful to myself, or harmful to others, or harmful to both; it will be an unwholesome action, producing suffering, resulting in suffering"—then you should certainly not perform that action.

'Also *while* you are preforming an action, by body, speech or mind, you should consider that action . . . If, in considering it, you realize: "This action which I am performing, is harmful to myself, or harmful to others, or harmful to both; it is an unwholesome action, producing suffering, resulting in suffering"—then you should desist from such an action.

'Also *after* you have performed an action, by body, speech or mind, you should consider that action . . . If, in considering it, you realize: "This action which I have performed, has been harmful to myself, or harmful to others, or harmful to both; it was an unwholesome action, producing suffering, resulting in suffering"—then you should in future refrain from it.' (*Majjh.* 61.)

2. *Tranquillity*. We shall now consider how the stopping for Bare Attention is also a helper in attaining or strengthening Tranquillity (*samatha*) in its double sense: of peace of mind in general, and of meditative concentration and calm.

By growing a habit of pausing and stopping for Bare Attention, it will become increasingly easier to withdraw into one's own stillness when unable to escape bodily from the loud and insistent noises of the outer world; it will be easier to forego useless reaction to foolish speech or deeds of others. Also when the blows of fate are particularly hard and incessant, a mind trained in Bare Attention will find it easier to take refuge in the haven of apparent passivity, or watchful non-action, and to wait patiently until the storms have passed. There are situations in life when it is best to allow things to come to their natural end. He who is able to keep still and wait will often succeed where aggressiveness or busy activity is vanquished. Not only in critical situations, but also in the normal course of life, the experience won by observant keeping still will convince us that it is not at all necessary to make an active response to every impression received, or to regard every encounter with people or things as a challenge to our interfering activity.

By refraining from busying ourselves unnecessarily, external frictions and, thereby, internal tensions will be reduced. Greater harmony and peace will pervade our everyday life, and the sometimes considerable contrast of normal life to the tranquillity of meditation will be reduced. Then there will be less of those disturbing inner reverberations of everyday restlessness which, in a coarse or suble form, invade the hours of meditation and produce bodily and mental unrest. Consequently, the Hindrance of Agitation (*uddhaccanīvaraṇa*), which is a chief obstacle of concentration, will be less often evident, or it will be easier to overcome it.

By cultivating the attitude of Bare Attention as often as opportunity offers, the centrifugal forces of mind, making for mental distraction, will be reduced, and the centripetal tendency, turning the mind inward and making for concentration, will be strengthened. The craving for a variety of changing objects of thought, or objects of desire, will be effectively checked.

Furthermore, regular practice of sustained attention to a continuous series of events will prepare for sustained concentration on a *single* object or a limited number of objects in the strict practice of meditation. Firmness, or steadiness, of mind, being another important factor in concentration, will likewise be cultivated in that way.

Thus, by keeping still, pausing and stopping for Bare Attention, several salient components of meditative tranquillity are fostered: calmness, concentration, firmness, reduction of the multiplicity of objects. The average level of normal consciousness is raised and brought closer to the level of the meditative mind. This is an important point, because it often happens that too wide a gap between these two levels of mind will again and again frustrate attempts at mental concentration or the achieving of smooth continuity in meditative practice.

In the sequence of the Seven Factors of Enlightenment we find that the enlightenment-factor Tranquillity (*passadhi-sambojjhaṅga*) precedes that of Concentration (*samādhi-sambojjhaṅga*): and, expressing the same fact, it was said; 'If tranquillized within, the mind will become concentrated'. Now, in the light of our previous remarks, we shall better understand these statements.

3. *Insight.* It has been said by the Exalted One: 'He whose mind is concentrated sees things as they really are.' Therefore all those ways by which Bare Attention strengthens concentration of mind, will also be a supporting condition of the development of insight. But there is also a more direct and specific help which Insight receives from 'Keeping still at Bare Attention'.

Apart from (supposedly) disinterested scholarly or scientific research, man is generally more concerned with 'handling' and utilizing things, or defining their relations to himself, than with knowing them in their true nature. He is therefore mostly satisfied with registering the very first signal conveyed to him by an outer or inner perception. Through deeply ingrained habit, that first signal will evoke standard responses by way of judgements like good–bad, pleasant–unpleasant, useful–harmful, right–wrong; which again will lead to further reactions by word or deed in accordance with these judgements. It is very rare that attention will dwell any longer upon an object of a common, or habitual type, than for receiving that very first signal, or the first few. Thus, mostly only one single aspect of the object, or a selected few, will be perceived (and sometimes misconceived), and only the very first phase (or little more) of the object's life-span will come into the focus of attention. One may not even be consciously aware that the process has an extension in time (origination and end); that it has many aspects and relations beyond those at first sight connected with the casual observer or the limited situation; that, in brief, it has a kind of evanescent individuality of its own. A world that has been perceived in that superficial way, will, to that extent, consist of rather shapeless little lumps of experiences marked by a few subjectively selected (and sometimes misapplied) signs or symbols which have significance mainly for the individual's self-interest. Parts of that rather shadow-like world are not only things and persons of one's environment, but even a good part of one's own bodily and mental processes which are often conceived in a similar superficial way. When thus the seal of self-reference is stamped again and again upon the world of everyday experience, the basic misconception 'This belongs to me' (attaniya) will steadily continue to grow subtle, but firm and wide-spread roots (comparable to the hair-roots of plants), which will scarcely be shaken by mere intellectual convictions about the non-existence of a self (anattā).

These grave consequences issue from that fundamental perceptual situation we have mentioned: on receiving a first signal from his perceptions, man rushes into hasty or habitual reactions which so often commit him to the four misapprehensions of reality: taking the impure for pure, the impermanent for lasting, the painful and pain-bringing for pleasant, and the impersonal for a self or something belonging to the self.

But if one musters the restraining forces of one's mind and pauses for Bare Attention, the material and mental processes that form the objects of mind at a given moment will reveal themselves more fully and more truly. If they are no longer dragged at once into the whirlpool of self-reference, but allowed to unfold themselves before the watchful eye of mindfulness, the diversity of their aspects and the wide net of their correlations and interconnections will appear: the narrow and often falsifying connection with self-interest will recede into the background and will be dwarfed by the wider view now gained. Birth and death, rise and fall of many of the observed processes will be clearly discerned, in their serial occurrence or in their component parts. Thereby the facts of Change and Impermanence will impress themselves on the mind with growing intensity. By the same discernment of rise and fall, many false conceptions of unity in the processes which had been created under the influence of the egocentric attitude will be dissolved. Self-reference uncritically overrides diversity, and lumps things together under the preconceptions of *being* a self (*attā*) or *belonging* to a self (*attaniya*). But Bare Attention reveals these sham unities as impersonal and conditioned phenomena. Facing thus again and again the evanescent, dependent and impersonal nature of life processes within and without, their monotony and unsatisfactory nature will become marked; in other words, the Truth of Suffering inherent in them will appear. In that way, all three Characteristics, or Signs, of Existence will open themselves to penetrative Insight (*Vipassanā*), by the simple device of slowing down, pausing and *keeping still* for Bare Attention.

SPONTANEITY

An acquired, or strengthened, habit of pausing mindfully before acting will not exclude or paralyse spontaneity of response where it is beneficial. On the contrary, the pausing, stopping and *keeping still* for Bare Attention will, through training, become quite spontaneous. They will grow into a 'selective mechanism' of the mind that, with an increasing reliability and swiftness of response, will prevent the upsurge of evil or unwise impulses which may have been intellectually realized by us as unwholesome, but which, by their own powerful spontaneity, still continue to defeat our better knowledge and nobler intentions. The practice of mindful pausing serves, therefore, to replace unwholesome spontaneity or habits, by wholesome ones.

Just as certain reflex moments are an automatically operating protection of the body, similarly a spontaneously working spiritual and moral self-protection will be a vital function of the mind. A person of average moral standard will instinctively shrink from theft or murder, without any long reflection. With the help of the method of Bare Attention, the range of such spontaneously functioning moral brakes can be greatly extended and ethical sensitivity heightened. Also false thought-habits can be broken in the same way and replaced by correct ones.

In an untrained mind, noble tendencies or right thoughts often succumb to the spontaneous outbreak of passions or prejudices, or they can assert themselves only with difficulty, after a struggle of motives. But if the spontaneity of the Unwholesome is checked or greatly reduced, as described above, our good impulses and wise reflections will have greater scope and they will be able to express themselves freely and spontaneously. Their spontaneous flow will give greater confidence in the power of the good within us and will carry more conviction for others. That spontaneity of the good will not be of an erratic nature, but will have deep and firm roots in previous methodical training. Here appears a way by which the 'premeditated good' (*sasankhārika-kusala*) may be transformed into 'spontaneously arising good thought' (*asankhārika-kusala-citta*) which, if combined with knowledge, takes the first place in the scale of ethical values, according to the psychology of the Abhidhamma. In this way we shall get practical understanding of a saying in *The Secret of the Golden Flower*[1]: 'If one attains intentionally to an unintentional state one has comprehension.' This saying

[1] A treatise of Chinese Mahāyāna, strongly influenced by Taoism.

just invites a paraphrase in Pāli terms: *Sasaṅkhārena asaṅkhā-rikaṁ pattabbaṁ.* 'By premeditated intentional effort sponta-neity can be won.'

If the numerous aids to mental growth and liberation, found in the Buddha's teachings, are wisely utilized, there is actually nothing that can finally withstand the Satipaṭṭhāna Method; and this method starts with the simple but in its effects far-reaching practice of learning to pause and stop for Bare Atten-tion.

SLOWING DOWN

Against the impetuosity, rashness and heedlessness of the untrained mind, practice of Pausing and Stopping sets a deli-berate slowing down. The demands of modern life, however, make it impracticable to introduce such a slowing down of functions into the routine of the average working-day. But as an antidote against the harmful consequences of the hectic speed of modern life, it is all the more important to cultivate that practice in one's leisure hours and especially in periods of strict Satipaṭṭhāna practice. It will also give the worldly benefits of greater calm, efficiency and skill in one's daily round of work.

For the purposes of meditative development, slowing down serves as an effective training in heedfulness, sense-control and concentration. But apart from that, it has also more specific significance for meditative practice. In the commentary to the *Satipaṭṭhāna Sutta,* for instance, it is told how the slowing down of movements may help in *regaining lost concentration* on a cho-sen object. A monk, so we read, had bent his arm quickly with-out remembering his subject of meditation, as his rule of practice demanded. On becoming aware of that omission, he took his arm back to its previous position and repeated the movement mindfully. The subject of meditation referred to was probably 'clearly comprehending action' (*sampajāna-kāra*), and especially the one mentioned in the *Satipaṭṭhāna Sutta* as follows: 'In bending and stretching he acts with clear comprehension' (*Sammiñjite pasārite sampajānakāri hoti*).

The slowing down of certain bodily movements during strict meditative training is also of great help in gaining Insight-knowledge (*Vipassanā-ñāṇa*) by one's own experience, and expecially the direct awareness of change (*anicca*) and impersonality (*anattā*). It is, to a great extent, the rapidity of movement that strengthens the illusion of unity, identity and substantiality of what is actually a complex and evanescent process. Therefore, in the strict practice of Satipaṭṭhāna, the slowing down of walking or bending and stretching and thereby discerning the several phases of each movement, is an exercise very helpful for direct insight into the three characteristics of all phenomena. It will make an impression of increasing force and significance on the meditator, to notice clearly how each partial phase of the process observed arises and ceases by itself, and nothing of it 'goes over' or 'transmigrates' to the next phase.

Also the average rhythm of our everyday actions, speech and thoughts will become more quiet and peaceful under the influence of that practice. Slowing down the hurried rhythm of life means that thoughts, feelings and perceptions will be able to complete the entire length of their natural life-time. Full awareness will extend up to their end-phase: to their last gentle vibrations and reverberations. Too often that end-phase is cut off by an impatient grasping at new impressions, or by hurrying on to the next stage of a line of thought before the earlier one has been clearly comprehended. This is one of the main reasons for the disorderly state of average consciousness which is burdened by a vast amount of indistinct or fragmentary perceptions, of stunned emotions and unfinished or undigested ideas. Slowing down will prove an effective device of recovering the fullness and clarity of consciousness. A fitting simile, and at the same time an actual example of it, is the procedure in the practice of Mindfulness on Breathing (*ānāpānasati*) where mindfulness has likewise to cover the whole extent of the breath, its beginning, middle and end. This is what is meant by the passage of the Discourse, saying 'Experiencing the *whole* (breath-) body, I shall breathe in and out'. Similarly, the entire 'breath', or rhythm of our life will become deeper and fuller, if, through slowing down, we get used to sustained attention.

The habit of prematurely cutting off processes of thought,

or slurring over them, has assumed serious proportions in the man of modern city civilization. His restlessness clamours for ever new stimuli, in an ever increasing speed of succession, having its counterpart in the increasing speed of our means of locomotion. This rapid bombardment of impressions will gradually blunt man's sensitivity, and consequently the new stimuli will have to be still more loud, coarse and variegated— a process which, if not checked, can only end in disaster. This state of affairs also explains the decrease of finer aesthetic susceptibility and the growing incapacity of genuine natural joy. The place of both is taken by a hectic, short-breathed excitement which does not leave any true aesthetic or emotional satisfaction. 'Shallow mental breath' is to a great extent responsible for the growing superficiality and coarseness of 'civilized man' and for the frightening spread of nervous disorders in the West. It may well become the start of a general deterioration of human consciousness in its qualitative level, its range and its strength. This danger threatens all those, in the East as well as in the West, whom the impact of technical civilization finds without an adequate spiritual protection. Satipaṭṭhāna can make an important contribution to remedying that situation, in the way we have indicated here briefly. Thus, also from the worldly point of view, the method will prove beneficial.

Here, however, we are chiefly concerned with the psychological aspects and their significance for meditative development. Sustained attention, being helped by slowing down, will affect the quality of consciousness mainly in three ways: (a) the *intensity* of consciousness, (b) the *clarity* of the object's characteristic features, and (c) it will reveal the object's *'relatedness'*.

(*a*) An object of *sustained* attention will exert a particularly strong and long-lasting impact on the mind, not only throughout the thought-series immediately following the perception, but its influence may also extend far into the future. It is that causal efficacy which is the measure of the *intensity of consciousness*.

(*b*) The first impression conveyed by any new sense-object or idea will be what is most striking in it, subjectively or objectively, and it will dominate the mind up to the culminating point of the impact. But there are sure to be other aspects, characteristics or functions of the object which may not be obvious or are less interesting to the cognizing subject but which are no less, or even more, important. There will also be cases where the first impression is entirely deceptive. Only if attention is sustained beyond that first impact, will the respective object reveal itself more fully. It is only at the downward course of the first perceptual wave (its end-phase), when the prejudicing force of the first impact lessens, that the object will yield a wider selection of detail, an all-round picture of itself. It is therefore, only by sustained attention that a greater *clarity of an object's characteristic features* can be obtained.

(c) Among the characteristic features of a physical or mental object there is one class which is often overlooked by hasty or superficial attention, and therefore we list it here separately: it is the *relatedness* of the object, extending to its past (origin, causes, reasons, logical precedents, etc.), and its present manifestation (environment, 'background', presently active influences, etc.). An event cannot be said to be fully understood if it is viewed in artificial isolation. It must be seen as a part of a wider pattern, in its conditioned and conditioning nature; and this can be done only with the help of sustained attention.

THE INFLUENCE OF SLOWING DOWN AND SUSTAINED ATTENTION OF SUBCONSCIOUSNESS, MEMORY AND INTUITION

It need hardly be pointed out how important all these three aforementioned points are for 'seeing things according to reality', in other words, for the development of Insight (*vipassanā*). Their *direct* influence is obvious, but there is also an *indirect* one which is no less powerful and important. Those three results of sustained attention, achieved with the help of slowing down, are also instrumental in influencing the quality and nature of *subconsciousness, memory* and *intuition* which, on their part, will again be aiding, nourishing and consolidating the progress of liberating Insight. Insight aided by them will be like the mountain lake (of the canonical simile) that is fed not only from without, by the rains, but also by springs welling up within its own depth. Similarly Insight will be nourished not only through external experience but also from the 'subterranean', i.e. subliminal resources of the mind: by memories, other subconscious material, and by the strengthened faculty of intuition. Meditative results of an Insight that has such deep roots will not be lost easily, even with unliberated worldlings (*puthujjana*) who are subject to relapse.

1. If perceptions or thoughts which have been objects of sustained attention, sink into *subconsciousness*, they will occupy there a special position by reason of their stronger impact on the mind and the greater distinctness of their characteristic features. As to the first reason: it will certainly not remain without any effect upon the structure of subconsciousness, if the end-phase of a moment of consciousness or of a cognitive-series, being immediately followed by subconsciousness, is not weak but of a strength equal to that of the preceding phases. As for the second reason: if an impression or idea, marked by numerous and distinct characteristics, sinks into subconsciousness, it will not so easily be absorbed into the vagueness of other subconscious contents or dragged into false subconscious associations with superficial similarities of passionate biases. And also, the last of the aforementioned three facts—the correct comprehension of the object's 'relatedness'—will have similar effects: there will be a greater resistance against a merging with inadequate subconscious material. If perceptions or thoughts of that level of intensity and clarity sink into subconsciousness, they will be more 'articulate' and more 'accessible' than contents of subconsciousness originating from hazy or 'stunned' impressions; they will be more easily 'convertible' into full consciousness, and less unaccountable in their hidden effects upon it. If, through an improvement in the quality and range of mindfulness, the number of such 'matured' impressions increases in the mind, it seems quite possible that a subtle change in the structure of subconsciousness can be achieved in that way.

2. It will be evident from our earlier remarks that those impressions which we have called 'matured' or 'more easily

accessible and convertible', will lend themselves more easily and more correctly to recollection. More easily: because of their greater intensity; more correctly: because of their clearly marked features which will give them a fair degree of protection against being distorted by false associative images or ideas. If, in addition, they are remembered in their 'context' and 'relatedness', it will work both ways, for easier and for more correct recollection. In that way, *Sati* in its meaning and function of Mindfulness, will help to strengthen *Sati* in its meaning and function of *Memory*.

3. From that very influence on subconsciousness and memory also a deepening and strengthening of the faculty of intuition will naturally follow, and particularly of intuitive insight, which here chiefly concerns us. Intuition is not 'a gift from the unknown', but, like any other mental faculty, it arises out of specific conditions which, in this case, are primarily the latent memories of perceptions and thoughts 'stored' in the subconscious. It is obvious that memories which have the aforementioned qualities of greater intensity, clarity and richness of distinctive marks, and thereby of greater accessibility, will provide the most fertile soil for the growth of intuition. Here too the preserved 'relatedness' of the respective impressions will contribute much. Recollections of that type will have a more organic character than memories of bare or vague, isolated facts, and they will more easily fall into new patterns of meanings and significance. These more 'articulate' memory-images will be a strong stimulation and aid for the intuitive faculty. Silently and in the hidden depths of the subliminal mental processes, the work of collecting and organizing the subconscious material of experience and knowledge goes on until it is ripe to emerge as what we call an *intuition*. The breaking-through of that intuition is sometimes occasioned by quite ordinary happenings which, however, may have a strong evocative power if, in previous occurrence, they had been made objects of sustained attention. Slowing down and pausing for Bare Attention will discover the depth-dimension of the simple things of every day, and will thus provide potential stimuli for the intuitive faculty. This applies also to the intuitive penetra-

tion (*paṭivedha*) of the four Noble Truths that culminates in Holiness (*arahatta*). Many instances are recorded of monks where the flash of intuitive penetration did not strike them when they were engaged in the meditative practice of insight proper, but on quite different occasions: when stumbling, when seeing a forest fire, a fata-morgana, a lump of froth in a river, etc.

We have met here another confirmation of that seemingly paradoxical saying that 'intentionally' an unintentional state may be won, or at least aided, by deliberately turning the full light of mindfulness even on the smallest events and actions of everyday life.

Sustained attention not only provides the nourishing soil for the *growth* of intuition, it also makes possible the fuller utilization and even repetition of the intuitive moment. Men of inspiration in various fields of creative activity have often related and deplored their common experience that the flash of intuition strikes so suddenly and vanishes so quickly that frequently the slow response of the mind scarcely catches the last glimpse of it. But if the mind has been trained in observant pausing, in slowing down and sustained attention, and if—as indicated above—the subconsciousness has also been influenced by it, then the intuitive moment, too, might gain that fuller, slower and stronger rhythm. This being the case, its impact will be strong and clear enough for making full use of that flash of intuitive insight. It might even be possible to lead its fading vibrations upward again to a new culmination, similar to the rhythmic repetition of a melody rising again, in harmonious development, out of the last notes of its first appearance.

The full utilization of a single moment of intuitive insight might be of decisive importance for one's progress toward full realization. If one's mental grip is too weak and those elusive moments of intuitive insight are allowed to slip away without being utilized fully for the work of liberation, then it might well happen that they will not recur before many years have passed, or perhaps not at all during the present life. Skill in sustained attention, however, will allow the full use of opportunities, and slowing down and Pausing during meditative practice, is an important aid in acquiring that skill.

136

Through our now concluded treatment of Pausing, Stopping and slowing down, one of the traditional definitions of Mindfulness found in the Pāli Scriptures will have become more intelligible in its far-reaching implications: that is its function of *anapilāpanatā*, meaning literally, 'not floating (or slipping) away'—'like pumpkin-pots on the surface of water', add the commentators; and they continue: 'Mindfulness enters deeply into its object', instead of hurrying over its surface only. Therefore 'non-superficiality' will be an appropriate rendering of the above Pāli term, and a befitting characterization of Mindfulness.

4. DIRECTNESS OF VISION

'I wish I could disaccustom myself from everything, so that I might see anew, hear anew, feel anew. Habit spoils our philosophy.'—G. Chr. Lichtenberg (1742–1799).

In an earlier section; we spoke about the impulsive spontaneity of the Unwholesome (*akusala*). We have seen how the stopping for bare and sustained attention is able to counter, or reduce, the occurrence of rash impulsive reactions, thus allowing us to face any situation with a fresh mind, with a *directness of vision*, unprejudiced by those first spontaneous responses.

By *directness of vision* we understand a direct view of reality, without any colouring or distorting lenses, without the intrusion of emotional or habitual prejudgement and intellectual biases. It means: coming face to face with the bare facts of actuality, seeing them as vivid and fresh as if they had occurred for the first time.

THE FORCE OF HABIT

Spontaneous reactions which so often stand in the way of direct vision, do not derive only from passionate impulses, but are very frequently the product of *habit*; and, in that form, they generally have an even stronger and more tenacious hold on man, which may work out either for the good and useful or for

137

the bad and harmful. The influence for the *good*, exercised by habits, is seen in the 'power of repeated practice' by which man's achievements and skills, of a manual or mental, worldly or spiritual kind, are protected against loss or forgetfulness, and are converted from a casual short-lived and imperfect acquisition into the more secure possession of a quality thoroughly mastered. The *detrimental* effect of habitual, spontaneous reactions is manifest in what is called, in a derogatory sense, the 'force of habit': its deadening, stultifying and narrowing influence, productive of compulsive behaviour of various kinds. In our present context, we shall be concerned only with that negative aspect of habit as impeding and obscuring the directness of vision.

As remarked earlier, the influence of habitual reactions is generally stronger than that of impulsive ones. Passionate impulses may disappear as suddenly as they have arisen. Though their consequences may well be very grave and extend far into the future, it is mostly the influence of habit which is longer-lasting and deeper-reaching. Habit spreads its vast and closely meshed net over wide areas of our life and thought, trying to drag in more and more of it. Passionate impulses too, might be caught into that net of habit and thus be transformed from passing outbursts into traits of character. A momentary impulse, an occasional indulgence, a passing whim may by repetition become a habit difficult to uproot, a desire hard to control, and finally an automatic function that is no longer questioned. By repeated gratification of a desire, habit is formed, and habit grows into a compulsion.

It may well be the case that some activity, behaviour or mental attitude to which one has become accustomed is, considered by itself, quite unimportant to the individual concerned, and also morally quite indifferent or inconsequential. At the start it might have been quite easy to abandon it or even to exchange it for its very opposite, since neither one's emotions nor reason had any strong bias towards either side of a possible choice. But by repetition, the continuance of the chosen way of acting, behaving or thinking will gradually become equated with 'pleasant', 'desirable', 'correct' or even 'righteous'; and it

138

will be finally identified, more or less consciously, with one's so-called character or personality. Consequently, any change in it—a break in that routine—will be felt as 'unpleasant' or as 'wrong', and any interference with it from outside will be greatly resented and even regarded as hostile towards 'one's vital interests and principles'. In fact, primitive minds, at all times, be they 'civilized' or not, have looked at a stranger with his 'strange customs' as an enemy, and have felt his mere unaggressive existence as a challenge or threat to themselves.

In the cases aforementioned, when the specific habit was originally not of great importance to the individual, the attachment which is gradually formed is not so much to the object proper, as to the pleasantness of undisturbed routine. The strength of that attachment to routine derives partly from the force of physical and mental inertia which is so powerful in man. By force of habit, the concern (any material object, activity, behaviour or way of thinking) is invested with such an increase of emotional emphasis that the attachment to quite unimportant or banal things may become as tenacious as that to the fundamental passions in man. Thus, even the smallest habits, if, by lack of conscious control, they become uncontested masters of their respective realms, may dangerously contribute to the rigidity and self-limitation of character, narrowing its 'freedom of movement' (environmental, intellectual and spiritual). Thus, often quite unnecessarily, new fetters are forged for the individual, and nourishing soil is provided for the growth of new attachments and aversions, prejudices and predilections, that is to say, for new suffering. Therefore when considering the following words of the *Satipaṭṭhāna Sutta*, we should also think of the important part played by habit in the formation of fetters:

. . . and whatever fetter arises dependent on both (i.e. the sense-organs and sense-objects), that he knows well. In what manner the arising of the not arisen fetter comes to be, that he knows well.'

In Buddhist parlance, it is pre-eminently the Hindrance of

Sloth and Torpor (*thīna-middha-nīvaraṇa*) which is strengthened by the 'force of habit'; and mental faculties like agility and pliancy of mind (*kāya-* and *citta-lahutā, mudutā,* etc.)[1] are correspondingly weakened.

The danger for spiritual development, involved in the dominating influence of habit, is all the more serious since its tendency towards expansion is particularly noticeable in our present age of increasing specialization and standardization in various spheres of life and thought.

The roots of that tendency of habits to extend their range, are anchored in the very nature of consciousness. Certain active types of consciousness, if possessing a fair degree of intensity, tend to repeat themselves, though that tendency is never quite undisputed, e.g. by new cognitions claiming attention. This tendency towards repetition stems not only from the aforementioned passive force of inertia, but in many cases from an active 'will to dominate and to conquer'. Even in quite peripheral or subordinate types of consciousness, there seems to exist an urge to gain ascendancy, to become by themselves ever so small centres around which other, weaker mental and physical states revolve, adapting themselves to that centre and becoming subservient to it. This is a striking parallel to the self-assertion and the domineering tendency of an egocentric individual in his contact with society. Among biological analogies, we may mention the tendency towards expansion by cancer and other pathological growths; and for the tendency towards repetition, we may think of the freak mutations which loom as a grave danger at the horizon of our atomic age.

Out of that 'will to dominate', inherent in many types of consciousness, a passing whim may grow into a relatively constant trait of character, and, if still not satisfied with its position, it may tend to break away entirely from the present combination of life forces till, finally, in the process of rebirths it becomes the very centre of a new so-called personality. There are within us countless seeds for new lives, for innumerable potential 'beings', all of which we should vow to liberate from

[1] About these important 'qualitative constituents' of good, wholesome (*kusala*) consciousness, see the author's *Abhidhamma Studies*, pp. 51f.

the wheel of Saṁsāra, as the Sixth Zen Patriarch expressed it.[1]

Detrimental physical or mental habits may grow strong, not only if fostered deliberately, but also if left unnoticed or unopposed. From minute seeds planted in a long-forgotten past, has grown much of what has now strong roots in our nature (see the Simile of the creeper in *Majjhima-Nik.* 45). This growth of morally bad or otherwise detrimental habits can be effectively checked by gradually developing another habit that will counter them: that of attending to them mindfully. Doing deliberately what had become a mechanical performance, and, perhaps, previous to it, pausing for a while for bare attention and reflection—this will give a chance for scrutinizing the habit in the light of Clear Comprehension of Purpose, and of Suitability (*sātthaka-*, and *sappāya-sampajañña*). It will allow a fresh assessment of the situation, a *direct vision* of it, unobscured by the mental haze surrounding a habitual activity, which conveys the feeling: 'It is right because it was done before.' Even if a detrimental habit cannot be broken at once, or soon, in this way, it will then lose a good deal of its unquestioned spontaneity of occurrence; it will carry the stamp of repeated scrutiny and resistance, and at its reoccurrence it will be weaker and prove more amenable to our attempts to change or abolish it.

It needs hardly to be mentioned that habit (which has rightly been called 'the wet-nurse of man') cannot and should not disappear from our life. Let us only remember what a relief it is, particularly in the crowded day and complex life of a city-dweller, that he can do a great number of things fairly mechanically, with, as it were, only 'half-powered attention'. It means a considerable simplification of his life. It would be an unbearable strain, if all that had to be done with deliberate effort and close attention. In fact, many products of manual labour, much of the *technique* in art, and even standard procedure in complex intellectual work, will generally bring better and more even results through skilled routine performance. Yet, that

[1] This may well be a somewhat ironical reference by that great sage to the fact that the well-known Mahāyānic Bodhisattva Vow of liberating all beings of the universe, is often taken much too light-heartedly by many of his fellow Mahāyānists.

evenness of habitual performance too will reach its dead point where it declines. It will show symptoms of fatigue, if it is not enlivened by the creation of new interest in it.

There is, of course, no question of our advocating here the abolishment of all our little habits as far as they are innocuous or even useful. But we should regularly assure ourselves whether we have still control over them, that is, whether we can give them up, or alter them, whenever wanted. We can make sure of it, firstly, by attending to them mindfully for a certain period of time, and secondly, by actually giving them up temporarily in cases where this will not have any harmful or disturbing effects upon ourselves or others. If we turn on them the light of *direct vision*, looking at them or performing them, as if seen or done for the first time, these little routine activities, and the habitual sights around us, will assume a new glow of interest and stimulation. This holds good also for our professional occupation and its environment, and for our close human relationships if they should have become stale by habit. The relations to one's marriage partner, to friends, colleagues, etc., may thus receive a great rejuvenation. A fresh and direct vision will also discover that one can react to people, or do things, in a different and more beneficial way, than done before habitually.

An acquired capacity to give up *little* habits will prove its worth in the fight against more dangerous proclivities, and also at times when we are faced with serious changes in our life which by force deprive us of very fundamental habits. Loosening the hardened soil of our routine behaviour and thoughts, will have an enlivening effect on our vital energy, our mental vigour, our power of imagination, and, what is most important, into that loosened soil we shall be able to plant the seeds of vigorous spiritual progress.

ASSOCIATIVE THOUGHT

Mental habituation to standard reactions, to sequences of activity, to judgements of people or things, etc., proceeds by way of associative thinking. From things or ideas, situations or people that we encounter, we select certain of their distinctive characteristics or marks, and associate, i.e. connect these marks with our own response to them. If these encounters recur, they are associated first with those marks selected earlier, and then with our original, or strongest, response. So these marks became a signal for releasing a standard reaction which may consist of quite a long sequence of connected acts or thoughts, well mastered or known through the repeated practice of experience. That way of functioning relieves man of the necessity to apply ever-renewed effort and painstaking scrutiny to each single step of such sequences of thought and action. This certainly means a great simplification of life and a release of energy for other tasks. In fact, in the evolution of the human mind, associative thinking has been a progressive step of decisive importance. It was indispensable for acquiring the capacity to learn from experience, and led up to the discovery and application of causal laws.

Yet, it is easy to see that, close to these benefits of associative thinking, there lurk, as many and grave dangers in this, now basic, procedure of mental activity, if it is faultily applied or not carefully watched. Let us draw up a list of these danger points (though not an exhaustive one):

1. Initial faulty or incomplete observations, errors of judgement, emotional prejudices (love, hate, pride), etc., may be easily perpetuated and strengthened by the mechanism of associative thinking, through being carried over to re-occurrences of similar situations.

2. Incomplete observations and restricted view-points in judgements, etc., which may have been sufficient for meeting a particular situation, may, if mechanically applied to changed circumstances, prove quite inadequate and may entail grave consequences.

3. Not infrequent are cases where, by misdirected associative thinking, a strong instinctive dislike is felt for things, places or persons which, in some way, are merely reminiscent of unpleasant experiences.

These but briefly stated instances show how vital it is to scrutinize from time to time these mental grooves of our associative thoughts, and the various habits and stereotype reactions deriving from them. In other words, we must step out of the ruts for a while, regain a direct vision of things and make a fresh appraisal of them in the light of that vision.

If we look once again over the list of potential dangers deriving from uncontrolled associative thinking, we shall better understand the Buddha's insistence of getting to the bedrock of experience. For instance, in these profound and terse stanzas called 'The Cave', included in the *Sutta Nipāta*, He says that the 'full penetration of *sense-impression (phassa)* will make one free from greed' and that, 'by understanding *perception (saññā)* one will be able to cross the flood of Saṁsāra' (stanza 778f).[1] By placing mindfulness, as a guard, at the very first gate through which experience enters, we shall be able to control the incomers much more easily, and shut out unwanted intruders. Thus the purity of 'luminous consciousness' can be maintained against 'adventitious defilements' (see *Aṅguttara-Nik.*, I).

The *Satipaṭṭhāna Sutta* provides a systematic training for inducing direct, fresh and undistorted vision, covering the entire personality in its physical and mental aspects, and including the entire world of experience. The methodical application of the several exercises to oneself (*ajjhatta*), to others (*bahiddhā*) and alternatingly to both, will be very helpful in discovering false conceptions due to misdirected associative thinking or misapplied analogies.

The principal types of false associative thinking are covered, in the terminology of the Dhamma, by the four kinds of *misapprehensions* or *perverted views (vipallāsa)* which wrongly take (1) what is impermanent, for permanent, (2) what is painful, or conducive to it, for happiness, (3) what is not-self and unsubstantial, for a self or an abiding substance, (4) what is impure, for beautiful. These perverted views of reality arise through a one-sided and incomplete selection, or entirely false apprehension, of the characteristic marks of things or ideas, and through 'associating' them closely with one's passions and false theories. By gradually 'dissociating' our perceptions and impressions from these misapprehensions, with the help of Bare

[1] Compare also the passage on the significance of sense impression (or contact; *phassa*) in the concluding sections of *Brahmajāla Sutta* (*Dīgha Nikāya*, Sutta 1).

Attention, we shall make steady progress in the *direct vision* of 'bare processes' (*suddha-dhammā*).

THE SENSE OF URGENCY (SAṀVEGA)

He who is stirred (*saṁvijja*) to a sense of urgency (*saṁvega*) by things which are deeply moving to one of clear and direct vision, will experience a release of energy and courage that is able to break through his timid hesitations and his rigid routine of life and thought. If that sense of urgency is kept alive, it will bestow the earnestness and persistence (*appamāda*) required for the work of liberation.

Thus said the teachers of old:

This very world here is our field of action.
It harbours the unfoldment of the Holy Path,
And many things to break complacency.
Be stirred by things which may well move the heart.
And being stirred strive wisely and fight on!'

Ayaṁ kammabhūmi, idha maggabhāvanā,
ṭhānāni saṁvejaniyā bahu idha,
Saṁvega saṁvejaniyesu vatthūsu,
saṁvegajāto'va payuñja yoniso.[1]

Our nearest neighbourhood is full of stirring things, but generally we do not perceive them as such, because habit has made our vision dull and our heart insensitive. Even the Buddha's teaching which, when we first encountered it consciously, was a powerful intellectual and emotional stimulation, will gradually lose for us its original freshness and impelling force, unless we constantly renew it by turning to the fullness of life around us which illustrates the Four Noble Truths in ever new variations. A direct vision will impart new life-blood even to the commonest experiences of everyday, so that their true nature appears through the dim haze of habit, and speaks to us with a fresh voice. It may well be just the long-accustomed sight of

[1] Quoted in the *Commentary* to the *Saṁyutta Nikāya, Salāyatana-Saṁyutta, Devadaha-vaggo catuttho* Sutta No. 2.

the beggar at the street-corner, or a weeping child or the illness of a friend, which startles us afresh, makes us think, and stirs our sense of urgency in treading resolutely the Path that leads to the Cessation of Suffering.

We know the beautiful old account of Prince Siddhattha's coming face to face with old-age, illness and death, when he drove in his chariot through the paternal city, after a long time of isolation in a make-believe world. This ancient story may well be historical fact, because we know that in the lives of many great ones there often occur events which gain a symbolic significance or have great consequences far beyond their ordinary appearances. Great minds find significance in the seemingly common and invest with far-reaching efficacy the fleeting moment. But, without conflicting with the inner truth of that old story, it may well have happened that the young prince had actually seen before, with his fleshly eye, old and sick people and those who had succumbed to death. But, on all these earlier occasions, it may not have touched him very deeply—as it is the case with most of us, most of the time. That earlier lack of sensitivity may have been due to the carefully protected, artificial seclusion of his petty (though princely) happiness into which his father—the hereditary routine of his life—had placed him. Only when he broke through that golden cage of easygoing habits, the facts of suffering struck him as forcibly as if he had seen them for the first time. Then only was he stirred by them to a sense of urgency that led him out of the home life and set his feet firmly on the road to Enlightenment.

The more *clearly* and *deeply* our minds and hearts respond to the Truth of Suffering as appearing in the very common facts of our existence, the less often we shall need a repetition of the lesson learned, the shorter will be our migration through Saṁsāra.[1] The *clarity* of perception evoking our response, will

[1] *Saṁsāra*: 'Round of Rebirth' lit, 'perpetual wandering', is a name for the sea of life ever restlessly heaving up down, the symbol of this continuous process of ever again and again being born, growing old, suffering and dying. More precisely put: Saṁsāra is the unbroken chain of the five-fold Khandha-combinations, which, constantly changing from moment to moment, follow continuously one upon the other through inconceivable periods of time. Of this Saṁsāra, a single lifetime constitutes only a tiny fraction; hence to be

come from an undeflected directness of vision, bestowed by Bare Attention (*sati*); and the *depth* of experience will come from wise reflection or Clear Comprehension (*sampajañña*).

THE ROAD TO INSIGHT

Directness of Vision is also a chief characteristic of the methodical practice of insight-meditation (*vipassanābhāvanā*). There it is identified with the direct or experiential knowledge (*paccakkha-ñāṇa*) bestowed by meditation, as distinguished from the inferential knowledge (*anumānañāṇa*) obtained by study and reflection. In the meditative development of insight, one's own physical and mental processes are directly viewed, without the interference of abstract concepts or the filtering screens of emotional evaluation, which, in this context, will only obscure, or camouflage, the naked facts, and detract from the immediate strong impact of reality. Conceptual generalizations from experience (though very useful elsewhere), if they interrupt the meditative practice of Bare Attention, tend to 'shove aside', or dispose of, the respective particular fact, by saying, as it were: 'It is nothing else but . . .'. Generalizing thought inclines to become impatient with a recurrent type, and soon finds it boring after having it classified. Bare Attention, however, being the key instrument of methodical insight, keeps to the particular. It follows keenly the rise and fall of successive physical and mental processes, and, though all phenomena of a given series may be 'true to type' (e.g. inhalations and exhalations), Bare Attention regards each of them as a distinct 'individual', and conscientiously registers, as it were, its separate birth and death. If mindfulness remains alert, these repetitions of type will, by their multiplication, exert not a reduced but an intensified impact on the mind. The three signs or characteristics (change, misery and voidness), inherent in the process observed, will stand out more and more clearly, appearing in the light shed by the phenomena themselves, and not in a *borrowed* light

---

able to comprehend the first Noble Truth of universal suffering, one must let one's gaze rest upon the Saṁsāra, upon this frightful chain of rebirths, and not merely upon one single lifetime, which, of course, may be sometimes less painful. (*Buddhist Dictionary*, Nyanatiloka).

147

(borrowed not even from the Buddha, though He is the peerless and indispensable guide to these experiences). These physical and mental phenomena, in their 'self-luminosity', will then convey a growing sense of urgency to the meditator: revulsion, dissatisfaction, awareness of danger will arise concerning them, followed by detachment—though, certainly, joy, happiness and calm, too, will not be absent throughout the practice. Then, if all other conditions of inner maturity are fulfilled, the first direct vision of final liberation will dawn, with the Stream-winner's (*sotāpanna*) indubitable knowledge: 'Whatever has the nature of arising, has the nature of vanishing.'

Thus, in the unfoldment of the four-fold power of mindfulness, Satipaṭṭhāna will prove itself as the true embodiment of the Dhamma of which it was said:

'Well proclaimed is the Dhamma by the Blessed One, visible here and now, not delayed, inviting of inspection, onward-leading, and directly experienceable by the wise.'

For further reading on Satipaṭṭhāna Meditation:

The Way of Mindfulness (the Satipaṭṭhāna Sutta and Commentary), transl., with Intro., by Soma Thera, 3rd edition, 152 pages (Kandy, Buddhist Publication Society).

The Foundations of Mindfulness (Satipaṭṭhāna Sutta), transl., with Intro. and Notes, by Nyanasatta Thera (The Wheel No. 19).

The Satipaṭṭhāna Sutta and its Application to Modern Life, V. F. Gunaratna (The Wheel No. 60).

Protection Through Satipaṭṭhāna, Nyanaponika Thera (Bodhi Leaves No. B.34).

The Progress of Insight through the Stages of Purification, Mahasi Sayadaw: Pali text, with Engl. transl. and Notes, by Nyanaponika Thera (Kandy, The Forest Hermitage).

The Heart of Buddhist Meditation, handbook of mental training based on the Buddha's Way of Mindfulness, Nyanaponika Thera (London, Rider & Co.).

V. ANATTA AND NIBBĀNA

THE VEN. NYĀNAPONIKA, MAHĀTHERA

'This world, Kaccāna, usually leans upon a duality: upon (the belief in) existence or non-existence . . . Avoiding these two extremes, the Perfect One shows the doctrine in the middle: Dependent on Ignorance are the Kamma-formations . . . By the cessation of Ignorance, Kamma-formations cease . . .'

—*Saṃyutta-Nikāya* 12, 15

The saying of the Buddha quoted here, speaks of the duality (*dvayatā*) of existence (*atthitā*) and non-existence (*natthitā*). These two terms refer to the theories of eternalism (*sassata-diṭṭhi*) and annihilationism (*uccheda-diṭṭhi*) which are the basic misconceptions of actuality that occur again and again in many variations, in the history of human thought. *Eternalism* is the belief in a permanent substance or entity, be it conceived as a multitude of individual souls or selves (created or not), as a monistic world-soul, a deity of any description, or as a combination of any of these notions. *Annihilationism*, on the other hand, believes in the temporary existence of separate selves or personalities, which are entirely destroyed or dissolved after death. Accordingly, the two key words of the text quoted above, refer (1) to the absolute, i.e. eternal, existence of any assumed substance or entity, and (2) to the ultimate, absolute annihilation of separate entities conceived as impermanent, i.e. their non-existence after the end of their life-span. These two extreme views stand and fall with the assumption of something static of either permanent or impermanent nature. They will lose their basis entirely if life is seen in its true nature, as a continuous flux of material and mental processes arising from their appropriate conditions—a process which will cease only when these conditions are removed. This will explain why our

149

text introduces here the formula of Dependent Origination (*paṭicca-samuppāda*) and its reversal, Dependent Cessation.

Dependent *Origination*, being an unbroken process, excludes the assumption of an absolute Non-existence, or Naught, that is supposed to terminate, by necessity, individual existence; while the qualifying word *dependent* indicates that there is also no absolute, i.e. independent existence, no static Being *per se*, but only an evanescent arising of phenomena, dependent on likewise evanescent conditions.

Dependent *Cessation* excludes the belief in absolute and permanent Existence, and shows, on the other hand, that there is no automatic lapse into Non-existence, but that the cessation of relative existence is likewise a conditioned occurrence.

Thus these teachings of Dependent Origination and Dependent Cessation are a true Doctrine in the Middle, transcending the extremes of Existence and Non-existence.

Thinking by way of such conceptual contrasts as Existence and Non-existence, has, however, a powerful hold on man because that way of thinking is perpetually nourished by several strong roots, deeply embedded in the human mind. The strongest of them is the practical and theoretical assumption of an Ego or self, the existence of which as a separate entity is taken for granted. It is the powerful wish for a preservation and perpetuation of the personality (or a refined version of it), which is at the background of all the numerous varieties of eternalistic belief. But even with people who have discarded eternalistic creeds or theories, the instinctive belief in the uniqueness and importance of their particular personalities is still so strong that for them the end of the personality, i.e. death, is tantamount to complete annihilation or non-existence. Thus the belief in a self is responsible not only for eternalism, but also for the annihilationist view (*uccheda-diṭṭhi*) which may express itself either in the popular unphilosophical materialism ('death is the end of it'), or in elaborate materialist theories.

There are also other contributory roots of these notions of existence and non-existence which, however, are closely connected with the main root of Ego-belief. There is, for instance, a *linguistic* root, consisting in the basic structure of language (subject and predicate, noun and adjective) and its tendency to simplify affirmative and negative statements for the sake of easy communication and orientation. The structural features of language and linguistic habits of simplified statements have exercised a subtle, but strong influence on our way of thinking, making us inclined to assume that 'there must be a thing, if there is a word for it'.

For holding these one-sided views, there may be also *emotional* reasons, expressive of basic attitudes to life. They may reflect the moods of optimism and pessimism, hope and despair, the wish to feel secure through metaphysical support, or the desire to live without inhibitions in a materialistically conceived universe. The theoretical views of eternalism and annihilationism may well change during life-time, together with the corresponding moods or emotional needs.

There is also an *intellectual* root: the speculative and theorizing preoccupation of certain minds,[1] creating various and elaborate philosophical systems in which these and other conceptual opposites are played off against each other with an ingenuity that provides great satisfaction to those engaged in these thought-constructions.

From these brief remarks, one will be able to appreciate the strength and variety of the forces which induce man to think, feel and speak in the way of these opposites, the belief in either absolute existence or absolute non-existence. It was, therefore, with good reason that the Buddha said, in our introductory passage, that men *usually* lean upon that duality. Hence we need not be surprised that even Nibbāna, the Buddhist's goal of deliverance, has been wrongly interpreted in the sense of either of these extremes: existence or non-existence. But these rigid conceptual terms cannot do justice to the dynamic nature of actuality, and still less to Nibbāna which has been declared to be supramundane (*lokuttara*) and beyond conceptual thinking (*atakkāvacara*).

In the early days, when knowledge of Buddhist teachings had just reached the West, most of the writers and scholars

---

[1] They correspond to the *diṭṭhi-carita*, the theorizing type of character, in Buddhist Psychology.

took Nibbāna as *non-existence*, pure and simple, with a few exceptions like Schopenhauer and Max Müller. Consequently, Western writers all too lightly condemned Buddhism as a nihilistic doctrine, teaching annihilation as its highest goal, which these writers described as philosophically absurd and ethically reprehensible. Similar statements can still be read nowadays in prejudiced non-Buddhist literature. The pendular reaction to that view was the conception of Nibbāna as *existence*, in the sense of Pure Being, Pure Being, Pure Consciousness, Pure Self, or any other metaphysical concept, seeing it in the light of religious and metaphysical notions familiar in the West and in the East alike.

But even Buddhist thought could not always keep clear of a lop-sided interpretation of Nibbāna. This happened even in early times: the sect of the Sautrantikas had a rather negativistic view of Nibbāna, while the Mahayanistic conceptions of Buddhafields (*Buddha-ksetra*), Primordial (*Ādi-*) Buddha, Tathāgatagarbha, etc., favoured a positive-metaphysical interpretation.

It is therefore not surprising that both these extremes are also advocated by modern Buddhist authors. In Buddhist countries of the East, however, there is now, as far as known to the writer, not a single Buddhist school or sect that favours a nihilistic interpretation of Nibbāna. Contrary to erroneous opinions, voiced mainly by uninformed or prejudiced Western authors, Theravāda, i.e. the tradition prevalent in Burma, Ceylon, Thailand, etc., is definitely averse to a view that regards Nibbāna as mere extinction. The first main section of this essay will substantiate this statement.

For reasons mentioned earlier, it is not easy, indeed, always to steer clear of those two opposite views of existence and non-existence, and to keep closely to the Middle Path shown by the Buddha, i.e. the teaching of Dependent Origination and Dependent Cessation. Until that way of thinking, i.e. in terms of conditionality, has been fully absorbed in the texture of one's mind, constant watchfulness will be required against the mind slipping unawares into either of the two extreme views of eternalism and annihilationism, or coming too close to them.

When discussing these questions there is the danger of being carried away by one's own arguments and countering one extreme by its opposite. Therefore, in the treatment of that problem, great caution and self-criticism is required lest one may lose sight of the Middle Path.

It is therefore the primary purpose of this treatise to offer material for a clear demarcation of the Buddha's doctrine of Nibbāna from both misinterpretations of it. It is not the intention of these pages to encourage any speculations on the nature of Nibbāna, which are bound to be futile and may even prove to be detrimental to the endeavours for an actual attainment of it. According to an elucidation of the four Noble Truths, as found in the texts, Nibbāna, the third Truth, is to be realized (*sacchikātabbaṃ*), not to be understood (as the first Truth), nor to be developed (as the fourth Truth). It must also be emphasized here that it will be improper to use the material presented here, in a one-sided manner as an argument in favour of either of the extremes against the other one. Each of the two main sections of this treatise requires the other for its qualification and completion. It is hoped that the material from canonical and commentarial sources collected in these pages, will at least reduce the points of conflict between the opposing interpretations, by clarifying the position of Theravāda.

1. THE NIHILISTIC-NEGATIVE EXTREME

PART I

We shall first consider the basic work of post-canonical Theravāda literature. 'The Path of Purification' (*Visuddhimagga*), compiled in the fifth century A. C. by the great commentator, Bhadantācariya Buddhaghosa. This monumental work furnishes a comprehensive and systematic exposition of the principal Buddhist doctrines, derived from the Pāli Canon and ancient commentarial literature which partly incorporates material that may well go back to the earliest times of the teaching.

In that work, in the chapter (XVI) on the Faculties and Truths, in the section dealing with the Third Noble Truth, we find a lengthy disquisition on Nibbāna. It is striking that the polemical part of it is exclusively directed against what we have called the 'nihilistic-negative extreme' in the interpretattion of Nibbāna. We cannot be sure about the reason for that limitation, since there is no explicit statement on it. It is, however, possible that the Venerable Buddhaghosa (or perhaps already the traditional material he used) was keen that the Theravāda teachings on that subject should be well distinguished from those of a prominent contemporary sect, the Sautrantikas, which, in other respects, was close to the general standpoint of Theravāda. It belonged to that group of schools which we suggest should be called *Sāvakayāna* (following the *early* Mahayanist nomenclature), instead of the derogatory Hinayāna. The Theravādins obviously did not want to be included in the accusation of nihilism, raised by the Mahayanists against the Sautrantikas. This might have been the external reason for the *Visuddhi-magga's* emphasis on the rejection of the nihilistic conception of Nibbāna. As to the positive-metaphysical view, the Venerable Buddhaghosa thought it, perhaps, sufficiently covered by the numerous passages in the *Visuddhi-magga* dealing with the rejection of the eternity-view and of a transcendental Self. However that may be, also nowadays Buddhism, and Theravāda in particular is quite often wrongly accused of nihilism. It is therefore apposite to reproduce here extracts from the relevant arguments found in the *Visuddhi-magga*, followed (in paragraph 2) by additions from the commentary to that work.[1] Many of the passages from the Suttanta (the Discourses of the Buddha) which are relevant to a rejection of nihilism, are quoted in both these extracts, making it unnecessary to deal with them separately.

In the aforementioned chapter of the *Visuddhi-magga*, the argument proper is preceded by a definition of Nibbāna, by way

[1] The rendering in the extracts from both works has mainly been taken, with a few alterations, from the excellent translation of the VisM, by Bhikkhu Nāṇamoli ('The Path of Purification'; XLIX, 886 pp; publ. by R. Semage, 1956. Explanatory additions by the writer of this essay are in [square brackets]: while those by Bhikkhu Nāṇamoli are in (curved brackets).

of three categories usually employed in commentarial literature for the purpose of definition.

'Nibbāna has peace as its characteristic. Its function is not to die; or its function is to comfort. It is manifested as the signless [i.e. without the "signs", or marks, of greed, hatred and delusion]; or it is manifested as non-diversification.'

[The first assertion about Nibbāna as non-existence, which follows now, is not a view about the *nature* of Nibbāna, but a simple denial of it, on account of the alleged illogical nature of the conception itself:]

'(Question 1.) [Is it not true that] Nibbāna is non-existent because it is unapprehensible like the hare's horn?
'(Answer.) That is not so, because it is apprehensible by the (right) means. For it is apprehensible by some (namely the Noble Ones) by the right means, in other words, by the way that is appropriate to it (the way of virtue, concentration, and understanding) . . . Therefore it should not be said that it is non-existent because unapprehensible; for it should not be said that what the foolish ordinary man does not apprehend is unapprehensible.'

[And for those who are followers of the Dhamma, it is added:]

'Again it should not be said that Nibbāna does not exist. Why not? Because it then follows that the way would be futile. For if Nibbāna were non-existent, then it would follow that the right way, which includes the three Aggregates beginning with Virtue, and is headed by right understanding, would be futile. And it is not futile because it reaches Nibbāna.
'(Q.2) But futility of the way does not follow because what is reached is absence [which has been aspired for] (that is, absence of the five aggregates, consequent upon the cutting off of the defilements)?
'(A.) That is not so. Because, though there is [always] absence

of past and future (aggregates), there is nevertheless no reaching of Nibbāna (simply because of that).

'(Q.3) Then is the absence of present (aggregates) as well Nibbāna? . . .

'(A.) That is not so. Because their absence is an impossibility (being self-contradictory), since their absence means that they are *not* present. (Besides if Nibbāna were absence of present aggregates too), that would entail the fault of excluding the arising of the Nibhāna element with result of past clinging left [*sopādisesanibbāna*; i.e. Nibbāna during lifetime], at the path moment which has present aggregates as its support.

'(Q.4) Then will there be no fault if it is the non-presence of defilements (that is Nibbāna)?

'(A.) That is not so. Because it would then follow that the noble path was meaningless. For if it were so, then, since defilements (can be) non-existent also before the moment of the noble path [of arahantship; e.g. temporarily, in every profitable (*kusala*) state of mind], it follows that the noble path would be meaningless. . . .

'(Q.5) But is not Nibbāna destruction (*khaya*), because of the passage beginning "That, friend, which is the destruction of greed . . . (of hate . . . of delusion . . . is Nibbāna)" (*S. IV*, 251)?

'(A.) That is not so, because it would follow that arahantship, also, was mere destruction. For that, too, is described in the (same) way beginning "That, friend, which is the destruction of greed . . . (of hate . . . of delusion . . . is arahantship)" (*S. IV*, 252).[1]

'And what is more, the fallacy then follows that Nibbāna would be temporary, etc.; for if it were so, it would follow that Nibbāna would be temporary [being limited to the moment of the destruction of greed, etc.], formed [conditioned (*saṅkhata*); because the destruction of greed, etc., is a conditioned phenomenon, but not Nibbāna]. . . .

'. . . Because [Nibbāna] serves figuratively speaking as

---

[1] 'But,' says the commentary, 'Arahantship is certainly not mere destruction, since it consists in the four mental aggregates having the highest fruition (of arahantship) as their foremost.'

decisive-support (*upanissaya*) for the kind of destruction called "cessation consisting in non-arising" (*anuppattini-rodha*), that (Nibbāna) is called "destruction" (*khaya*) as a metaphor for it. . . .

'(Q.7) Why is Nibbāna not described in its own nature [but only by circumlocutions and negations]?

'(A.) Because of its extreme subtlety. And its extreme subtlety is established because it inclined the Blessed One to inaction (that is, to not teaching the Dhamma; see *M*. I, 186) and because a Noble One's eye is needed to see it (*M*. I, 510). It is not shared by all because it can only be reached by one who is possessed of the path. And it is uncreated because it has no first beginning.

'(Q.8) Since it *is*, when the path is, then it is not un-created?

'(A.) That is not so, because it is not arousable by the path; it is only reachable, not arousable, by the path; that is why it is uncreated. It is because it is uncreated that it is free from ageing and death. It is because of the absence of its creation and of its ageing and death that it is permanent. . . .

'. . . The Buddha's goal is one and has no plurality. But this (single goal, Nibbāna), is firstly called "with result of past clinging left" (*sa-upādisesa*) since it is made known to-gether with the (aggregates resulting from past) clinging still remaining (during the Arahant's life), being thus made known in terms of the stilling of defilement and the remaining (result of past) clinging that are present in one who has reached it by means of development. But (secondly, it is called "without result of past clinging left" (*anupādisesa*) since after the last consciousness of the Arahant, who has abandoned arousing (future aggregates) and so prevented kamma from giving result in a future (existence), there is no further arising of aggregates of existence, and those already arisen have dis-appeared. So the (result of past) clinging that remained is non-existent, and it is in terms of this non-existence, in the sense that "there is no (result of past) clinging here" that that (same goal) is called "without result of past clinging left" (see *Itivuttaka* 38).

'Because it can be arrived at by distinction of knowledge that succeeds through untiring perseverance,[1] and because it is the word of the Omniscient One,[2] Nibbāna is not non-existent as regards its nature in the ultimate sense (*paramatthena nāvijjamānaṁ sabhāvato nibbānaṁ*); for this is said: "Bhikkhus, there is an unborn, an unbecome, an unmade, an unformed" (*It.* 37; *Ud.* 80).'

PART II

Taking up the last quotation, the Commentary to the *Visuddhimagga* (*Paramattha-mañjusā*),[3] says:

*'By these words the Master proclaimed the actual existence of Nibbāna in the ultimate sense. But he did not proclaim it as a mere injunction of his [i.e. as a creedal dogma], saying: "I am the Lord and Master of the Dhamma"; but, in his compassion for those to whom intellectual understanding is the highest that is attainable (*padaparama*), he also stated it as a reasoned conclusion (*yuttito*), in the continuation of the passage quoted above (*Ud.* 80): "If bhikkhus, there were not the unborn, etc., an escape from what is born, etc., could not be perceived (*na paññāyetha*). But because, bhikkhus, there is an unborn, etc., and escape from what is born, etc., can be perceived." This is the meaning: if the Unformed Element (*asaṅkhata-dhātu*=Nibbāna), having the nature of being unborn, etc., did not exist, no escape from the formed (or conditioned; *saṅkhata*), i.e. the five aggregates, could be perceived in this world; their final coming-to-rest (i.e. cessation) could not be perceived (*na paññāyeyya*), could not be found (or apprehended; *na upalabheyya*), would not be possible (*na sambhaveyya*). But if Right Understanding and the other path factors, each performing its own function, take Nibbāna

---

[1] Comy: 'This is to show that, for Arahants, Nibbāna is established by their own experience (*paccakkhasiddhatam*).'

[2] Comy: 'For others it is established by inference [based on the words of the Master (*anumāna-siddhatam*)].'

[3] The paragraphs beginning with * are translated by the author of this essay; those without, by Bhikkhu Nāṇamoli (taken from the notes to his translation of the *Visuddhi-magga*).

as object, then they will completely destroy the defilements. Therefore one can perceive here a getting-away, an escape from the suffering of existence in its entirety.

'Now in the ultimate sense the existingness of the Nibbāna-element has been demonstrated by the Fully Enlightened One, compassionate for the whole world, by many Sutta passages such as "Dhammas without condition," "Unformed dhammas" (see *Dhammasaṅganī*), "Bhikkhus, there is that sphere (*āyatana*) where neither earth. . . " (*Ud.* 80) "This state is very hard to see, that is to say, the stilling of all formations, the relinquishing of all substance of becoming" (*D.* II, 36; *M.* I, 167), "Bhikkhus, I shall teach you the unformed and the way leading to the unformed" (*S.* IV, 362), and so on, and in this Sutta "Bhikkhus, there is an unborn . . ." (*It.* 37; *Ud.* 80). . . .

'. . . the words "Bhikkhus, there is an unborn, an unmade, an unformed" and so on, which demonstrate the existingness of Nibbāna in the ultimate sense, are not misleading [or: have not an ambiguous meaning; *aviparītattha*] because they are spoken by the Omniscient One, like the words "All formations are impermanent, all formations are painful, all *dhammas* (states) are not-self" (*Dh.* 277–9; *A.* I, 286; etc.).

*'If Nibbāna were mere non-existence (or absence; *abhavamattaṁ eva*), it could not be described by terms as "profound [deep, hard to see, hard to comprehend, peaceful, lofty, inaccessible to ratiocination, subtle to be known by the wise]" etc.; or as "the unformed, [the cankerless, the true, the other shore]", etc.[1]; "kammically neutral (without condition, unincluded [within the three realms of existence]", etc.'[2]

PART III

The references to Sutta-texts, quoted in the extracts from the *Visuddhi-magga* and its commentary, make it quite clear that

---

[1] These are some of the altogether 33 designations of Nibbāna, in *Saṁyutta Nikāya* 43, 12–44.

[2] This infers to Abhidhammic classifications in which Nibbāna is included, occurring, for instance, in the *Dhammasaṅgani*.

the Buddha declared Nibbāna to be an attainable entity (see paragraph 1, Q. 1; paragraph 8) and did not conceive it as the mere fact of extinction or cessation (see paragraph 1, Q. 5). All negatively formulated statements on Nibbāna should be understood in the light of the Sutta passages quoted here, and do not admit an interpretation contradictory to these texts. Any forced or far-fetched interpretation of them will be contrary to the whole straightforward way of the Buddha's exposition.

If we have spoken above of Nibbāna as an 'entity', it should be taken just as a word-label meant to exclude 'non-existence'. It is used in the same restricted sense of a linguistic convention in the emphatic words in the *Udāna*: 'There *is* an unborn . . .', 'There *is* that sphere where neither earth . . .'. It is not meant to convey the meaning of 'existence' in the strict sense, which should be kept limited to 'the five aggregates or any of them'. Nibbāna is indescribable in the strictest sense (*avacanīya, avyākata*).

Our extracts from such an authoritative work as the *Visuddhi-magga* will have shown how emphatically the Theravāda tradition has rejected a nihilistic conception of its highest ideal, Nibbāna. This fact may perhaps help to remove one of the points of controversy among modern writers and Buddhist schools: the prejudice that Theravāda, or even the Pāli Canon, advocates 'annihilation' as its highest goal.

There is, however, another principal point of difference in the interpretation of Buddhism, and of the Pāli Canon in particular which is likewise closely connected with the conception of Nibbāna. It is the question of the range of validity, or application, of the *Anattā* doctrine, i.e. the doctrine of impersonality. It applies not only to the world of conditioned phenomena, but also to Nibbāna. The denial of its application to the latter falls under the heading of the 'positive-metaphysical extreme' which will be treated in the following section.

2. THE POSITIVE-METAPHYSICAL EXTREME

PART IV

In India, a country so deeply religious and philosophically so creative, the far greater danger to the preservation of the Dhamma's character as a 'Middle Way', consisted in identifying, or connecting, the concept of Nibbāna with any of the numerous theistic, pantheistic or other speculative ideas of a positive-metaphysical type and, chiefly, with various conceptions of an abiding self. According to the penetrative analysis in the *Brahmajāla Sutta* (*Dīgha Nik.* I), all these various notions of a self (and this applies also to other metaphysical or theological statements) arise from either of two sources: (I) from a limited and misinterpreted meditative experience (where we may also include supposed revelations, prophetic inspirations, etc.), (2) from bare reasoning (speculative philosophy and theology). But as the driving force behind all these metaphysical and theological productions of the human mind looms the powerful urge in man to preserve, in some way or other, his belief in an abiding individuality, or in any mental projection of that urge which he can invest, by proxy, with all his longings for permanency, security, eternal happiness, etc. It is therefore not surprising that, yielding to that powerful instinctive urge for 'self'-preservation, and under the influence of long-cherished and widely held views, there are also nowadays advocates of the positive-metaphysical interpretation of Nibbāna and *Anattā*, who sincerely believe themselves to be true Buddhists; and among them are many who have a genuine devotion towards the Buddha and a fair appreciation of other aspects of his teachings. With these views we shall now be concerned.

In the spirit of the Middle Way, the following refutation of the positive-metaphysical extreme is also meant to guard against any metaphysical conclusions which may be wrongly derived from our rejection of nihilism, in the first section of this essay. In the reverse, that first section may serve to counter an excessive 'defence-reaction' against the metaphysical views to be treated now.

L

The positive-metaphysical extreme in the interpretation of Nibbāna consists in the identification, or metaphysical association, of a refined or purified self (attā) with what, in the context of this view, is held to be Nibbāna. Two main types of the metaphysical view can be distinguished which are already implied in the preceding sentence.

(1) The assumption of a universal and unitary (non-dual and non-pluralistic) principle with which a purified self, i.e. one thought to be liberated from the aggregates (khandhā), either merges, or is assumed to be basically one. These views might differ in details, according to their being influenced either by Theosophy, Vedānta or Mahāyāna (the latter, with varying degrees of justification).[1]

(2) The assumption that the transcendental 'selves' of the Arahants, freed from the aggregates, enter Nibbāna which is regarded as their 'eternal home' and as 'the only state adequate to them'. Nibbāna itself is admitted to be not-self (anattā), while the Holy Ones (Arahants) are supposed to retain 'in Nibbāna' some kind of individuality, in a way unexplained and unexplainable. This view is, to our knowledge, advocated in such a way only by the German author Dr Georg Grimm and his followers.

PART V

(a) Common to both views is the assumption of an eternal self supposed to exist beyond the five aggregates (khandhā) that

---

[1] The *theosophical* variant is, e.g. represented by neo-buddhistic groups in Britain and elsewhere which otherwise have done good work in introducing Westerners to Buddhism or to their conception of it.—The *vedantic* influence is conspicuous, e.g. in utterances of well-meaning Indians, among them men of eminence, maintaining the basic identity or similarity, of the vedantic and buddhistic position concerning *Ātman*. This is, by the way, quite in contrast to the opinion on that subject, expressed by the great classical exponents of Vedānta. See *Vedānta and Buddhism*, By H. v. Glasenapp ('The Wheel', Publ. No. 2),—*Mahāyānistic* influence may be noticeable in some representatives of the former two variants. But also in Mahāyāna literature itself, the positive-metaphysical extreme is met with, in varying degrees: ranging from the Mādhyamika scriptures where it is comparatively negligible, up to the Yogā-cāra school where Asaṅga uses even the terms *mahātma* and *paramātma* in an approving sense (see *Mahāyāna-sutrālankāra-sāstra* and Asaṅga's own commentary).

make up personality and existence in its entirety. The supposition that the Buddha should have taught anything like that, is clearly and sufficiently refuted alone by the following saying:

'Any ascetics or brāhmans who conceive manifold (things or ideas) as the self, all of them conceive the five aggregates (as the self) or any one of them.'
Ye hi keci bhikkhave samaṇā vā brāhmaṇā vā anekavihitaṁ attānaṁ samanupassamānā samanupassanti, sabbe te pañcupādānakkhandhe samanupassanti etesaṁ vā aññataraṁ (*Samyutta-Nikāya* 22, 47).

This textual passage also excludes any misinterpretation of the standard formulation of the *Anattā* doctrine: 'This does not belong to me, this I am not, this is not my self.' Some writers believe that this statement permits the conclusion that the Buddha supposed a self to exist outside, or beyond, the five aggregates to which the above formula usually refers. This wrong deduction is finally disposed of by the words of the Buddha quoted above, which clearly say that all the manifold conceptions of a self can have reference only to the five aggregates or to any one, or several, of them. How else could any idea of a self or a personality be formed, if not from the material of the five aggregates and from a misconception of them? On what else could notions about a self be based alternatively? This fact about the only possible way how ideas of a self can be formed was expressed by the Buddha Himself, in the continuation of the text quoted above:

'There is bhikkhus, an uninstructed worldling . . . He regards corporeality as self, or the self as possessing corporeality, or the corporeality as being within the self, or the self within corporeality [similarly with the four mental aggregates].[1] In this way he arrives at that very conception "I am" (*iti ayañ-c'eva samanupassanā asmī'ti c'assa adhigataṁ hoti*).' (*Samy.* 22, 47).

Further it was said: 'If there are corporeality, feeling, per-

[1] These are the twenty kinds of individuality-belief (*vīsati sakkāya-diṭṭhi*).

ception, formations and consciousness, on account of them and dependent on them arises the belief in individuality . . . and speculations about a self' (*Saṁy.* 22, 154, 155).

(*b*) If the words 'I', 'ego', 'personality', 'self', etc., should have a meaning at all, any form of an ego-conception, even the most abstract and diluted one, must necessarily be connected with the idea of particularity or separateness, i.e. with a differentiation from what is regarded as *not* 'ego'. But from what could that particularity or differentiation be derived if not from the only available data of experience, i.e. the physical and mental phenomena which have been comprised by the Buddha under the classification of the five aggregates?

In the Discourse called 'The Simile of the Serpent' (*Majjh,* 22), it is said:

' "If, bhikkhus, there is a self, will there also be something belonging to a self?"—"Certainly, Lord".—"If there is something belonging to a self, will there also be (the view) 'My self'?"—"Certainly, Lord".—"But since, bhikkhus, a self and anything belonging to a self cannot truly and really be found, is it not a perfectly foolish doctrine to hold the point of view 'This is the world. This is the self. Permanent, abiding, eternal and immutable shall I be after death, in eternal identity shall I persist'?"—"What else should it be, O Lord, than a perfectly foolish doctrine." '

The first sentence of that text expresses, in a manner as simple as emphatic, the fact pointed out before: that the assumption of a self requires also something 'belonging to a self' (*attaniya*), i.e. properties by which that self receives its distinguishing characteristics. To speak of a self devoid of such differentiating attributes, having therefore nothing to characterize it and to give meaningful contents to the word, will be entirely senseless and in contradiction to the accepted usage of these terms 'self', 'ego', etc. But this very thing is done by those who advocate the first of the two main-types of the 'positive-metaphysical extreme': that is, the assumption of a 'great, universal self, or over-self' (*mahātman*) supposed to merge, or be basically

164

identical with, a universal and undifferentiated (*nirguṇa*) metaphysical principle which is sometimes equated with Nibbāna. Those who hold these views are sometimes found to make the bold claim that the Buddha wanted to deny only a 'separate self' and that, in none of His utterances, He rejected the existence of a 'transcendental self'. What has been said before in this section, may serve as an answer to these beliefs.

Those views, however, which we have assigned to the second category, insist on the separate existence of liberated, transcendental 'selves' within the Nibbāna-element. They leave quite a number of issues unexplained: how they arrive at any idea of separateness without reference to the world of experience; in what that 'separateness' actually consists and how it can be said to persist in the Nibbāna-element, which, by definition, is undifferentiated (*nippapañca*), that is, the very reverse of separateness.

Both varieties of individuality-belief wish to combine various conceptions of self with the Buddhist teaching of Nibbāna. They are, at the very outset, refuted by the philosophically very significant statement in the Discourse on the 'Simile of the Serpent', implying that I and Mine, owner and property, substance and attribute, subject and predication are inseparable correlative terms, which, however, lack reality in the ultimate sense.

PART VI

The two main-types of a positive-metaphysical interpretation of Nibbāna can be easily included in a considerable number of false views, mentioned, classified and rejected by the Buddha. A selection of applicable classifications will be presented in what follows. This material, additional to the fundamental remarks in the preceding section, will furnish an abundance of documentation for the fact that not a single eternalistic conception of self and Nibbāna, of any conceivable variety, is reconcilable with the teachings of the Buddha as found in their oldest available presentation, in the Pāli Canon.

(*a*) In the *Saṁyutta Nikāya* (22, 86; 44, 2) we read:

' "Do you think, Anurādha, that the Perfect One is apart from corporeality (*aññatra rūpā*) . . . apart from consciousness?"[1]—"Certainly not, O Lord."—"Do you think that the Perfect One is someone without corporeality (*arūpī*) . . . someone (*tathāgata*) without consciousness?"[2]—"Certainly not, O Lord."—"Since the Perfect One, Anurādha, cannot, truly and really, be found by you even during lifetime, is it befitting to declare: 'He who is the Perfect One, the highest being . . . that Perfect One can be made known outside of these four possibilities. The Perfect One exists after death . . . does not exist . . . exists in some way and in another way not . . . neither can be said to exist nor not to exist."—"Certainly not, O Lord." '

This text applies to both main-types which assume a self beyond the aggregates. It deserves to be mentioned here that the Commentary paraphrases the words 'the Perfect One' (*tathāgato*) by 'living being' (*satto*). That is probably meant to convey that the statements in the text are valid not only for the conventional term 'the Perfect One', but that they hold true also for any other terms designating an individuality.

(*b*) Since the concept of a self is necessarily linked with that of an ownership of qualities and possessions (see paragraph 5b), both main-types come under the following headings of the twenty kinds of individuality-belief (*sakkāyadiṭṭhi*; see paragraph 5a): 'He regards the self as possessing corporeality . . . as possessing feeling . . . perception . . . formations . . . consciousness.'

This applies, in particular, to the second main-type advocated by Dr Georg Grimm who expressly speaks of the five aggregates as 'attributions' ('Beilegungen') of the self. It does not make here any difference that these 'attributions' are regarded by Grimm as 'incommensurate' to the self and as capable of being discarded. What matters, here, is the fact that such a

---

[1] i.e. outside the aggregates taken singly.
[2] i.e. outside the aggregates as a whole.

relationship between the self and the aggregates is assumed, and this justifies the inclusion of that view in the aforementioned type of individuality-belief.

(c) From the 'Discourse on the Root Cause' (*Mūlapariyāya Sutta*; *Majjh*, 1), the following categories apply to both types: 'He thinks (himself) different from (or: beyond) the four material elements, the heavenly worlds, the uncorporeal spheres; from anything seen, heard, (differently) sensed and cognized; from the whole (universe), (*sabbato*); to the second type is applicable: 'He thinks (himself) in Nibbāna (*nibbānasmiṁ*) or as different from Nibbāna (*nibbānato maññnati*; that is, he believes that the liberated self supposed to enter the Nibbāna element, is different from it).'

(d) In the Sutta 'All Cankers' (*Sabb'āsava Sutta*; *Majjh*, 2), the following instances of unwise and superficial thinking (*ayoniso manasikāra*) are mentioned and rejected:

Six theories about the self, from which the following are applicable here: 'I have a self', 'By the self I know the self.'[1]

Sixteen kinds of doubt about the existence and nature of the self, with reference to the past, present and future, e.g. 'Am I or am I not?', 'What am I?', 'Shall I be or not?', 'What shall be?'

Hereby any type of speculation about an alleged self is rejected.

(e) In the *Brahmajāla Sutta* (*Dīgh*, 1), the theories about a self are specified as to their details. Those, however, who advocate the two main-types of the positive-metaphysical extreme, with which we are here concerned, generally avoid or reject detailed statements on the nature of Nibbāna and the self. But if, by them, an eternal and transcendental self is assumed, it must be thought as being of a passive nature (Pāli *vañjho*, barren, unproductive) and motionless, i.e. immutable. For, any creative or other relationship to the world would involve an abandonment of the transcendental state assumed. Therefore both main-types fall under the eternalist view, characterized in the *Brahmajāla Sutta* as follows: 'Eternal are self and world;

---

[1] Pāli: *attanā'va attānam sanjanāmi*. This refers to vedantic conceptions. Quite similar formulations are found already in the *Saṁhita*, the pre-Buddhist *Upaniṣads*, later in the *Bhagavadgīta*.

barren (*vañjho*), motionless like a mountain peak, steadfast like a pillar.'

(*f*) The rejection of any belief in a self (as abiding or temporarily identical) and of the extremes of existence and not-existence cannot be better concluded then by quoting the continuation of the saying that forms the motto of this treatise:

'For him, Kaccāna, who considers, according to reality and with true wisdom, the origination of (and in) the world, there is not what in the world (is called) "non-existence" (*natthitā*). For him, Kaccanā, who considers, according to reality and with true wisdom, the cessation of (and in) the world there is not what in the world (is called) "existence" (*atthitā*). This world, in general, Kaccāna, is fettered by propensities, clingings and biases. But he (the man of right understanding, *sammā-diṭṭhi*) concerning these propensities, clingings, fixed mental attitudes, biases and deep-rooted inclinations, he does not come near, does not cling, does not have the mental attitude "I have a self" (*n'adhiṭṭhāti attā me'ti*). He has no doubt or uncertainty that it is suffering, indeed, that arises, and suffering that ceases. Herein his knowledge does not rely on others. In so far, Kaccāna, is one a man of right understanding.' (*Saṁy*, 12, 15.)

3. TRANSCENDING THE EXTREMES

If we examine the utterances on Nibbāna, in the Pāli Canon, we find that it is described (or better: paraphrased) in positive and negative terms. Statements of a positive nature are, e.g. designations like 'the profound, the true, the pure, the permanent, the marvellous', etc. (*Saṁy*, 43; see paragraph 2); further, texts such as those quoted above (paragraph 2); 'There is that sphere . . .', 'There is an unborn . . .', etc. Statements in the form of negative terms are, e.g. definitions of Nibbāna as 'the destruction of greed, hatred and delusion', as cessation of existence' (*bhavanirodha*; *Saṁy*, 12, 68). If the Buddhist doctrine of Nibbāna is to be understood correctly, one will have to give full weight to the significance of both types of utterance. If one were to quote only one group of them, as a vindication of one's own one-sided opinion, it would result in a lop-sided view.

To the utterances of positive character we may ascribe the following purposes: (1) to exclude the nihilistic extreme, (2) to allay the fears of those who are still without an adequate grasp of the truths of Suffering and *Anattā* and consequently shrink back from the final cessation of suffering, i.e. of rebirth, as if recoiling from a threatening fall into a bottomless abyss, (3) for showing Nibbāna as a goal capable of attainment and truly desirable.

The emphatic 'There is' that opens the two well-known texts on Nibbāna, in the *Udāna*, leaves no doubt that Nibbāna is not conceived as bare extinction or as a camouflage for an absolute Zero. But, on the other hand, as a precaution against a metaphysical misinterpretation of that solemn enunciation '*There is . . . (atthi)*', we have that likewise emphatic rejection of the extremes of existence (*atthitā*) and non-existence (*natthitā*).

But even those utterances on Nibbāna which are phrased positively, include mostly negative terms too;

'There is that sphere where there is neither earth . . . neither this world nor the next, neither coming nor going . . .'.

'There is an *un*born, an *un*become . . .'

'I shall teach you the Unformed . . . the Profound . . . , and way to it. What now is the Unformed . . . the Profound? . . . It is the destruction of greed, the destruction of hatred, the destruction of delusion.'

These texts, combining positive and negative statements, illustrate our earlier remark that both the positive and the negative utterances on Nibbāna require mutual qualification, as a precaution against sliding into an extremist position.

Negative utterances are meant to emphasize the supramundane and undepictable nature of Nibbāna that eludes any adequate description in positive terms. Our language is basically unsuited for it, since it is necessarily related to our world

169

of experience, and its structure and terms are derived from it. Therefore the positive statements in the Suttas cannot be more than allusions or metaphors (*pariyāyadesanā*), making use of emotional values intelligible to us, and of experiences and reactions known to those who have trodden the path to the Pathless. In brief, they are evocative, and not truly descriptive; but they have nevertheless great practical value for the reasons mentioned above. Negative statements, however, are quite sound and legitimate in themselves. They relate Nibbāna to the world of experience only by negations. The negating method of approach consists in a process of eliminating what is inapplicable to Nibbāna and incommensurate with it. It enables us to make much more definite statements about the supramundane state of Nibbāna than by the use of abstract terms, the positive character of which can be only metaphorical. Negative statements are also the most appropriate and reverential way to speak of that which has been called the Marvellous (*acchariya*) and the Extraordinary (*abbhuta*).

Negative ways of expressions have also another important advantage. Statements like those defining Nibbāna as 'the destruction of greed, hatred and delusion', at the same time, indicate the direction to be taken, and the work to be done, for actually *reaching* Nibbāna. And it is this which matters most. These words on the overcoming of greed, hatred and delusion set a clear and convincing task which can be taken up here and now. Further they do not only point to a way that is practicable, and is worthwhile for its own sake, but they also speak of the lofty goal itself which likewise can be experienced here and now, and not only in an unknown Beyond. For it has been said: 'If greed, hatred and delusion have been completely destroyed, insofar is Nibbāna visible here and now, not delayed, inviting of inspection, and directly experienceable by the wise' (*Aṅguttara Nik.* III, No. 55).

That visible Nibbāna has been lauded by those who attained to it, as an unalloyed and unalienable happiness, as the highest solace, as the unspeakable relief of being freed from burden and bondage. A faint foretaste of it may be experienced in each act of joyful renunciation and in moments of serene detachment.

To know oneself, if but temporarily and partially, free from the slavery of passions and the blindness of self-deception; to be master of oneself and to live and think in the light of knowledge, if but for a time and to a limited extent—these are truly not 'mere negative facts', but are the most positive and elevating experiences for those who know more than the fleeting and deceptive happiness of the senses. 'There are two kinds of happiness, O monks: the happiness of the sense-pleasures, and the happiness of renunciation. But the greater of them is the happiness of renunciation' (*Anguttara-Nikāya, Duka-nipāta*).

Thus, these seemingly negative words of the destruction of greed, hatred and delusion, will convey to the thoughtful and energetic a stirring positive message: of a way that can here be trodden, of a goal that can here be reached, of a happiness that can here be experienced.

That aspect of a lofty happiness attainable here and now, should, however, not be allowed to cover for us the fact that the attainment of Nibbāna is the end of rebirth, the cessation of becoming. This end or cessation is, however, in no way the destruction or annihilation of anything. What actually takes place is the ending of new origination owing to the stopping of its root-causes: ignorance and craving.

He who sees the Truth of Suffering deeply and thoroughly, is 'no longer carried away by the unreal, and no longer shrinks back from the real'. He knows, 'It is suffering, indeed, that arises, it is suffering that ceases.' With a mind unswerving, he strives after the deathless state, the final cessation of suffering—Nibbāna.

The Holy Ones know it as bliss:
    the personality's cessation;
Repugnant to the worldly folk,
    but not to those who clearly see.
What others count as highest bliss,
    as pain regard it Holy Ones;
What those as painful do regard
    is for the Holy Ones sheer bliss.'

        (*Sutta-nipāta*, 761/2)

VI. NIRVANA, NIHILISM AND SATORI[1]

DOUGLAS M. BURNS, M.D.

---

1. CARDINAL FEATURES OF BUDDHIST THOUGHT

THE REALM OF CHANGE

To understand the word 'Nirvāna' one must be acquainted with the other major tenets of Buddhism. For on a conceptual level (but not on an experiental level) Nirvāna is an important part of a well-integrated philosophical system. Thus to begin our discussion of Nirvāna let us first speak of its antithesis, *saṁsāra*, the so-called 'world of becoming'. In Buddhism the word '*saṁsāra*' designates the entire universe of physical and psychological existence—time, space, matter, thought, emotion, volition, perception, karma, etc.

The Buddhist version of the beginning of existence is unique among the world's religions. For it teaches that there is no discernible beginning; there never was a Primal Cause which at a given instant in eternity produced or began to produce the universe. Rather the Buddha taught that every object and condition is the result of other objects and conditions which preceded it; and these in turn are the results of still earlier ones, and so on back into the beginningless past. We live in a world governed by impersonal laws of cause and effect; so it has been throughout all eternity, and so shall it be into the unending future. But while *saṁsāra* may endure forever, not one of its components can do the same. Accompanying the Buddhist

---

[1] *Note:* In the subsequent footnotes the numbering of the Pāli Canon references follows that of the Pāli Text Society, London, but not all translations are taken from this source.

172

doctrine of cause and effect is the equally important teaching of *anicca* or impermanence. Every living being; every thought, mood and feeling; every hill, mountain and river is a temporary phenomenon which in time will give way to new conditions, which it has helped to create. The universe then is eternally dynamic, a never-ending process of interacting and inter-dependent forces and factors no one of which is eternal, static, immortal, self-formed or self-willed. Within *samsāra* it is only the law of change which does not change. The earth and sun themselves will in the course of time perish and be no more, but the Buddha further taught that as old earth-sun systems die out new ones evolve and come into being.[1]

But cosmology is a relatively insignificant facet of the Dhamma (the teaching of the Buddha). The primary significance of the eternal principles, change and cause and effect, is the way they relate to the process of human existence; to the hopes, fears, sorrows and joys which give meaning and purpose to the lives of all conscious beings. This brings us to another important feature of *samsāra*—i.e. *anattā* or soullessness. The anattā doctrine states that all thought, emotion, memory, sensation, perception, and all other forms of our consciousness are temporary, dynamic and interdependent. Without such mental states the notion of oneself can have no meaning, and yet there is not one of these states which alone can be called one's true self, 'the real I'. Oneself is the composite of all of these, and at no place within these dynamic aggregates does one find some unchanging essence or other stable entity that can be designated as a soul or immutable being.

Buddhism does not deny the existence of the personality; it only states that the personality is compounded and dynamic —a process rather than an entity. Our moods, thoughts, expectations and emotions change from day to day, hour to hour, minute to minute. Is oneself at the age of two the same self one finds 10 years later at the age of 12? And is one's 12-year-old self the same person as the 20-year-old self or the 40 or 60-year-old selves? Thus from the Buddhist viewpoint, it

[1] *Buddhism, Science and Atheism*, by Douglas M. Burns (Bangkok, World Fellowship of Buddhists, 1965), pp. 47–56.

is more accurate to say that the two-year-old is a psycho-physical phenomenon which in the course of time will be modified by its interactions with other phenomena as well as the interactions of its own internal components. This evolution will result in the respective personalities of ages 12, 20, 40 and so forth.

When asked 'Who, Lord, is it who feels?' the Buddha replied:

'It is not a fit question. I am not saying (someone) feels. If I were saying so, the question would be a fit one. But I am not saying that. If you were to ask thus: "Conditioned now by what, Lord, is feeling?" this were a fit question. And the fit answer would be: "Feeling is conditioned by (sense) contact." '

—*Saṁyutta-Nikāya* II, 13 (XII, 2; 12)

And again he is quoted:

'He who does the deed and he who experiences (its result) are the same: This, Brahmin, is one extreme. He who does the deed is not the same as he who experiences: This, Brahmin, is the other extreme. The Buddha, not approaching either of these extremes, teaches a middle doctrine.'

—*Saṁyutta-Nikāya* II, 76 (XII, 5; 46)

The Dhamma teaches that mind and body are interdependent. Neither can come about or endure without the other.[1] When the body dies the mental states which preceded death become the causes of new mental conditions that occur with the birth of a new personality. This is the Buddhist concept of post-mortem survival and is termed 'rebirth'. Those psychological factors preceding death which determine the time, place and form of the new birth are known as '*karma*' (or *kamma* in Pāli).

However, karma (*kamma-vipāka*)[2] is not confined to the process of rebirth. Rather it is an ever-present principle of

[1] *Samyutta-Nikāya* II, 113–114 (XII, 7; 67).

[2] In proper Pāli usage *kamma* refers only to volitional actions, i.e. causes, while the effects of such actions are termed *vipāka*. However, in Hindu and recent popular Buddhist writings *karma* has widely come to mean the whole universal law of cause and effect. Thus I have used the word '*karma*' in instances where *vipāka* or *karma-vipāka* would technically be correct.

psychological cause and effect, and it can be explained by saying that each state of mind is a condition which becomes the cause of other states of mind that will arise in the future. Karma may be classified as wholesome, unwholesome and neutral (*avyākata*) which means that a given mental state is of such a nature that its results will be either pleasant, unpleasant or neutral (*adukkha-m-asukha*) respectively. Examples of unwholesome karma are greed and hatred, while wholesome karma is seen in compassion and kindness.[1]

Because one's karma is complex and must act interdependently with other aspects of saṁsāra, some of its results will be immediate, while others will be delayed for days, months or years. Or in some cases, karma is rendered inoperative by other portions of the karma of that same personality and thus produces no effect. Thus Buddhism teaches that each man is the product of what he has done or thought in the past, and his present thoughts and actions will determine the future.[1] Though karma is often explained in an ethical context, it must not be confused with social mores or other cultural standards of good and evil, for it operates independently of these. Also it should not be assumed that karma accounts for all pleasant and unpleasant experiences. In addition to one's karma, factors external to oneself act upon personality with pleasurable and displeasurable consequences.[2]

Buddhism uses the word 'rebirth' to distinguish its position from the Hindu doctrine of reincarnation via an immortal soul. The distinction between the two religious teachings is best illustrated in terms of an analogy. To understand the Hindu position one may imagine a row of various kinds of containers such as a drinking glass, a cup, a bowl, a pot, etc. One takes a marble and deposits it in the first container; then lifts it out and puts it in the second and so on down to the end of the row. The marble represents the soul and the containers the various bodies successively inhabited by the soul. Though each container is different, the marble is essentially unchanged throughout the

---

[1] *Karma and Rebirth*, by Nyānatiloka Mahāthera (Kandy, Buddhist Publication Society).

[2] *Anguttara-Nikāya* I, 173 (III, 7; 61).

entire process. To contrast the Buddhist view, imagine that one lights a match and then with the match lights a candle at the same time extinguishing the match. Then with the candle one lights a Coleman lantern (pressure lantern) and extinguishes the candle. Now we ask the question: Is the flame which once burned in the match the same flame now burning in the lantern? One can answer the question either 'yes' or 'no', both replies being equally appropriate.

While the child is not the same as the adult, the food the child eats, the values he incorporates and the education he receives will strongly determine the nature of his adult existence. And similarly for successive births.

LIFE, LIVING AND EMPIRICISM

The above paragraphs briefly describe the Buddhist world view; that is, the conceptual or theoretical framework in which Buddhism has traditionally explained samsāra. In addition there is the empirical, experiential approach to samsāra as explained in the following paragraphs. This latter approach is actually the more important, as it transcends any need for faith, dogma and theory. It is possible to explain Buddhism from either an exclusively conceptual, theoretical approach or from an exclusively experiental one. To give a complete picture, both should be mentioned. It is said that one who pursues Buddhist mental development to its maximum possible degree can have experiential certainty of the theoretical concepts.

Buddhism begins its understanding of samsāra on a strictly empirical basis—i.e. one's immediate conscious experience. Direct experience is the only absolute certainty of which man is capable, and whatever lies beyond experience can only be inferred with varying degrees of probability. For example, no matter how strongly one may believe in God (be it the Moslem Allah, the Hindu Brahma or the Christian Jehovah) one does not have complete certainty that that god exists. But the one thing of which the believer can be sure is that he believes; that is, he experiences the state of mind known as believing. Likewise a scientist may formulate a theory about the structure of a certain molecule. Since he has never seen this molecule (or

any molecule), the validity of his theory is a matter of probability derived from inductive reasoning. The real certainty which
the scientist has is first the existence of his *idea* or *belief* as
to the molecular structure and second the existence of the
memories of the facts and observations (which he assumes to
be correct) that led to his theory. Or finally any given sensory
experience may be either a dream, hallucination, illusion or an
actual physical reality, but the one thing of which the recipient
can be certain is the conscious experience itself. Or as expressed
in the Buddha's own words:

> 'What, brethren, is everything? The eye and forms, the ear
> and sounds, the nose and smells, the tongue and tastes, the
> body and touch, the mind and objects of mind. This, brethren,
> is called everything. Whoso, brethren, should say: "Rejecting
> this everything, I will proclaim another everything,"—it
> would be mere talk on his part, and when questioned he
> could not make good his boast, and further would come to
> an ill pass. Why so? Because, brethren, it would be beyond his
> scope to do so.'
>
> —*Samyutta-Nikāya* IV, 15 (XXXV 3; 23)

From this it should not be assumed that Buddhism denies the
reality of physical existence apart from human awareness. For
such is not the case. Nor does the Dhamma state that consciousness is some sort of metaphysical absolute upon which all else
is founded. On the contrary, the Buddha clearly stated that
human consciousness is dependent upon a physical substrate,
i.e. a body.[1] Furthermore, while it is true that memory, emotion,
sensation and thought cannot exist without consciousness, it is
equally true that consciousness cannot exist without at least
one of these other four (i.e. memory, etc.). To have consciousness
one must be conscious *of* something. Pure consciousness is not
to be found.[2] In other words consciousness is an interdependent
phenomenon, as are all other aspects of samsāra.

[1] *Majjhima-Nikāya* I, 259 (No. 38, *Mahātanhāsankhaya Sutta*).
[2] *Fundamentals of Buddhism*, by Nyānatiloka Mahāthera (Colombo, Bauddha Sāhitya Sabhā, 1949), p. 65.

M

However, the most important aspect of conscious existence, the most significant thing in life, is that we have feelings both pleasant and unpleasant. The human mind is far more than a computer which gathers and analyses information. From the dim awareness of an insect, fish or reptile to the most highly complex and sensitive realizations of humanity, one feature alone is paramount; that is, the pursuit of happiness, pleasure and enjoyment and conversely the avoidance of pain, sorrow, frustration and fear. Without such feelings there would be no such thing as value, purpose, meaning and significance; motive and incentive could not exist, and there would be no reason to think, speak or act. Man is unique in this regard only in his relative ability to experience a greater diversity and complexity of pleasurable experiences, such as creativity, music and abstract contemplation. Even the most dedicated rationalists and the most self-sacrificing idealists assume their respective roles because they find some level of satisfaction, happiness or peace of mind in so doing. The Christian and Moslem conceptions of Heaven and Hell are but symbolic simplifications of this pleasure-pain principle.

According to Buddhist doctrine, it is man's thirst for pleasurable experiences that generates new karma (*vipāka*) and perpetuates his existence. Enjoyable experience itself is karmically neutral, but what does produce karma (*vipāka*) is our craving (*taṇhā*), the unquenchable yearning for repeated sensory and emotional stimulations of whatever sorts they may be.

It is craving that sustains our existence. But what does it mean to exist? In terms of experience life is nothing more than each conscious moment; the moments of reading this manuscript, of travelling, of bathing, of studying, of day-dreaming, of planning, of worrying, of rejoicing, of striving, of relaxing, of talking, of working. All these and more are life. Each endures for an instant and never again returns exactly the same as before. Which ones do we live for? Which are the ones that justify our desires for continued existence? And conversely how many are of negative value—painful, irritating, disappointing, worrisome, boring, frustrating, empty or any of the other

178

displeasurable states of mind all of which Buddhism groups under the one word 'dukkha'?

All manifestations of samsāra come about through cause and effect, and the nature of life is to avoid or minimize dukkha while endeavouring to realize a maximum of rewarding or meaningful experiences. Therefore it follows that the key to living is to discover, understand and eliminate those factors which are causes of dukkha while at the same time developing and cultivating those which lead to true happiness and well-being.

On the basis of the above the Buddha repeatedly summarized his doctrine in terms of the Four Noble Truths:

1. Dukkha is an inherent aspect of samsāra.
2. The cause of dukkha is *taṇhā* or misdirected pleasure seeking.
3. It is possible to realize an end of dukkha.
4. This end is achieved by means of the Eightfold Path—the multidimensional Buddhist practice of spiritual and psychological maturation.

Thus the essence of Buddhism is its way of life. It is the fourth of the Four Noble Truths, that is, the techniques, the practices, the insights and the disciplines that restructure the personality to produce either a relative or a total end of dukkha. However, in this writing I wish to give primary concern to the Third Truth, the goal toward which the Fourth Truth is directed.

A study of the Suttas of the Pāli Canon (which are the most authentic existing records of the teachings of the Buddha) reveals that the Buddha taught there are *two* ways in which one can deal with the problem of existence. One is to continually act in such a manner as to create wholesome karma; in other words, to constantly produce conditions which will enhance satisfaction, happiness and well-being. The other is to totally and completely end one's existence within samsāra, i.e. to achieve Nirvāna. The two are not entirely separate paths, for to a considerable extent they overlap. The further one progresses towards a complete realization of the former, the closer one will come to attaining the latter. However, the Buddha placed major emphasis and importance on the latter goal, the cessation of one's being in samsāra. For while dukkha can be minimized within samsāra, it can never be totally eliminated, and every situation in which one may invest one's hopes, affections and feelings will eventually perish. Furthermore, let us imagine that one acquires an understanding of samsāra and how to deal with it and is then able to carry this knowledge over into successive lives for one's continual happiness and prosperity. But even such knowledge itself is created and temporary, and thus like all other creations eventually will perish leaving the personality once again to act blindly towards those laws which mould human destiny.

Thus the Buddhist version of salvation, either of the relative or absolute sort, is something resulting primarily from one's own volitions and can neither be imposed upon one nor granted to one by some external agent. The Buddha's mission was to enlighten men as to the nature of existence and advise them as to how best to behave for their own benefits and the benefits of others. Consequently Buddhist ethics are not founded upon commandments which men are compelled to follow. From the Buddhist viewpoint each conscious being is an individual free to act as it sees fit. The Buddha only advised men as to which conditions were most wholesome and conducive to long-term benefit. Rather than addressing sinners with such words as 'shameful', 'wicked', 'wretched', 'unworthy' and 'blasphemous', he would merely say: 'You are foolish and acting in such a way as to bring sorrow upon yourselves and others.' Often he said, 'You yourselves must make the effort. Buddhas are only teachers.'[1] Consequently the Buddha did not condemn those who chose to enjoy sensuality and the pleasures of worldly existence. He even advised such persons on how to achieve their ends providing no harm would come to others, but he also cautioned them as to the dangers and reminded them that to maintain such pleasures they must be willing to pay the price. The price being continual effort and diligence. A good example is related in the *Vyagghapajja Sutta*:

[1] *Dhammapada* 276.

'Once the Exalted One was dwelling amongst the Koliyans in their market town named Kakkarapatta. Then Dighajānu, a Koliyan, approached the Exalted One, respectfully saluted him and sat on one side. Thus seated, he addressed the Exalted One as follows:

' "We, Lord, are laymen who enjoy worldly pleasure. We lead a life encumbered by wife and children. We use sandalwood of Kāsi. We deck ourselves with garlands, perfume and unguents. We use gold and silver. To those like us, O Lord, let the Exalted One preach the Doctrine, teach those things that lead to weal and happiness in this life and weal and happiness in future life.' "

To this Buddha replied:

' "Four conditions, Vyagghapajja, conduce to a householder's weal and happiness in this very life. Which four? The accomplishment of persistent effort, the accomplishment of watchfulness, good friendship and balanced livelihood.
' "What is the accomplishment of persistent effort?
' "Herein, Vyagghapajja, by whatsoever activity a householder earns his living, whether by farming, by trading, by rearing cattle, by archery, by service under the king, or by any other kind of craft—at that he becomes skilful and is not lazy. He is endowed with the power of discernment as to the proper ways and means; he is able to carry out and allocate (duties). This is called the accomplishment of persistent effort.
' "What is the accomplishment of watchfulness?
' "Herein, Vyagghapajja, whatsoever wealth a householder is in possession of, obtained by dint of effort, collected by strength of arm, by the sweat of his brow, justly acquired by right means—such he husbands well by guarding and watching so that kings would not seize it, thieves would not steal, fire would not burn, water would not carry away, nor ill-disposed heirs remove. This is the accomplishment of watchfulness.
' "What is good friendship?

' "Herein, Vyagghapajja, in whatsoever village or market town a householder dwells, he associates, converses, engages in discussions with householders or householders' sons, whether young and highly cultured or old and highly cultured, full of faith, full of virtue, full of charity, full of wisdom. He acts in accordance with the faith of the faithful, with the virtue of the virtuous, with the charity of the charitable, with the wisdom of the wise. This is called good friendship.

' "What is balanced livelihood?

' "Herein, Vyagghapajja, a householder knowing his income and expenses leads a balanced life, neither extravagant nor miserly, knowing that thus his income will stand in excess of his expenses, but not his expenses in excess of his income. . . .

' "The wealth thus amassed, Vyagghapajja, has four sources of destruction: Debauchery; drunkenness; gambling; and friendship, companionship and intimacy with evildoers. . . ." '

Anguttara-Nikāya IV, 280–282 (VIII 6; 54)

2. THE NATURE OF NIRVANA

We now come to what is one of the most frequently asked questions in Buddhism: What is Nirvāna? In the above paragraphs we have already stated that it is the ending of rebirth, the final termination of one's existence within samsāra. And in the Pāli Canon we read 'The ceasing of becoming is Nirvāna'.[1] The origin of the word itself carries this same implication. One common etymological explanation is: '*Nir*' means 'not', and '*vāna*' can be rendered as 'the effort of blowing'. This was probably a simile referring to a smith's fire which goes out if not repeatedly blown upon; the implication being the extinction of the fire of greed, hatred and delusion.[2] Thus it is not surprising that many critics of Buddhism have considered Nirvāna to be a sophisticated version of suicide, a goal of self-extinction, complete nihilism, and absolute zero.

[1] *Samyutta-Nikāya* II, 117 (XII, 7; 68).
[2] *Three Cardinal Discourses of the Buddha*, by Ñānamoli Thera (Kandy, Buddhist Publication Society), p. 15.

Such a conclusion, however, is one-sided and superficial. The Buddha himself rejected and cautioned against the two extremes of philosophical dualism. One extreme being eternalism or existence and the other being annihilationism or non-existence. Though this was usually taught with reference to the existence or non-existence of the personality after death, it is equally appropriate to Nirvāna. The whole tradition of Theravāda Buddhism has emphatically rejected the nihilistic interpretation of Nirvāna, and a significant portion of the writings of the famed Fifth Century Theravādin scholar, Buddhaghosa, was directed at refuting the notion of Nirvāna as non-existence.[1]

Perhaps most significant is that the Buddha and many of his disciples *experienced* Nirvāna; that is, they were aware of it, as the Buddha said, 'here and now in this present life'. And in the suttas we find statements that the Buddha and the other arahants[2] 'enjoyed the peace of Nirvāna'. It is referred to by such terms as 'profound', 'deep', 'hard to see', 'hard to comprehend', 'peaceful', 'lofty', 'inaccessible to ratiocination', 'subtle', 'the true', 'the other shore', 'to be known by the wise'.[3] In the *Dhammapada* the Buddha is quoted:

'There is no fire like lust,
No crime like hatred;
There is no misery like the constituents of existence,
No happiness higher than the Peace of Nirvāna.

'Hunger is the worst of diseases,
Component existence is the worst of distresses;
Knowing this as it really is (the wise realize)
Nirvāna the highest bliss.

Health is the highest gain;
Contentment is the greatest wealth.
A trusty friend is the best of kinsmen;
Nirvāna is the supreme bliss.

—*Dhammapada* 202–204

---

[1] *Visuddhimagga* XVI, 67–74.
[2] *Arahant*—one who has fully realized Nirvāna.
[3] *Anattā and Nibbāna*, by Nyānaponika Thera (Kandy, Buddhist Publication Society, 1959). [See Section V.]

Arahantship is said to be an irreversible condition, for once achieved it is impossible that one can fall back into lust and delusion. Thus an arahant is completely incapable of greed, anger and egotism and generates no unwholesome karma. In many respects he (or she) will continue to act, think and feel as any normal person until the time of death, and his demise is sometimes termed 'Parinirvāna' the complete cessation of existence in samsāra, the final end of rebirth. Nirvāna has nothing to do with occult powers or supernatural wonders, and many of the arahants at the time of the Buddha stated that they had no such abilities.[1] While with Nirvāna one is liberated from grief, sorrow, despair, worry, frustration and all other psychological forms of dukkha, one is still subject to physical discomforts until such time as the body passes away. Throughout the Suttas we read of occasions when the Buddha sustained a back ache,[2] fell ill with intestinal wind,[3] had his foot pierced by a stone splinter,[4] etc., and in each instance there was accompanying physical pain. But never was there an emotional reaction or psychological discomfort resulting from the pain.

As best can be determined from the scriptural sources, an arahant is not experiencing Nirvāna in every waking moment but is capable of experiencing it at will. Persons who have had such an experience but are not at all times able to reproduce it and may still fall back into greed, anger and delusion are not designated as arahants; though eventually they will become such. They are known as 'sotāpanna' or 'streamwinners', ones who have entered the stream that eventually leads to Nirvāna.

Rather than the end of craving per se, Nirvāna is that which is realized when craving is ended. Nirvāna is nothing only in that it is no thing. It is neither matter nor energy, and it has no location in space and time. It is not perceived by the senses, nor is it a thought, concept, mood or emotion. Though an arahant is conscious of Nirvāna, it is not consciousness in any

---

[1] *Samyutta-Nikāya* II, 121–123 (No. 70, *Susimāparibbājaka Sutta*).
[2] *Anguttara-Nikāya* IV, 358–359 (IX, 1, 4).
[3] *Samyutta-Nikāya* I, 174 (VII, 2; 3).
[4] *Ibid.*, 27 (I, 4; 8).

sense by which we normally understand that word. It is indivisible, timeless, changeless, unborn and not compounded; in other words the very antithesis of samsāra. It is thoroughly apart from samsāra and thus neither influences nor is influenced by karma. In no way does it interact with samsāra or intervene into samsāra in the way Brahma or Jehovah is said to answer prayers or manifest divine intervention.

Much of the above is reiterated in the Buddha's famous 'Discourse on the Snake Simile':

'A Noble One who has abandoned the conceit of self, has cut it off at the root, removed it from its soil like a palmyrah tree, brought it to utter extinction, incapable of arising again. Thus is the monk a Noble One who has taken down the flag, put down the burden, become unfettered. When a monk's mind is thus freed, O monks, neither the devas with Indra, nor those with Brahma, nor those with Pajāpati, when searching will find on what the consciousness of one thus gone (*tathāgata*) is based. Why is that? One who has thus gone is no longer traceable here and now, so I say.

'So teaching, so proclaiming, O monks, there are some recluses and brahmans who misrepresent me untruly, vainly, falsely, not in accordance with fact, saying: "A nihilist is the ascetic Gotama; he teaches the annihilation, the destruction, the non-being of an existing individual." As I am not and as I do not teach, therefore these worthy recluses and brahmans misrepresent me untruly, vainly, falsely, and not in accordance with fact when they say: "A nihilist is the ascetic Gotama; he teaches the annihilation, the destruction, the non-being of an existing individual." What I teach now as before, O monks, is suffering and the cessation of suffering.

'If for that others revile, abuse, scold and insult the Tathāgata (i.e. the Buddha), on that account, O monks, the Tathāgata will not feel annoyance, nor dejection, nor displeasure in his heart. And if for that others respect, revere, honour and venerate the Tathāgata, on that account the Tathāgata will not feel delight, nor joy, nor elation in his heart. If for that others respect, revere, honour and venerate

185

the Tathāgata, he will think: It is towards this (mind-body aggreate) which was formerly fully comprehended, that they perform such acts.'

(The Buddha then repeats the above paragraph advising the monks to do the same when they too receive blame or praise. He then continued:)

'Therefore, monks, relinquish whatever is not yours. Your relinquishment of it will for a long time bring you welfare and happiness. What is it that is not yours? Material shape is not yours. Relinquish it. Your relinquishment of it will for a long time bring you welfare and happiness. Feeling is not yours. Relinquish it. Your relinquishment of it will for a long time bring you welfare and happiness. . . . (And likewise for perception, mental formations and consciousness.)'

—*Majjhima-Nikāya* I, 139–141
(No. 22 *Alagaddūpama Sutta*)

A common source of misunderstanding about the Buddha's use of the word 'Nirvāna' originates from the Hindu usage of the same word. The Hindus give it a positive metaphysical and mystical meaning stating that Nirvāna is Union with Brahma or God, a condition of Oneness with the Cosmic Absolute in which the soul of man merges with the Infinite Soul of the Universe. Such a misconception is furthered by the fact that some centuries after the Buddha, various schools of Mahāyāna Buddhism began to develop along mystical and metaphysical paths unknown to or even refuted by the Buddha. Consequently Mahāyāna Buddhist writings often abound with such terms as Buddha Nature, Universal Mind, the Tri-kāya and Primordial Buddha. Thus the concept of Nirvāna now has a host of mystical religious and psychological usages quite different from its original Buddhist meaning.

The Buddha spoke relatively little about Nirvāna. One reason being that there is little which is meaningful that one can say. Within the Pāli Canon the most detailed dissertation on Nirvāna given by the Buddha is quoted as follows:

'There is, monks, a realm where there is neither earth, water, fire nor air, nor the sphere of infinite space, nor the sphere of infinite consciousness, nor the sphere of nothingness, nor the sphere of neither-perception-nor-non-perception; neither this world nor a world beyond nor sun and moon.

'There, monks, I say, there is neither coming to birth nor going nor staying nor passing away nor arising. It is without support or mobility or basis. It is the end of dukkha (suffering).

> That which is selfless, hard it is to see;
> Not easy is it to perceive the truth.
> But who has ended craving utterly
> Has naught to cling to, he alone can see.

'There is, monks, an unborn, a not-become, a not-made, a not-compounded. If, monks, there were not this unborn, not-become, not-made, not-compounded, there would not be an escape from the born, the become, the made, the compounded. But because there is an unborn . . . therefore there is an escape . . .'

—*Udāna* VIII, 2–3; 80–81 (*Pātaligāma*)

The outstanding feature of this quotation is that it is a series of negatives. Other than the simple affirmation 'there is', not one positive description is used. Why?

The answer is not hard to find. Since Nirvāna is in no way related to anything within normal human experience, we have no words adequate to describe it. Even if we should adopt some word or phrase such as 'Ultimate Reality' or 'Pure Being' such would more likely than not create an illusion of understanding rather than give any true insight. Such terms would tell us no more about Nirvāna than the word 'music' tells to a man born deaf, the word 'passion' tells to a young child or the word 'beatnik' tells to an Eskimo. Thus the value of negative terms is that they discourage one from holding to verbal symbols which quickly become illusions of reality. Or in the language of Zen: The finger pointing at the moon must not be confused with the moon itself.

As was explained on pages 176 f., the only true certainty man can have is direct experience. Consequently, the Buddha did not attempt to describe the indescribable. Rather than talk about Nirvāna, the great majority of his teachings were concerned with the techniques of psychological development, which proceed from the empirical data of one's own states of consciousness in the immediate present. If such practices are done properly, the dimensions of one's awareness progressively expand until Nirvāna becomes a reality on the basis of direct experience. When that happens explanations become unnecessary. Attempts at verbal descriptions only lead to useless metaphysical conjectures which may divert one's attention and energies from the practices necessary for true realization. Consequently, when questioned on transcendental matters the Buddha would either show the futility of such inquiries or remain silent. We have for example his encounter with the young Brahman, Udāyi:

'Well then, Udāyi, what is your own teacher's doctrine?'

'Our own teacher's doctrine, venerable sir, says thus: "This is the highest splendour! This is the highest splendour!" '

'But what is that highest splendour, Udāyi, of which your teacher's doctrine speaks?'

'It is, venerable sir, a splendour greater and loftier than which there is none. That is the Highest Splendour.'

'But, Udāyi, what is that splendour greater and loftier than which there is none?'

'It is, venerable sir, the Highest Splendour greater and loftier than which there is none.'

'For a long time, Udāyi, you can continue in this way, saying, "A splendour greater and loftier than which there is none, that is the Highest Splendour". But still you will not have explained that splendour. Suppose a man were to say: "I love and desire the most beautiful woman in this land", and then he is asked: "Good man, that most beautiful woman whom you love and desire, do you know whether she is a lady from nobility or from a Brahman family or from the trader class or Sudra?" And he replied "no"—"Then, good man, do not know her name and that of her clan? Or whether she is tall, short or of middle height, whether she is dark, brunette or golden-skinned, or in what village or town or city she dwells?" And he replied "no". And then he is asked: "Hence, good man, you love and desire what you neither know nor see?", and he answers "yes".—What do you think, Udāyi, that being so, would not that man's talk amount to nonsense?'

'Certainly, venerable Sir, that being so, that man's talk would amount to nonsense.'

'But in the same way, you, Udāyi, say, "A splendour greater and loftier than which there is none, that is the Highest Splendour", and yet you have not explained that splendour.'
—*Majjhima-Nikāya* II, 32–33 (*No. 79, Cūla-Sakuludāyi Sutta*)

The Buddha had acquired an insight totally unrelated to that of normal persons and which in no way could be equated with any experiences in samsāra, yet he wished to reveal his discovery. The problem can be described in terms of an analogy. Let us imagine there is a man who has been blindfolded from the moment of birth and thus has never had an experience of light, vision or colour. But from the words of others he comes to know that there is something which he has never realized. He may then attempt to discover this unknown quality by meditating upon God or thinking of Ultimate Being. But at best he can only echo in his mind the words 'vision', 'colour', and 'light' or intensify some subjective impression of what he thinks these things may be. On the other hand our blindfolded man may reason as follows: 'There is something which I don't realize and is beyond me. Since it is beyond me it must be greater than I, and if it is greater than I, it must be able to help me.—Oh Vision! Oh Light! Please come to me. Make Thyself known unto me, Thy humble servant.' This, of course, is the devotional approach. The metaphysical approach, the approach of philosophy, is to attempt to verbally describe vision with positive phrases, skilful similes and inventive metaphors. But what words can enable a blind man to realize the difference between red

189

and green or to comprehend any other features of visual experience? Words cannot, and to avoid creating misconceptions and illusions it is best to say either nothing at all or give only negative descriptions. Consequently, the Buddha talked about one thing and one thing only—i.e. how to take off the blindfold.

In line with the above it should be noted that the Suttas of Theravāda Buddhism make little mention of meditating upon Nirvāna. This strongly contrasts with the Hindu practice of meditating upon Brahma and similar meditations in other schools of mysticism. Buddhist meditation is of two major sorts. One is tranquillity or *samatha* in which the practitioner concentrates upon a clay or colour disk, a flame, the thought of equanimity, one's own quiet breathing or any one of several similar things, all for the sake of stilling the mind.[1] More important than samatha are the insight meditations or *vipassanā*, which are based on the development of full awareness of one's actions, thoughts, feelings and emotions.[2]

The one exception to the preceding paragraph concerns the peace meditation. In the early Pāli writings Nirvāna is often termed 'the peaceful', and peace is considered to be one feature of Nirvāna. Peace is also listed among the forty prescribed meditation subjects, and it is thus inferred that meditating upon peace is meditating upon an attribute of Nirvāna. This meditation, however, is but one of forty, and meditation instructors would assign it only to selected students. According to the *Visuddhimagga*, it can be of full benefit only to persons who have already glimpsed Nirvāna.[3]

3. THEORIES REGARDING NIRVANA

Can Nirvāna be explained as a trance state such as occurs in deep hypnosis? Or is it a state of ecstasy as seen in mystical

---

[1] *Path to Deliverance*, by Nyānatiloka Mahāthera (Colombo, Bauddha Sāhitya Sabhā, 1959), pp. 73–118.

[2] *The Heart of Buddhist Meditation*, by Nyānaponika Thera (London, Rider & Co.), 1962.

[3] *Visuddhimagga* VIII, 245–251.

practices or under the effect of psychedelic drugs? Or is it regression of the personality back to prenatal existence? All three of these hypotheses have been used to explain Nirvāna. And while such contentions are distasteful to devout Buddhists, it must be admitted that one cannot flatly and dogmatically reject any one of them unless oneself has experienced Nirvāna. For how can we prove that one man's subjective experiences are either identical to or different from another's? We cannot; for as stated before, the only reality and certainty that one has is one's own immediate states of consciousness, be they of subjective or objective origins. However, on the basis of the available evidence it is possible to throw serious doubt on all three of the above.

TRANCE

The concept of trance includes a variety and spectrum of different but overlapping states which can be classified into somewhat arbitrary groupings and which sometimes merge imperceptibly into states of ecstasy. The most common and readily observed condition of trance is hypnosis. However, as yet psychology has no satisfactory explanation for hypnosis. The best that can be done is merely to describe what happens, and that is that the subject becomes extremely suggestible to the instructions of others even to the extent of having hallucinations and some degree of control of the autonomic nervous system (which is normally beyond conscious control). Usually there is either partial or complete amnesia for the period of hypnosis, but paradoxically one can often recall detailed events of the past not normally accessible to one's memory. So far as the subject's subjective experience is concerned, there is no characteristic feature of the trance per se. Some subjects find it mildly pleasant, others discomforting and others neutral, and the experience can be different for the same subject on different occasions. Strong emotional reactions and states of euphoria may occur but usually not unless induced by the hypnotist. Hypnosis is an alteration in one's normal states of consciousness, but since we do not know what consciousness is in the first place, it is impossible to explain its deviations and alterations.

Hypnotic trance differs from Nirvāna in several important ways. Hypnosis can be rapidly produced and produced in a wide variety of different kinds of personalities. It rarely lasts more than a few hours at most and usually produces no enduring alteration in one's psyche. Nirvāna, on the other hand, can only be achieved by a long period of restructuring the total personality with certain very definite character traits as prerequisites (absence of lust, etc.). It is an irreversible state of which one is fully conscious and is very much a unique experience. In the deepest stages of hypnosis one is unconscious, has total amnesia for the event, and subjectively the hypnotic experience has no unique features of its own.

Another category of trance states and one quite well known in Buddhism are the eight absorptions or *jhānas*. In the lower four jhānas one is said to be fully conscious but to have shut off awareness of all sensory impressions, stilled discursive and verbal thinking and temporarily abandoned lust, anger, agitation, torpor and doubt. Thus upon reaching the fourth jhāna one dwells in a state of pure equanimity and concentration. Having achieved the fourth jhāna, one may then progress to the four *arūpajjhānas*. These are states of deep samatha meditation as described on page 190 and in their successive orders of attainment they are termed 'the sphere of infinite space', 'the sphere of infinite consciousness', 'the sphere of nothingness' and 'the sphere of neither-perception-nor-non-perception'.[1] Though years of practice may be required to attain these states, they do not represent the complete abolition of craving nor true insight into one's own nature. They are actually pre-Buddhist practices known to the Hindu faith as well as to Buddhism, and the Buddha himself achieved them before realizing Nirvāna.[2] Though the jhānas are taught in Buddhism and though the lower four are even included in the eighth step of the Eightfold Path, they are, though often helpful, not strictly necessary to

---

[1] *Majjhima-Nikāya* I, 174–175 (No. 26 *Ariyapariyesana Sutta*).
[2] *Ibid.*, I, 164–168.

the attainment of Liberation. (Highly developed mental concentration, however, is indispensable.)

ECSTASY

Like trance, the states of ecstasy also embrace a wide variety of experiences and occur in such diverse situations as the rites and rituals of cults and primitive societies, acute psychotic reactions, epilepsy, moments of solitude in forests and mountains, artistic absorption, deep contemplation, romance, religious fervour and the intoxications of various drugs such as LSD-25, mescaline and hashish.[1] Spontaneous cases are not uncommon, but here the word 'spontaneous' must be taken to mean that the precipitating factors are not immediately discernible. All of these experiences do not belong to the same order of mental phenomena, but our very limited understanding of such states, the inadequacy of language to fully relate them, the great spectrum of human feelings which seems to lack clearly defined boundaries, and the ability of the mind to mix various levels of feelings into one experience all warrant grouping such phenomena under one heading.

What these states have in common is an intense or unusual feeling of bliss, well-being or euphoria. (Though fear or other negative emotions may also be present.) All of one's usual preoccupations and emotions are swept aside, and for the moment only the ecstasy itself seems important. One may gain the impression of a new and deeper insight into existence. Atheists and agnostics in describing the effects of LSD often use such words as 'divine', 'mystical' and 'religious'.

Like hypnosis these states differ from Nirvāna in their sudden onset, relatively brief duration and (with infrequent exceptions) the lack of any lasting influence upon the personality. Also, like hypnosis, they contrast with Nirvāna by appearing in numerous and diverse types of people regardless of the extent to which one has relinquished greed, hatred and delusion or resolved emotional conflicts. The paramount feature of ecstasy is that one is so enamoured in bliss that for the moment all else

[1] *Modern Clinical Psychiatry*, by Arthur P. Noyes and Lawrence C. Kolb (Philadelphia, W. B. Saunders Co., 1963), p. 80.

is either forgotten or seems unimportant or unreal. Consequently, at such times it is almost impossible to make sound and realistic judgements. Thus it is significant that the accounts we have of the Buddha and the other arahants reveal that they were unusually realistic and objective. Were this not the case it is unlikely that Buddhism could have won out over numerous competing systems and existed to the present day. The Suttas reveal that it was not only necessary for the Buddha and his chief disciples to maintain the order and discipline of the continually expanding body of monks; they also had to be proficient in lecture, debate, systematizing the doctrine and managing the affairs of everyday life.

REGRESSION

Another hypothesis about Nirvāna is the psychoanalytic belief that it is a state of regression to intra-uterine existence; that is, a psychological return to one's prenatal life, when the foetus floated effortlessly in the timeless, black silence of the amniotic fluid, a time free of frustration, thought, anxiety, sensory impressions or awareness of time-space relationships. Perhaps the major proponent of this hypothesis was the well-known psychoanalyst, Dr Franz Alexander. Two paragraphs from his manuscript, 'Buddhistic Training as an Artificial Catatonia', are quoted here:

'From our present psychoanalytical knowledge it is clear that Buddhistic self-absorption is a libidinal, narcissistic turning of the urge for knowing inward, a sort of artificial schizo-phrenia with complete withdrawal of libidinal interest from the outside world. The catatonic conditions of the Hindu ascetics in self-absorption prove quite clearly the correctness of this contention. The mastery of the world is given up and there remains as an exclusive goal of the libido the mastery of the self. In the older pre-Buddha Yogi practice the aim is clearly a mastery of the body, while the absorption of Buddha is directed toward the psychic personality, i.e. the ego.'

194

'The Yoga self-absorption, however, has no therapeutic goal; the mastery of the body is an end in itself. Likewise, in Buddhistic self-absorption the turning of the perceptive consciousness inward is an end in itself, a narcissistic-masochistic affair shown by the fact that the way to it leads through asceticism. Psychoanalysis turns inward in order to help the instincts to accommodate themselves to reality; it wishes to effect an alliance between consciousness and instinct, in order to make experience with the outer world useful to the instincts. The Buddhistic theory sets itself an easier task: it eliminates reality and attempts to turn the entire instinctual life away from the world, inwards, towards itself.'[1]

Dr Alexander's thesis was published in 1931 and written with a limited knowledge of Buddhism. Consequently from the Buddhist position it is easy to refute several of the arguments on which he built his case. For example, he equated the lotus position of Buddhist meditation with the foetal position (in which the entire neck and trunk are curled and the wrists and knees brought up over the face). He believed the sole purpose of yogi meditation to be mastery of the body. He mistakenly believed it is only biological forms of suffering (such as old age, sickness and death) which motivate Buddhist training and not any social or emotional forms. He spoke at the end of the Buddha's doctrine 'which came with a tragic crash', but since Buddhism is still very much alive in the world today, it is difficult to know just what historical event Dr Alexander was referring to. On extremely limited data he analysed the Buddha's disciple, Ānanda, as acting under the influence of an unresolved Oedipus complex. But perhaps most important is that his case rests heavily upon explaining Nirvāna as attained via the jhānas, and he inferred that Nirvāna is but an intensification of the fourth jhāna. As already mentioned, Buddhist doctrine teaches that attaining the jhānas is not necessary for the realization of

---

[1] *The Scope of Psychoanalysis*, 'Buddhistic Training as an Artificial Catatonia', by Franz Alexander (New York, Basic Books Publishing Co. Inc., 1961), pp. 75–76.

Nirvāna,[1] and the Buddha clearly stated that Nirvāna is of a totally different order of being even up to the eighth (the highest) jhāna.

But regardless of the errors in Dr Alexander's thesis, we are still confronted with his basic hypothesis that Nirvāna is regression to intra-uterine life. Several considerations make this assumption appear doubtful.

First Alexander believed that regression can go back to the very moment of conception. Yet it is questionable whether or not such a degree of regression is possible in terms of present-day biological theory. The concept of regression presupposes memory, and on good evidence it is generally assumed that human memory is the product of a matured and highly developed nervous system. Yet even at the time of birth the infant human brain is still undeveloped and largely non-functional. If early prenatal memory is possible, we then have evidence to support the Buddhist belief in a non-physical component of the psyche which is present from the time of conception.

Second, if we assume that Nirvāna is the complete withdrawal of libido from the outside world (i.e. a total lack of feeling for persons and things outside oneself), then we are at a loss to explain the great emphasis which the Buddha gave to love, ethics and social improvements. Dr Alexander himself was aware of this and states the following:

'Nowhere in the Buddhistic literature has sufficient account been taken of the deep contradiction between the absorption doctrine and Buddha's practical ethics, so far as I am able to follow. The goal of absorption, Nirvāna, is a completely asocial condition and is difficult to combine with ethical precepts.'

However, no contradiction exists if one assumes the Buddhist interpretation of Nirvāna (see section 7, p. 242). Only if one takes Dr Alexander's position does a problem arise. Thus it was up to Dr Alexander and not Buddhism to explain the discrepancy. This he did not do.

[1] *The Word of the Buddha*, by Nyānatiloka Mahāthera (Kandy, Buddhist Publication Society, 1959), p. 79.

While the Buddha advocated a state of non-craving and non-attachment, this did not mean a condition devoid of feeling, sensory perception or other forms of experience. We have, for example, the record of his encounter with Uttara, a disciple of a Brahmin teacher named Parasariya. The Buddha inquires of Uttara as to his teacher's doctrine, to which the latter replies:

'As to this, good Gotama, one should not see material shapes with the eye; one should not hear sounds with ear. It is thus, good Gotama, that the brahman Parasariya teaches the development of the sense-organs to his disciples.'

To this the Buddha replied:

'This being so, Uttara, then according to what Parasariya the brahman says a blind man must have his sense-organ developed; a deaf man must have his sense-organ developed. For a blind man, Uttara, does not see material shape with this eye, nor does a deaf man hear a sound with his ear . . .'

He then explains his own position on this matter:

'When a monk has seen a material shape with the eye there arises what is liked; there arises what is disliked; there arises what is both liked and disliked. He comprehends thus: "This that is liked is arising in me; this that is disliked is arising, and this that arises is because it is constructed, is gross. (But) this is the real, this the excellent, that is to say equanimity." So whether what is arising in him is liked, disliked or both liked and disliked, it is (all the same) stopped in him and equanimity remains.'
—*Majjhima-Nikāya* III, 298–299
(*No.* 152 *Indriyabhāvanā Sutta*)

An arahant is said to be wise, oriented to his environment and compassionate towards others. We need only consider the life and personality of the Buddha himself. Had he vegetated by retreating into purely subjective existence, it would have been

197

impossible for him to produce the very strong and lasting effect which he has made upon world history. Alexander explains this by saying that his withdrawal was not complete; one bond remained unsevered, his spiritual attachment to his disciples. Yet we must remember that at the time of his enlightenment the Buddha was living completely alone and had no disciples or companions of any sort. Also, from both the Suttas and the Vinaya it is clearly apparent that he made great efforts to assure that his doctrine would reach all levels of humanity and last for many generations. After his enlightenment and the enlightenment of sixty of his followers, he gave his well-known missionary address:

'I am freed, monks, from all fetters both divine and human. You also, monks, are freed from all fetters both divine and human. Wander for the welfare and happiness of many, out of compassion for the world, for the gain, for the welfare and happiness of gods and men. Let not two take the same course. Proclaim the Dhamma excellent in the beginning, excellent in the middle and excellent in the end, in the spirit and in the letter. Proclaim ye the life of consummate purity.'
—*Saṁyutta-Nikāya* I, 105 (IV, 1; 5)

If we equate the psychoanalytic concept of libido with the Buddhist concept of *taṇhā* or craving, then it may not be far from wrong to say that withdrawing libido from the world is either the same as Nirvāna or a forerunner of Nirvāna. And if we assume that because the embryo or foetus has not yet experienced the outside world, it thus has not yet invested libido into this world; then we can understand the rationale behind Dr Alexander's reasoning: Libido remains invested in the self; hence narcissism. We must remember, however, that Buddhist training requires the withdrawal of libido from oneself as well as from the world of sensory experience, and all states of one's thoughts and feelings must be regarded with the same detached objectivity as is the world at large. At this point the concept of 'withdrawing libido' comes under question; for into what is it withdrawn? Thus Buddhism does not use such a concept, but rather deals with individual states of mind and the causative factors which produce those states.

Even though the concept of embryonic libido is somewhat problematic, Dr Alexander's hypothesis does warrant consideration. However, in presenting his case his repeated use of the words 'narcissistic', 'masochistic' and 'schizophrenic' gives a rather distorted and unpleasant flavour to the whole idea. Apparently his use of the word 'masochistic' comes from the mistaken notion that Buddhism is a type of asceticism. Actually the Buddha rejected self-inflicted pain as being spiritually futile and as unwholesome as sensual indulgence.

The word schizophrenia covers a variety of mental disorders and certainly its most common forms do not in any way apply to an arahant. Among the prime features of most schizophrenias is a distorted perception of external reality (often with delusions and hallucinations) and a marked confusion and deterioration of logical thinking. Speech is often irrelevant, fragmented and inconsistent. This contrasts sharply with the eloquence, clarity and consistency of the Buddha's logic and oratory. Perhaps most significant was his unusual ability to see through semantic problems and thus resolve matters which were purely linguistic in origin; a feature quite opposite that of schizophrenic thinking. On a feeling level schizophrenics are often characterized by great emotional lability, inappropriate responses and difficulty in accepting and handling emotional impulses. Again this stands in sharp contrast to the personality of the arahants. It is almost inconceivable that a schizophrenic, at least of the usual sort, could successfully institute, manage and perpetuate a complex and highly organized religious order.

It is the catatonic form of schizophrenia which Alexander specifically equates with Nirvāna; a condition of prolonged trancelike stupor, immobility and seeming unresponsiveness to the outside world. One may remain in such a state for weeks at a time without changing position, not feeding oneself and not even tending to toilet needs. At such times one is usually indifferent to pin-pricks and other forms of pain. But even catatonia manifests in a variety of ways and quite commonly is interspersed with episodes of excitement, rambling speech and hyperactivity. Persons who have recovered from catatonic stupor do not describe any particular mental state as being characteristic of this condition, nor is it necessarily pleasant. Usually thought disorders characteristic of other forms of schizophrenia are also present. Perhaps most important is that the descriptions given of the catatonic experience bear little in common with the arahants' accounts of Nirvāna. Catatonia is not a condition which one enters voluntarily; rather it is the result of social, psychological and environmental forces which overpower and are beyond one's control; such a person is a victim of samsāra, and his stupor is a prison which he cannot leave at will. If the depth and tranquillity of Buddhist meditation is a state of catatonia, then it is a condition of catatonia which one enters and leaves mindfully and wilfully at one's own discretion—something unknown in the history of psychiatry. Thus Nirvāna is so different from the usual forms of catatonia, that it is doubtful that the word 'catatonia' can be applied.

THE PRACTICAL SOLUTION

As stated at the beginning of this chapter, logically and scientifically, one can neither prove nor disprove with complete certainty that Nirvāna either is or is not a condition akin to trace, ecstasy or regression. But putting aside all such speculations, the best information we have about Nirvāna is the Pāli Canon of Theravāda Buddhism. If Nirvāna is real and if any person in history has actually realized Nirvāna then in all probability that person was the Buddha himself. And on the basis of the historical record we find the Buddha to be a man who dedicated over 40 years of his life to the untiring service of his fellow beings; who was widely respected for his wisdom, compassion and moral character, and who apparently did not display anger, greed or prejudice. He was a man noted for his calm and equanimity and who has strongly influenced the lives of many hundreds of millions of people during the past 2,500 years. Thus on the historical record alone one can reasonably conclude that whatever Nirvāna may be, most likely it is not undesirable.

4. ZEN ENLIGHTENMENT

Another category of experience, which appears to belong to a class of its own is the enlightenment of Zen Buddhism, usually termed 'satori'. Since Zen is a school of Buddhism and employs some of the same terminology and concepts as early Buddhism, it is often assumed that Zen enlightenment (satori) and Theravāda enlightenment (Nirvāna) are the same. But apparently such is not the case. It is difficult to give a satisfactory account of satori, not only because of the elusive and paradoxical features of Zen, but also because of the different versions of enlightenment and Zen in general as presented by the various Zen sects and masters of the past 1,400 years. One can quote selected passages of Zen scriptures and other Zen writings to support just about any interpretation of Zen that one may choose to formulate. On the basis of Zen literature, however, satori seems to be very much a product of samsāra and to contain two essential features. One is a true insight into the nature of things and oneself beyond intellectual knowing. The other is a total restructuring of the psyche so that even though one remains very much involved in samsāra, one's whole perception of life and response to life situations are so radically altered that life becomes something quite different than it ever was before.[1] There is in Zen only scant mention of ending one's existence in samsāra. While Zen has given much concern to freeing onself from the restrictions of intellectualizing and conceptual thinking, it says much less about altering one's feelings, motives and emotions. One occasionally reads of great Zen masters expressing anger and of persons who have realized satori and yet are more selfish than many who have not.[2] We are told that there are degrees of satori, and one must ripen it and grow in it.[3] The renowned Zen scholar D. T. Suzuki comments on the Zen version of jhāna or *dhyāna* in these words:

[1] *Zen Buddhism*, by D. T. Suzuki (Garden City, New York, Doubleday & Co., Inc., 1956), p. 84.
[2] *The Three Pillars of Zen*, by Philip Kapleau (Tokyo, John Weatherhill, Inc., 1965), pp. 103–104.
[3] *Ibid.*, p. 228.

'Dhyāna is not quietism, nor is it tranquillization; it is rather acting, moving, performing deeds, seeing, hearing, thinking, remembering.'[1]

One may question whether or not satori is a real experience or merely a philosophical ideal which evolved in the history of Zen thought. Two independent sources of evidence indicate that there is such an experience. One source is the recent electroencephalographic (EEG or brain wave) studies of Zen meditators.[2] The other source is the case histories and testimonies of persons allegedly realizing satori in recent years. Both these two areas of study require further investigation before any definite conclusions can be made, and probably the characteristic Zen EEG tracings are not akin to the subjective experiences described in the case histories. In other words they appear to be two unrelated phenomena. Also, it may be that both of these recently-studied phenomena are quite different from the satori experiences of the Zen masters of old or of those Zen monks residing today in secluded and highly disciplined meditation centres.

ELECTROENCEPHALOGRAPHIC STUDIES

The EEG investigations have been conducted in Japan since 1953. The subjects studied included monks with many years of meditation experience as well as non-meditators. Two significant findings have been noted. First, during meditation in a well-lighted room and with eyes open, accomplished Zen practitioners produce a rhythmic slowing of the EEG pattern to cycles of seven or eight per second.[3] Usually this is seen in non-meditators only when the eyes are closed and is termed 'alpha wave pattern'. As a rule it occurs in meditators with open eyes only during and for a few minutes following medita-

---

[1] *Zen Buddhism, op. cit.,* p. 181–182.

[2] *Folia Psychiatrica et Neurologica Japonica,* Vol. 20, No. 4, 'An Electroencephalographic Study of the Zen Meditation (Zazen)' by Akira Kasamatsu and Tomio Hirai. December, 1966, pp. 315–336. (Supplementary data obtained by correspondence with the authors.)

[3] This occurs in all areas but is most pronounced in the frontal and central regions of the scalp.

tion. However, it has occasionally been seen in non-meditators, and as yet no studies have been done to establish a correlation between this EEG pattern and personality structure. It is known that some meditators who produce this pattern are not free of a normal intensity of sexual impulses. The Zen EEG pattern is distinctly different from those of sleep and hypnotic trance, and the meditators said that during meditation they were free from sleepiness, confusion and other mental disturbances. Normally an EEG cannot reveal a person's exact emotions, and people with identical EEG patterns may be experiencing very different states of thought and feeling. However, it was 'fairly constant' that the Zen practitioners described their subjective experiences during meditation as 'calm, undisturbed and serene'. It is noteworthy that no mention is made of 'religious', mystical, indescribable, transcendental or otherwise unusual states.

The second finding of the EEG studies revealed an alteration in the Zen practitioner's response to sensory stimuli, which suggests an alteration in the perception of one's environment. In normal persons a sudden sensory stimulus, such as a loud noise, draws attention for a brief period, but if the stimulus is repeated at regular and frequent intervals, one eventually becomes oblivious to it and takes no notice. EEG tracings taken on such occasions reveal that in normal subjects the first stimulus produces an alteration in EEG of seven seconds or more; this duration shortens with each successive distraction (in this case noises produced at 15-second intervals) until the fifth stimulus when virtually no EEG effect is seen. It is different, however, with advanced Zen practitioners. The EEG response to the first stimulus lasts only two to three seconds and then continues to last for two to three seconds for every succeeding stimulus up to the twentieth. This suggests a greater total awareness of one's environment but with fewer strong reactions to individual stimuli. This phenomenon has been observed only during meditation and only in persons experienced in Zen training.[1]

Satori is said to be present both in and out of meditation, and the reports of the above EEG studies make no mention of

[1] *Folia Psychiatrica et Neurologica Japonica*, Vol. 20, No. 4.

whether or not the subjects had had enlightenment. This writer knows of no EEG investigations of Theravāda meditators or Mahāyānists apart from Zen.

CASE STUDIES OF THE SATORI EXPERIENCE

Perhaps the best published examples of alleged satori experiences are those described by Mr Philip Kapleau in his book, *The Three Pillars of Zen*. Mr Kapleau presents eight case histories in the form of personal testimonies, which describe in varying amounts of detail the experiences preceding and during enlightenment. His subjects, including himself and his wife, range from 25 to 60 years of age and include three women and five men. Four are Japanese; three are American; one is Canadian. All are laypeople, i.e. not monks or priests. In the following paragraphs I shall discuss satori as described and explained in Kapleau's writing. All eight of his cases occurred to persons who were practising under the guidance of experienced Zen masters and most, if not all, were tested and affirmed by these masters to be genuine instances of satori. However, the reader should be aware that some reputable and long-experiened Zen practitioners reject the validity of these cases.[1]

As a psychiatrist, I find it tempting to speculate on the psychological mechanisms which produced Kapleau's case histories, though such speculations can be hazardous on two counts. First, it may be presumptuous to assume that western psychology in its present forms is fully capable of explaining the satori experience. Perhaps it is capable, but having no close contact with persons claiming satori I cannot venture to say. Second, Kapleau's case histories do not furnish enough information to enable one to speculate with certainty as to individual psychodynamics and personality structures. Some furnish almost no such information, and it is not the primary purpose of his writing to provide this sort of data.

[1] *Editorial Note:* It would appear that the term *satori* is used in Japan to cover a considerable range of experiences, from some of a relatively low order right up to 'supreme enlightenment'. I would assume that the latter, when it occurs, cannot be different from the attainment of arahantship as referred to in the Theravāda school.

But while there are insufficient data to analyse most of the individual case histories of Kapleau's series, I feel that collectively there is enough information to formulate a reasonable hypothesis for explaining his examples of satori on psychological grounds. Before presenting such a hypothesis, let us first note the nature of Zen training and its subsequent satori experiences.

All but one of Kapleau's eight cases give clear indication of significant emotional disturbances which resulted in the subjects taking up Zen training. In some cases these were relatively normal reactions to stressful situations such as the death of a loved one, serious illness and the insecurity of life in Japan following the war. Other cases indicated more basic personality disturbances such as alcoholism and psychosomatic symptoms. However, in all accounts of Zen training known to this writer very little concern is given to uncovering the psychological causes of one's disturbances. The Zen practitioner is repeatedly told to see his 'true self'; that is, to behold his Buddha Nature, his Oneness with the whole universe, and this must be done by dropping dualistic (i.e. subject-object) thinking and abandoning conceptualizing. For example, we read of one dialogue between a Zen trainee and a master. The trainee says she has had several insights into herself and 'felt extremely elated'. She is therefore puzzled that the master has told her that insights are *makyo* (i.e. mental distractions such as visions and fantasies). In response to this the master makes no inquiry as to what these insights are but responds 'In themselves they (insights) are not harmful, they may even be beneficial in some measure. But if you become attached to or ensnared by them, they can hinder you.'[1]

Perhaps the best example of this apparent indifference to motives and personality traits is displayed in the last case of Kapleau's series. The subject relates that while her childhood could be called almost 'ideal'. 'Even from the first, though, there were recurrent periods of despair and loneliness which used to seep up from no apparent source, overflowing into streams of tears and engulfing me to the exclusion of everything else.' This is not the behaviour of a normal child, and though

[1] *The Three Pillars of Zen*, p. 99.

the source may not have been 'apparent' it would be naïve to assume there was no source at all. Then again 'Within a few months our marriage took place and almost immediately after I awoke to find myself a widow. The violent, self-inflicted death of my husband was a shock more severe than anything I had ever experienced.'[1] One can only wonder what more had taken place but was left unmentioned. It is extremely unusual for a normal well-adjusted man to commit violent, self-inflicted death shortly after his marriage. And it is also unusual for a normal well-adjusted woman to marry a person predisposed to such action. Later the subject enters Zen training in Japan. We are given detailed accounts of her Zen experiences but told in only five words that during this period she marries again. There is no mention of her feelings towards her fiancé, her desires for companionship or the nature of the marital relationship. It is as though these aspects of oneself are a world apart from Zen practice and not directly concerned with 'seeing into one's True Nature'.

The essence of Zen training is *zazen* or the sitting meditation. This one practises at frequent and regular intervals often for hours at a time and extended over a period of months or years. On such occasions one sits in the company of others and gazes at a blank wall or other blank object. One is repeatedly subjected to great pressures and persuasions to strive with the utmost efforts to empty the mind, abandon intellectualizing and realize the Oneness of all things. Deliberate humiliations and painful brief beatings may be employed to encourage diligence and effort. One is told not to think about the Oneness or to have any ideas about one's yet-unrealized Buddha Nature. Nevertheless, the practitioner has already heard much about it and knows something of the enlightenment experiences of others before him.

The reactions to one's initial satori experience vary between different individuals, and it is questionable that all of these 'enlightenments' represent the same mental phenomenon. Often persons break out in uncontrollable laughter and/or sobbing. Some do neither. Usually there is a sense of joy, calm-

[1] *The Three Pillars of Zen*, p. 255.

ness or euphoria and often a feeling of oneness with all things. How enduring these states may be is uncertain and probably varies considerably between different individuals. To determine the real value of such experiences it would be necessary to have long-term follow-up reports at regular intervals. A mystical or uplifting emotional experience can be worthwhile in itself, but if years of arduous training have been required to produce it, one should hope for a reward lasting more than a few days or weeks. In the first case of Kapleau's series (which is also the only case that gives no history of previous emotional stress) we are told only of a 48-hour period in which a Japanese executive breaks out with tears, crying and a loud uncontrollable laughter described as 'inhuman'. With this are great feelings of peace, happiness and freedom. This is most likely akin to the states of euphoria described earlier, and we are given no previous history of this person and no report of his condition following the 'enlightenment'.

What then is the satori experience? Probably it is more than one thing, depending on whose experience we are talking about. Also, it may be presumptuous to assume that one not having had satori can fully account for it. Nevertheless, I feel that two types of phenomena are responsible for most of these experiences and such probably occur in varying degrees and combinations in different instances.

SATORI AND CONVERSION

The most striking feature of the recorded satori experiences is their strong resemblance to Christian conversion and/or salvation experiences. Readers of Buddhist writings are often predisposed to stereotyped and negative impressions of Christian experiences based mostly upon the extremely emotional and fanatic conversions so often witnessed at evangelistic revivals. But Christian conversions include a much deeper and wider range of experiences than these. William James in his well-known classic, *The Varieties of Religious Experience*, covers this topic with remarkable perspicacity, drawing his material both from numerous personal testimonies and case histories as well as the psychological studies of other researchers. While each conversion is a unique experience which reflects the convictions and emotional constitution of the person involved, one cannot avoid being impressed by the number of recurrent features in Christian conversions which are equally common in alleged satoris. Usually the moment of conversion is preceded by a duration (often several years) of unhappiness, emotional conflict or a general dissatisfaction with oneself and life in general. Often there has been a great (usually frustrated) striving to find God and to be pure and good. Yet the moment of salvation often comes at the instant one lets go and stops trying.

' "Lord, I have done all I can, I leave the whole matter with thee." Immediately there came to me a great peace. . . .'[1]

Such moments often occur when one's emotions or efforts have built up to a point that might be called a spiritual crisis. While this occurs more or less fortuitously in a Christian life, Zen induces it deliberately. In his own account of zazen meditation Kapleau relates the following.

'Suddenly the sun's streaming into the window in front of me! The rain's stopped! It's become warmer! At last the gods are with me! Now I can't miss satori! . . . Mu, Mu, Mu! . . . Again Roshi (the Zen master) leaned over but only to whisper: "You are panting and disturbing the others, try to breathe quietly. . . ." But I can't stop. My heart's pumping wildly, I'm trembling from head to toe, tears are streaming down uncontrollably. . . . Godo cracks me but I hardly feel it. He whacks my neighbour and I suddenly think: "Why's he so mean, he's hurting him." . . . More tears. . . . Godo returns and clouts me again and again, shouting: "Empty your mind of every single thought, become like a baby again. Just Mu, Mu! right from your guts!"—crack, crack, crack! . . .' [All the spacings, . . . are Kapleau's].[2]

---

[1] *The Varieties of Religious Experience*, by William James (London, Longmans, Green & Co., 1952), p. 249.
[2] *The Three Pillars of Zen*, p. 218.

And returning to Christianity we read:

'I have been through the experience which is known as conversion. My explanation of it is this: the subject works his emotions up to the breaking point, at the same time resisting their physical manifestations, such as quickened pulse, etc., and then suddenly lets them have their full sway over his body. The relief is something wonderful, and the pleasurable effects of the emotions are experienced to the highest degree.'[1]

As in Zen, the Christian experience is direct and immediate. Theology and philosophy fade out of sight at least for the moment, and in their place one may experience what appears to be a new insight into the nature of things:

'My emotional nature was stirred to its depths, confessions of depravity and pleading with God for salvation from sin made me oblivious of all surroundings. I pleaded for mercy, and had a vivid realization of forgiveness and renewal of my nature. When rising from my knees I exclaimed, "Old things have passed away, all things have become new." It was like entering another world, a new state of existence. Natural objects were glorified, my spiritual vision was so clarified that I saw beauty in every material object in the universe, the woods were vocal with heavenly music; my soul exulted in the love of God, and I wanted everybody to share in my joy.'[2]

'Not for a moment only, but all day and night, floods of light and glory seemed to pour through my soul, and oh, how I was changed, and everything became new. My horses and hogs and even everybody seemed changed.'[3]

And now as described by Zen devotees:

'Never before had the road been so roadlike, the shops such perfect shops, nor the winter sky so unutterably a starry sky. Joy bubbled up like a fresh spring. . . .

[1] *The Varieties of Religious Experience*, p. 246.
[2] *Ibid.*, p. 244.   [3] *Ibid.*, p. 245.

'The days and weeks that followed were the most deeply happy and serene of my life.'[1]

And from another Zen practitioner:

Am totally at peace at peace at peace.
Feel numb throughout body, yet hands and feet
    jumped for joy for almost half an hour.
Am supremely free free free free free.
Should I be so happy?
There is no common man.
The big clock chimes—not the clock but Mind chimes. The universe itself chimes.
There is neither Mind nor universe. Dong, dong, dong!
I've totally disappeared. Buddha is![2]

Also, as in Zen, Christian experiences can be precipitated by a simple word, a passage of scripture or non-verbal sensory experience.

It is difficult at this point to assert any essential difference between the Christian and Zen experiences. Both claim a state of certainty, a direct knowing beyond logic and argument. Perhaps the basic differences are the respective vocabularies, religious convictions and cultural settings that determine the manner in which one describes and explains them.

While such religious experiences are usually brief and of little consequence, in both the Zen and Christian traditions one finds examples of profound and long-lasting (often permanent) personality changes, usually for the better. Such instances most often are preceded by an unsatisfactory life pattern of either overt or repressed unhappiness—drunkenness, sensuality, cynicism, insecurity, etc. Apparently one's inner conflicts build up to such a point that there occurs a radical restructuring of the personality. The old, selfish, guilt-ridden and unrewarding tendencies are repressed and their existence denied. Simultaneously the previously denied or undeveloped feelings of companionship and love are brought into focus. Thus one indeed is reborn

[1] *The Three Pillars of Zen*, pp. 266–267.   [2] *Ibid.*, p. 207.

and is now manifesting a personality pattern which brings much greater personal rewards and brings a previously unknown sense of purpose in life. James states:

> 'Another American psychologist, Prof. George A. Coe, has analysed the cases of seventy-seven converts or ex-candidates for conversion, known to him, and the results strikingly confirm the view that sudden conversion is connected with the possession of an active subliminal (i.e. unconscious) self. Examining his subjects with reference to their hypnotic sensibility and to such automatisms as hypnagogic hallucinations, odd impulses, religious dreams about the time of their conversion, etc., he found these relatively much more frequent in the group of converts whose transformation had been "striking", "striking" transformation being defined as a change which, though not necessarily instantaneous, seems to the subject of it to be distinctly different from a process of growth, however rapid.'[1]

Obviously in many instances the fruits of both Zen and Christian experiences are highly beneficial in terms of morality, social productivity and one's internal well-being. Yet these remarkable transformations take place with an almost total lack of insight into oneself. The old, neurotic, unwholesome tendencies are more often repressed than resolved and thus may manifest in more covert ways such as evangelical fervour, 'a hatred for sin', or religious fanaticism. This is more apt to occur in the Christian tradition where the religious experience is made a part of a rigidly defined dogma, and the devotee is often unable to separate the experience itself from such concepts as God, salvation and Bible. One knows of examples of saintly, elderly Christians, self-sacrificing and compassionate, who for decades have won the hearts of many and epitomized Christian virtue. Yet if caught in a discussion where the fallacies of their theological convictions are laid bare, fear, anxiety and even unmasked anger break forth until again repressed in conformity with Christian ideals. This also appears to occur to some extent

[1] *The Varieties of Religious Experience*, p. 235.

in Zen. We read, for example, of a dialogue between a highly respected Zen master and a pupil. The student raises a doubt about an extremely unlikely Zen teaching which claims that Zen was the Buddha's highest doctrine and was passed on by special transmission down to the present. After the student asks if this is not really a myth, the master unconditionally replies: 'No, it is true. If you don't believe it, that's too bad.'[1]

Other features of Zen training can also produce desirable personality changes: there is the factor of suggestion; one hears over and over again what should happen, and thus eventually it does. The introspective nature of Zen and especially of meditation can make one aware of mental changes and states of mind which might otherwise go unnoticed though be no less present in non-meditators. (This same can apply in part to the claims for success of all of the other numerous and divergent schools of psychotherapy besides Zen.) The move to a new environment (either to a new culture for Westerners or into a monastery for Japanese laymen) can in itself change the person and make old concerns seem unimportant; transplanted to a new world it is easier to abandon old habits, to form a new identity and to relinquish attachments. The process of growing up and maturing regardless of religion and practice must be taken into account, especially when we consider that Zen training often requires several years. And finally there is the fact that Zen training is a long and arduous discipline; just as one who has survived a long journey through a wilderness or scaled a difficult mountain or withstood any prolonged stress, the sheer fact of successful endurance gives one self-confidence and a feeling of worth.

PERCEPTUAL ALTERATION

In addition to the above-mentioned causes of Zen experiences, the nature of Zen meditation probably produces an additional state of mind not normally present in Christian conversions. This state can occur either singly or in combination with any of the other Zen experiences already noted.

Recent psychological studies have shown that prolonged

---

[1] *The Three Pillars of Zen*, p. 133.

concentration on simple visual objects can produce striking temporary alterations of feeling and perception. Perhaps most noteworthy are the studies of Dr Arthur J. Deikman of Austen Riggs Center, Stockbridge, Massachusetts, U.S.A.[1,2]

Dr Deikman's subjects were seated in front of a blue vase and instructed:

'Your aim is to concentrate on the blue vase. By concentration I do not mean analysing the different parts of the vase, or thinking a series of thoughts about the vase, or associating ideas to the vase, but rather, trying to see the vase as it exists in itself, without any connections to other things. Exclude all other thoughts or feelings or sounds or body sensations. Do not let them distract you but keep them out so that you can concentrate all your attention, all your awareness on the vase itself. Let the perception of the vase fill your entire mind.'

It is significant that of the more than eight persons selected for these studies apparently none had had any previous exposure to meditation nor had any contact with mystical literature. Subjects were described as 'normal adults in their thirties and forties, well educated and intelligent'. After a few introductory sessions of about 10 minutes' duration, the sessions were increased to 30 minutes each and held three times a week. Four of the subjects completed 30 to 40 sessions; one completed 78 sessions, and one was still continuing after 106. Though marked individual variations were noted, most, if not all, subjects experienced perceptual changes relating to the vase, modification of the state of consciousness and a general feeling that the sessions were pleasurable and valuable. Quite commonly the vase became more vivid or luminous; a loss of the third dimension was often noted. Some subjects felt a loss of ego boundaries,

[1] *The Journal of Nervous and Mental Disease*, Vol. 136, No. 4, 'Experimental Meditation', by Arthur J. Deikman (U.S.A., Williams & Walkins Co., April 1963).

[2] *The Journal of Nervous and Mental Disease*, Vol. 142, No. 2, 'Implications of Experimentally Induced Contemplative Meditation', by Arthur J. Deikman, 1966, pp. 101–116.

a confusion of the subject-object relationship as though they and the vase were merging. Such experiences occurred spontaneously and unexpectedly and were sometimes frightening. The degree of success in achieving such states appeared to correlate with one's ability to relinquish control and accept whatever happens. In general the subjects found it difficult to describe their feelings and perceptions—'it's very hard to put into words' was a frequent comment. This difficulty seemed due in part to the difficulty of describing their experiences without contradictions.

Immediately following the meditation sessions, the subjects were asked to describe the experience and also to look out the window and describe the way things now appeared to them. A few of their comments are quoted below:

'One of the points that I remember most vividly is when I really began to feel, you know, almost as though the blue and I were perhaps merging, or that the vase and I were. I almost got scared to the point where I found myself bringing myself back in some way from it. . . .'

'The building is a kind of very white . . . a kind of luminescence that the fields have and the trees are really swaying, it's very nice . . . lean way over and bounce back with a nice spring-like movement. . . .'

'The movements are nice, the brightness is. I would have thought it was a terribly overcast day but it isn't. It's a perception filled with light and movement both of which are very pleasurable. Nobody knows what a nice day it is except me.'

'I am looking differently than I have ever looked before. I mean it's almost as though I have a different way of seeing. It's like something to do with dimensions. It's as though I am feeling what I am looking at. It's as though I have an extension of myself reaching out and seeing something by feeling it. It's as though somebody added something, another factor to my seeing.'

'. . . I've experienced . . . new experiences and I have no
vehicle to communicate them to you. I expect that this is
probably the way a baby feels when he is full of something
to say about an experience or an awareness and he has not
learned to use the words yet.'

'. . . It's so completely and totally outside of anything else
I've experienced.'

'It was like a parallel world or parallel time. . . .'

The similarities between these descriptions and the descriptions of Zen experiences are so striking that little comment is
needed.

Dr Deikman lists several factors which he believes account for
these experiences, three of which warrant discussion here. They
are de-automatization, perceptual expansion and reality transfer.

In order to explain de-automatization and perceptual expansion it is first necessary to explain the word 'perception' as
used in modern psychology. For simplicity, our dicussion will
be confined to visual perception, but the same principles also
apply to auditory, tactile and olfactory perception.

Visual perception is dependent upon, but must be distinguished from, simple visual sensation. Sensation is the patterns
of colours which we behold upon opening our eyes. Perception is
the way in which we understand or interpret these patterns.
Contrary to popular assumption, human visual perception is not
innate in visual experience but rather is gradually acquired by
learning as the result of repeatedly seeing visual patterns. The
best and most convincing illustration of this is noted in the case
of persons born blind but who in later life receive eye surgery.
For all practical purposes these people obtain instant and near-
perfect vision for the first time in what has been a lifetime of
total blindness. They are overwhelmed by a mass of confusing
colours and shapes, which they are totally at a loss to understand. They are unable to determine the difference in distance,
size and quality between a full moon in the sky, a light bulb on
the ceiling or a white ball placed two feet in front of them. They

are just as likely to try and reach for a cloud as to reach for a piece of paper near at hand. A pencil seen from its end will not be recognized as the same object as the same pencil seen from its side. But only when the pencil has been examined over and over in one's hands (in the same manner and for the same reason as a very young child) will one come to know that these very different visual patterns actually are the same object, i.e. a pencil.[1]

Any person raised in a Western culture who in later life learns to read a non-Romanized language, such as Chinese, Thai, Sanskrit or Arabic, will recall that in the beginning great attention had to be given to the details of shape and form of each letter or character. But once fluency is achieved, one scarcely is aware of individual letters let alone their details of shape. One can now glance at whole patterns of words and immediately comprehend the meanings; just as one competent in English reads these pages.[2]

[1] *Space and Sight*, by M. Von Senden (Glencoe, Illinois, Free Press, 1960).

[2] Thus perception is dependent upon memory and is inseparable from it. In Theravāda Buddhism mind (*nāma*) is divided into four groups, one of which is consciousness. Consciousness in turn is interdependent with the other three (see page 174). Of these other three the first is termed sensation or feeling (*vedanā*); the second (*saññā*) means both 'memory' and 'perception' and is translated into English as either one of these two words, usually the latter. The third group is mental formations (*sankhāra*) and includes conceptional formations (thinking), willing, planning.[3] The corresponding classification used in Western psychology is sensations, perceptions, and concepts arising in that order. After perceptions have become established, the mind is able to use sound (i.e. spoken words) and figures (i.e. written words) to serve as symbols to represent respective objects, feelings and abstract relationships; this is the formation of concepts. Thus once conceptualization has developed, it no longer is necessary to see or touch a tree, for example, to know that a tree exists at a given site; the simple sound 'tree' will bring to mind the perceptions which occur in actually experiencing a tree. The word 'sankhāra' has a range of usages, but as applied to the above aspect of Buddhist psychology it includes conceptualization as understood in Western psychology but also includes aspects of volition and motivation.

If the reader will refer back to the instructions given to the experimental meditation subjects (page 213), it will be noted that their field of awareness is narrowed in two ways. First is by concentration on a given object to the exclusion of other concerns. Second is suppression of verbal thinking and all other forms of conceptualization. Thus the mind approaches a preconceptual level,

[3] *Buddhist Dictionary*, by Nyanatiloka Mahāthera (Colombo, Island Hermitage Publication, 1956).

Psychology uses the word 'automatization' for referring to the natural loss of awareness of the intermediate steps in perception. For example, one does not consciously give attention to the shape of each letter in the words one is reading. Automatization thus increases our mental efficiency by freeing the mind from concern for repetitious details. De-automatization is the undoing of automatization; that is, attention is again focused on minor sensory details. Perceptually, de-automatization puts one's mind momentarily on the same level as a young child. Colours become more vivid; previously unnoticed details hold the attention. Commonplace objects such as boxes, brooms and key chains may seem fascinating and beautiful.[2] Concentrative meditation is not the only way of inducing this phenomenon; sensory deprivation and drugs such as marijuana, peyote and LSD-25 are equally if not more effective de-automatizers.

The response of Zen practitioners in meditation to repeated stimuli as shown by EEG (page 203) may well be the result of de-automatization. However, it cannot at this time be concluded that the phenomena of Deikman's relatively inexperienced meditation subjects are either qualitatively or quantitatively the same as the EEG phenomena observed in Zen monks. Control studies on 22 non-meditators failed to produce these same EEG findings. Also, the degree of EEG change correlated directly with the number of years in practice, and the most striking change (i.e. 6–7/second theta waves) was rarely if ever seen in monks with less than 20 years of experience.

Following and dependent upon de-automatization is perceptual expansion. So strong is the process of automatization that

---

i.e. a predominantly sensation-perception level presumably similar to that of an animal or one-year old child. Psychological studies have shown that as a child matures the *vividness* of visual experience is reduced because vision becomes modified by the presence of perception and reflective thought.[3] Thus alteration or diminution of perception and conceptual thinking (as occurs in concentrative meditation and under LSD) increases the vividness of visual experience.

[3] *The Journal of Nervous and Mental Disease*, Vol. 142, pp. 111–113.

[2] *The Doors of Perception and Heaven and Hell*, by Aldous Huxley (London, Penguin Books, 1959).

it is virtually impossible for one to see visual patterns in their true form independently of perceptual conditioning. η, for example, will be seen as the written form of N by an American, but to a Thai it is the Siamese equivalent of a T. And what does the English-trained mind make of น, ค, or ญ?

The figure below will immediately be recognized as a cube. If one stares at the extreme upper right-hand corner of this cube, some people will perceive this corner as belonging to the front (near) side of the cube; others will see it as belonging to the back (far) side. Most people who stare at the cube for a minute or two will perceive the position of the upper right-hand corner as constantly changing; that is, first it is forward, and then back, and then forward again and so on. In reality there is no front or back side; in fact there is no third dimension at all.

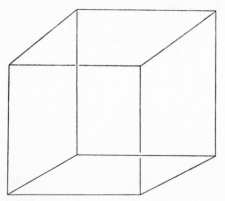

Perception compels us to see a third dimension that is not really there. Under de-automatizing drugs such as hashish and LSD the figure above may appear flat, i.e. have no third dimension, and yet a moment later one may see all three possibilities (forward, backward and flat) simultaneously. This is but one example of perceptual expansion.

The artistic value of perceptual expansion, whether obtained through drugs or through concentrative meditation, is not to be denied. No doubt it enables an artist to see previously unnoticed patterns and thus can enhance creativity. Also the experience is often accompanied by pleasant and uplifting emotions. However, it is questionable whether or not such experiences have any lasting value in terms of emotional well-being, long-term happiness or adjustment to life problems. The failures of numerous persons who have long tried Zen and/ or LSD to resolve emotional and neurotic problems testifies to this fact.[1] Of the two subjects in Deikman's meditation experiments who both practised the longest and got the most striking results, both showed evidence of neurotic conflicts on the basis of personal history and psychological testing, though they were functioning relatively well in their environments. De-automatization experiences, whether induced through chemistry or zazen, are quite brief—a few hours at most in the case of drugs and only a few minutes following meditation. Also, we must not forget that normal perception (i.e. automatization) has a definite biological value or it would not have evolved. Its presence allows us greater efficiency in dealing with the problems of daily living. The man who quickly reads through a menu will be farther along the road to survival than one who becomes enamoured with the shape and form of the ABCs.

The reader should keep in mind that the above statements regarding meditation are concerned with only one type of meditation and do not apply to insight meditation (*vipassanā*) as practised in Pāli Buddhism. Nor do these statements apply to the deeper tranquillity practices (jhāna) nor to the various discursive meditations.

Dr Deikman's third factor used to explain the above meditation experiences he terms 'reality transfer'. This phrase refers to the fact that actual physical reality and the *sensation* or *feeling* of reality are not the same. In the interests of biological survival, the normal state of the mind is to invest a feeling of reality into the objects of everyday experience. However, factors which alter the mind (such as hypnosis, LSD, psychotic

[1] This is not to imply that LSD and related drugs have no psychotherapeutic potential at all. There are instances in which they have produced valid psychological insights and thus facilitated personality growth. However, such growth will take place only if one is emotionally and intellectually prepared to confront, understand and make use of the acquired insights.[2]

[2] *The Drug Experience*, edited by David Ebin (New York, The Orion Press, 1961), pp. 368–384.

states and prolonged concentration) can displace this reality sensation. At such times the real world may seem unreal, while subjective states and minor sensory perceptions may appear more real than normal reality.

5. THE OCCURRENCE OF ARAHANTS

If Nirvāna is real, why are arahants so hard to find? Has even one lived within the past century? We are told that at the time of the Buddha over 1,000 of the monks realized Nirvāna. But despite this impressive figure we are also told that the occurrence of arahants is rare in the world, and even more rare is the occurrence of an enlightened teacher who warrants the title of 'Buddha'.[1]

> Few among men are there indeed
> Who cross to the Further Shore.
> The remaining men, most of mankind
> Run up and down this hither shore.
>
> But they who Dhamma practice
> In this Dhamma well-expounded,
> It is such among mankind
> Who will reach the Further Shore,
> Who will cross old Death's dominions
> So difficult to cross.[1]

—*Dhammapada*, 85–86

It goes without saying that the realization of Nirvāna is no easy achievement, for it requires the complete and final abolition of all attachment and craving. What is not fully appreciated, however, is that the desire to remove attachments will not in and of itself effect their removal. Wanting to abandon passion only means that one is in a state of ambivalence; that is, two contradictory or opposing feelings coexist. We have for example the well-known prayer of St Augustine:

[1] *Dīgha-Nikāya* II, 149 (No. 16 *Mahāparinibbāna Sutta* Ch. V, 23).

'I had begged chastity of Thee, and said, "Give me chastity and continency, only not yet!" For I feared lest Thou shouldest hear me soon, and soon cure me of the disease of concupiscence, which I wished to have satisfied, rather than extinguished.'[1]

The problem is compounded by the fact that if the desire to be free of hatred or passion is significantly stronger than the hatred or passion itself, one may unwittingly repress these unwanted feelings so as to hide them from awareness and thus not realize that they still exist. This brings us to the second major barrier to Nirvāna, which is delusion (moha). Delusion and desire are interdependent. It is because of desires of one sort or another that we structure delusions and unconsciously resist their relinquishment. As an example, the desire to be rid of passion is as often as not motivated by a more subtle form of pleasure seeking, which is the egotistical wish to be pure, virtuous and holy. This in turn originates in part from the delusion that one has an Ego, a true unchanging self, something special and unique which is the essence of one's true being. But the level of self-deception goes even deeper than this; in the light of modern science and psychology many persons have come to accept that there is no immortal soul; rather man is a compounded and highly complex psycho-physical phenomenon. However, an intellectual acceptance is something quite different from a thorough emotional acceptance. Quite likely many of the most ardent materialists retain some lingering notion of a soul or even of personal immortality no matter how strongly they may repress such feelings or find them intellectually unpalatable. The same is equally true of great scholars of Buddhist thought, if their scholastic achievements have not been accompanied by successful insight (vipassanā) practice. Thus the realization of Nirvāna requires the maximum possible goal of psychoanalysis—a complete laying bare of the subconscious, the total removal of repression, rationalization and all other unconscious defence mechanisms. Ardent discipline, religious

[1] Confessions, Book VIII, 17, by St Augustine (Chicago, Henry Regnery Co., 1948), p. 144.

dedication and deep faith no matter how strong they may be do not guarantee that true insight will be achieved. For quite often discipline, dedication and faith originate from the very factors that obstruct one's progress towards enlightenment; common among such factors are bigotry, compulsiveness, ethnocentrism, egotism and insecurity. Thus discipline, dedication and faith are double-edged swords. Though they can be assets towards realizing Nirvāna, they must be subjected to close scrutiny and questioning.

> The faults of others are easy to see,
> While hard indeed to see are one's own;
> Like chaff one winnows others' faults,
> Concealing carefully those of one's own;
> Just as a cheating gambler hides
> The ill-thrown dice from others' eyes.

—*Dhammapada*, 252

But even allowing for the great difficulty in realizing Nirvāna, one might think that among the many millions of Buddhists in the world today at least a few should win the ultimate goal. In this regard two facts must be kept in mind. First, many Buddhist regions are Buddhist in name only. During the past 2,500 years the Dhamma has spread to many lands and become mixed with numerous indigenous beliefs and superstitions, while at the same time its teachings have been radically modified by priests and scholars. Thus many millions of Buddhists have followed and are still following beliefs and practices that are the direct antithesis of the Buddha's teachings, too often these teachings have been either obscured by folklore, mythology and ecclesiasticism or buried in a deluge of metaphysics, meticulous categorizations and philosophizing. Then again, when one does encounter the apparently valid teachings of the Buddha, one occasionally finds that the major emphasis is either upon the correct intonations for chanting these teachings in Pāli (which has been a dead language for two millenniums) or else the primary concern is upon scriptural hair splitting, rote memorizing or argumentation.

All of this is not meant to imply that there are very few persons with an extensive and profound grasp of the Dhamma. For such is not the case. The point to be made, however, is that the quoted number of world Buddhists is a figure many times greater than the number of those who truly understand what the Buddha taught. And smaller still is the number of those who both understand and practise.

Persons not usually credulous and who are in close contact with advanced centres of Buddhist training, have stated that there are indeed arahants alive in the world today. This writer can neither deny nor affirm such claims, but two facts must be mentioned. First, the Vinaya rules, by which all Theravādin monks are bound, state that a monk must not tell a lay person of his attainment of either Jhāna or Nirvāna even though such be true.[1] Second, there are very good reasons for establishing such a rule. One familiar with Asian society need only reflect a moment on what would happen were an Arahant to make his attainment known. The results would be little short of disastrous. In the minds of uneducated lay Buddhists he would be regarded as a god and in possession of almost limitless supernatural powers. There would be pleas for cures of ailments, requests for prophecies and demands for blessings to protect one from ghosts, ill fortune and injury. Should the announced arahant utter any statement contrary to either popular tradition or the letter of Buddhist scriptures, there would be a wail of protests rejecting his claims to enlightenment and accusing him of fraud. Undoubtedly he would be repeatedly approached by fanatics and by persons intent on challenging and testing his claim.

How then can one who has not achieved Nirvāna be assured of the attainment of one who has? This same question was once put to the Buddha:

'The king, the Kosalan Pasenadi, came to visit the Exalted One, and having saluted him, took a seat at one side. Now just then there passed by, not far from the Exalted One seven ascetics of those who wore the hair matted, seven of the

[1] *Vinaya, Suttavibhanga, Pācittiya* 8.

Niganthas (Jains), seven naked ascetics, seven of the Single Vestment class, and seven Wanderers, all with hairy bodies and long nails, carrying friars' kit. Then the king, rising from his seat, and draping his robe over one shoulder, knelt down on his right knee, and holding forth clasped hands, thrice called out his name to those ascetics: "I am the king, your reverences, the Kosalan Pasenadi." And when they were gone by, he came back to the Exalted One, and saluting him, sat down as before. So seated, he asked the Exalted One:

' "Are those persons, lord, either among the world's arahants, or among those who are in the Path of arahant-ship?" '

To this the Buddha replied:

' "Hard is it, sire, for you who are a layman holding worldly possessions, dwelling amidst the encumbrances of children, accustomed to Benares sandalwood, arrayed in garlands and perfumed unguents, using gold and silver, to know whether those are arahants, or are in the Path of arahantship."

' "It is by life in common with a person, sire, that we learn his moral character; and then only after a long interval if we pay good heed and are not heedless, if we have insight and are not unintelligent. It is by converse with another, sire, that we learn whether he is pure-minded; and then only after a long interval if we pay good heed and are not heedless, if we have insight and are not unintelligent. It is in time of trouble, sire, that we learn to know a man's fortitude and then only after a long interval, if we pay good heed and are not heedless, if we have insight and are not unintelligent.' "

—*Saṁyutta-Nikāya* I, 77–78 (III, 2; 1)

Among the commentaries to the Pāli Canon is the following story:

'At the monastery on the Cittala Hill, there lived an elder who was a canker-freed Saint (i.e. an arahant). As his personal

attendant he had a novice who got ordained in old age. One day the old novice went on almsround together with the elder, and carrying the elder's alms bowl and outer robe, he walked behind him. While they so went, the old novice asked the elder: "Those who are Saints, how do they look? How can we recognize them?" The elder said: "There is an old person who carries a Saint's bowl and robe, fulfils all duties towards him, and even goes along with him—yet he cannot recognize Saints. So hard to know, friend, are the Saints!" And not even then did the old novice understand.'
—Commentary to the *Saṁyutta-Nikāya*

At this point one may ask whether or not Buddhism is a satisfactory religion, for it offers salvation to so few. But the problem is not one of 'offering' salvation but rather of pointing the way for those who are able and willing to tread the path. What then of persons apparently unable to reach the goal? In this regard we must first remember that Buddhism is empirical; it is dealing with things as they are, not as we would like them to be. A religion which promises universal or easy salvation may be more emotionally satisfying, but in the long run it will tend to be an opiate which diverts our efforts from truly constructive endeavours. But the Buddha was fully aware of the needs and capabilities of the common people. Repeatedly he gave them instructions for finding comfort and happiness in everyday life.[1] Even those who strive for Nirvāna without fully attaining the goal have not wasted their efforts; for the extent to which one has freed one's mind from greed, hatred and delusion and developed compassion and equanimity is the extent to which one finds emotional well-being and peace of mind in the present. Furthermore, such achievements are said to result in good karma, which in turn brings happiness in the future. And in the next birth, which allegedly arises as the result of the present one, one would be that much closer to Nirvāna should one choose to continue the journey. If we consider the great infinity of time as taught in Buddhism and also

[1] *Dīgha-Nikāya* III, 180–193 (No. 31 *Sigālovāda Sutta*).

the fact that Nirvāna is said to be obtainable after several life-
times of patient endeavour, then perhaps the percentage of
beings reaching Nirvāna is much greater than realized. Also,
the Buddha is quoted as saying that some persons who make
sufficient progress towards Nirvāna will not be reborn in this
world. Rather they will continue their existence on some other
dimension within samsāra and in that realm attain the final
goal.[1]

6. AESTHETIC AND MORAL
CRITICISMS

APATHY AND NEGATION

As Nirvāna can be realized only by the abolition of desire and
craving, it is often viewed as a condition of emotional death,
a state of emptiness and apathy. Even in the minds of many
Theravādin Buddhists it seems depressing, as if to say one never
wins in samsāra, so the only solution is suicide. Yet suicide of
the usual sort is almost invariably preceded by severe and inescapable depression. Before concluding that the quest for Nirvāna is motivated by a death-wish, we should note that the
Buddha divided the types of craving one should overcome into
three categories. The first two are cravings for sense pleasures
and for continued existence. The third craving to be relinquished
is craving for annihilation after death.[2]

An arahant is not in a state of chronic apathy. In the Suttas
the Buddha is often referred to as 'the Happy One',[3] and of the
seven states of mind listed as conducive to Nirvāna one is
happiness and two of the others are tranquillity and equanimity.
(The remaining four are mindfulness, investigation of reality,
energy and concentration.)[4] The Buddha is quoted:

[1] *Majjhima-Nikāya* III, 80 (No. 118 *Anāpānasati Sutta*).
[2] *Saṁyutta-Nikāya* V, 421 (*Dhamma-cakka-ppavattana Sutta*).
[3] *Dīgha-Nikāya* II, 93 (No. 16 *Mahāparinibbāna Sutta* Ch. II, 9).
[4] *The Seven Factors of Englightenment*, by Piyadassi Thera (Kandy, Buddhist
Publication Society, 1960).

Happy is he contented in solitude,
Seeing the truth he has learned.
Happy is he who abstains from harming,
Living restrained towards all that lives.
Happiness true is freedom from passion
If senses' cravings are left behind.
But highest happiness is his
Who has removed the self-conceit.

Udāna II, 1 (*Mucaliṇḍa*)

The Buddha's statement 'happiness is won by happiness'
stands in sharp contrast to the Jain teaching that happiness is
won by suffering.[1] Too often Buddhism is misunderstood as a
practice of rigid asceticism intended to induce a state of euphoria. In his first sermon the Buddha contradicted this notion
by advocating the famed Middle Way, the avoidance of the two
extremes; one extreme being sensual indulgence and the other
self-torture.[2] And in the *Kassapa-Sihanāda Sutta* the Buddha
asks:

'If a man, O Kassapa, should go naked, and be of loose habits,
and lick his hands clean with his tongue, and do and be all
those things you gave in detail, down to his being addicted
to the practice of taking food, according to rule, at regular
intervals up to even half a month—if he does all this, and
the state of blissful attainment in conduct, in heart, in intellect, have not been practised by him, realized by him, then
is he far from Samanaship, far from Brahmanship. But from
the time, O Kassapa, when a Bhikkhu has cultivated the
heart of love that knows no anger, that knows no ill-will—
from the time when by the destruction of the deadly intoxications (the lusts of the flesh, the lust after future life, and the
defilements of delusion and ignorance), he dwells in that
emancipation of heart, that emancipation of mind, that is
free from those intoxications, and that he, while yet in this

---

[1] *The Book of the Gradual Sayings*, Vol. II (*Anguttara-Nikāya* II), translated
by F. L. Woodward (London, The Pāli Text Society, 1952), pp. 2–3.
[2] *Saṁyutta-Nikāya* V, 421 (*Dhamma-cakka-ppavattana Sutta*).

visible world, has come to realize and know—from that time,
O Kassapa, is it that the Bhikkhu is called a Samana, is
called a Brahmana.'

—*Dīgha-Nikāya* I, 167 (No. 8 *Kassapa-Sīhanāda Sutta*)

And again he is quoted:

'Now it may well be, Potthapāda, that you think: "Evil
dispositions may be put away, the dispositions that tend to
purification may increase, one may continue to see face to
face, and by himself come to realize, the full perfection and
grandeur of wisdom, but one may continue sad." Now that,
Potthapāda, would not be accurate judgement. When such
conditions are fulfilled, then there will be joy, and happiness,
and peace, and in continual mindfulness and self-mastery,
one will dwell at ease.

'And outsiders, Potthapāda, might question us thus:
"What then, sir, is that material (or that mental, or that
formless) mode of personality for the putting away of which
you preach such a doctrine. . . ." And to that I should reply:
"Why this very personality that you see before you is what
I mean." '

—*Dīgha-Nikāya* I, 196–197 (No. 9 *Potthapāda Sutta*)

The Buddha never taught that the abolition of all feelings is
a prerequisite to Nirvāna. Only those states of mind which are
unwholesome (i.e. conducive to dukkha and undesirable karma)
need be abandoned. Usually he classified such states into
greed, hatred and delusion. On other occasions they were
termed the 'five mental hindrances' and enumerated as:
Sensual lust, anger, sloth and torpor, agitation and worry and
sceptical doubt. Sometimes the list was expanded to ten:
Belief that oneself is an unchanging soul, scepticism, belief in
salvation through rules and ceremonies, sensual lust, hatred,
craving for existence in a heaven world, craving for the bliss
of deep meditation (i.e. arūpajjhāna, see pages 188–189, conceit, restlessness and ignorance.[1]

[1] *Samyutta-Nikāya* V, 61 (XLV, I, VIII, 9–10).

In place of the unwholesome levels of feeling the Buddha advocated the cultivation and development of the four *Brahma-vihāras*: Love (*mettā*), compassion, sympathetic joy (i.e. the happiness one experiences in perceiving the happiness of others) and equanimity.[1] The first of these four, mettā, is usually translated into English as 'love' or 'loving-kindness', but there is no precise English equivalent. By simultaneously thinking of love, kindness and friendship we can best understand its meaning.

In Buddhist teaching there is no moral or psychological wrong in encountering and acknowledging an enjoyable experience *per se*. The pleasures which accompany the sweet taste of sugar and the beauty of a mountain scene are not in themselves barriers to Nirvāna. But danger arises from the craving or attachment that such experiences may produce. That is, the notion 'I must have this. I must re-experience it.' Thus the Buddha said:

> 'If he (an arahant) feels a pleasant feeling he knows it is transient, he knows it is not clung to, he knows it has no lure for him . . . (The same is then repeated for painful and neutral feelings). . . . If he feels a pleasant feeling, he feels that feeling with detachment. If he feels a painful feeling, he feels that feeling with detachment.'
> —*Saṁyutta-Nikāya* II, 82 (XII, 6: 51)

Referring to the place at which he first realized Nirvāna, the Buddha spoke:

> 'Pleasant indeed and delightful is the forest grove with a flowing river of clear water, a pleasant and delightful ford and a village near by for procuring food. Indeed it is a most suitable place for a noble youth intent on spiritual exertion.'
> —*Majjhima-Nikāya* I, 167
> (No. 26 *Ariyapariyesana Sutta*)

And on an occasion shortly before the Buddha's demise:

[1] *The Four Sublime States*, by Nyānaponika Thera (Kandy, Buddhist Publication Society, 1960).

'So the Exalted One proceeded to the Cāpala Shrine, and when he had come there he sat down on the mat spread out for him, and the venerable Ānanda took his seat respectfully beside him. Then the Exalted One addressed the venerable Ananda, and said: "How delightful a spot, Ānanda, is Vesāli, and how charming the Udena Shrine, and the Gotamaka Shrine, and the Shrine of the Seven Mangoes, and the Shrine of Many Sons, and the Sarandada Shrine, and the Cāpala Shrine!" '

—Dīgha-Nikāya II, 102
(No. 16 *Mahāparinibbāna Sutta*, Ch. III)

And at another time he is quoted:

'Now I, Bhaggava, being of such an opinion, certain recluses and brahmins have falsely, emptily, mendaciously and unfairly accused me, saying: Gotama, the recluse, is all wrong, and so are his monks. He has said: Whenever one has attained to the stage of deliverance entitled the Beautiful (*subha*, a condition below both Nirvāna and arupajjhāna), one then considers all things as repulsive. But this, Bhaggava, I have not said. What I do say is this: Whenever one attains to the stage of deliverance, entitled the Beautiful, one is then aware: 'Tis lovely!'

—Dīgha-Nikāya III, 34 (No. 24 *Pātika Sutta*)

This same appreciation of beauty was also expressed by others among the arahants. There is, for example, a poem attributed to Sabbaka after his enlightenment:

Whene'er I see the crane, her clear bright wings
Outstretched in fear to flee the black stormcloud,
A shelter seeking, to safe shelter borne,
Then doth the river Ajakarani give joy to me.

Who doth not love to see on either bank
Clustered rose-apple trees in fair array
Behind the great cave (of my hermitage)
Or hear the soft croak of the frogs, well rid

Of their undying mortal foes, proclaim:
'Not from the mountain streams is't time today
To flit. Safe is the Ajakarani.
She brings us luck. Here is it good to be.'
—'Psalms of the Brethren', *Thera Gāthā* IV, 196

And Kassapa, another of the arahants, is allegedly the author
of the following:

Those upland glades delightful to the soul,
Where the kareri spreads its wildering wreaths,
Where sound the trumpet-calls of elephants:
Those rocky heights with hue of dark blue clouds,
Where lies embosomed many a shining tarn
Of crystal-clear, cool waters, and whose slopes
The 'herds of Indra' cover and bedeck: . . .
Here is enough for me who fain would dwell
In meditation rapt, mindful and tense.
—'Psalms of the Brethren', *Thera Gāthā* XVIII, 261, 4

However, it is only the hand which has no wound that can
safely handle poison. Not uncommonly we mistakenly consider
ourselves free of addictions simply because we have not been
separated from the objects of gratification enough to experience
the full intensity of our desires. Cigarette smoking is one obvious
example. Thus for one treading the path to Nirvāna a considerable amount of renunciation and discipline is imperative.

This brings us to another feature of the Dhamma which has
given many the impression that it is life-negating, depressing
and morbid. That is those passages of scripture which refer to
the body or the world in general as 'disgusting' or 'impure' or
else advocate the development of 'disgust'. This is especially
characteristic of the cemetery meditations that occur in
satipaṭṭhāna practice. Here a monk is advised to meditate upon
a human corpse in various stages of decay and putrification,
'swollen, blue and festering' or 'being eaten by crows, hawks,
cultures, dogs, jackals or by different kinds of worms'. And
with each of these mental pictures the monk 'then applies his

231

perception to his own body thus: "Verily, also my own body is of the same nature: such it will become and will not escape it." [1] Likewise one finds meditations on food in which the meditator visualizes the digestion and decomposition of food as it proceeds through the intestines. [2]

The point to remember is that Buddhism is first and foremost a series of techniques for psychological maturation rather than a philosophy about the nature of the world. Furthermore, these techniques must be varied from person to person and also varied from time to time for any one person, depending upon one's particular state of mind. [3] Thus the above meditations are specific techniques intended as antidotes for specific types of craving (in the above instances the cravings of narcissism, immortality, passion and gluttony). Their function is one of negative conditioning. It is like a man who is repeatedly told while under hypnosis that cigarette smoke tastes like ammonia. This produces the post-hypnotic hallucination that cigarettes do taste like ammonia, and he eventually loses his desire for cigarettes. Or again it is like Pavlov's dog which is given a painful electric shock every time it sees a certain food. In time all desire for that food is lost. When reading of these meditations one often gets a very depressing view of them. But if they induce depression, one has either misperceived them or one's present mental condition is not one for which these meditations are intended. In this regard the Buddha has said:

'If in the contemplation of the body, bodily agitation, or mental lassitude or distraction should arise in the meditator; then, Ānanda, he should turn his mind to a gladdening subject. Having done so, joy will arise in him.'

—*Saṃyutta-Nikāya* V, 155 (XLVII, III, I, X)

A SELFISH GOAL

Is the goal of Nirvāna a selfish one? Perhaps the most common criticism directed against Buddhism and Theravāda Buddhism

[1] *Majjhima-Nikāya* I, 58 (No. 10 *Satipaṭṭhāna Sutta*).
[2] *Visuddhimagga* XI, 1–26.
[3] *Saṃyutta-Nikāya* V, 112–115 (XLVI, II, VI, 3).

in particular is that one's primary concern is one's own salvation. The whole effort and purpose of the Eightfold Path is self-development, self-purification, one's personal liberation.

In reply to the question 'Is Buddhism selfish?' the answer must be 'yes' in the sense that every wilful action is selfish. Referring to our previous discussion of the pleasure-pain principle (pages 177–178), all human endeavours (unless purely habitual) are motivated by some attempt at achieving happiness, pleasure, love, self-respect, social approval, beauty and other enjoyable experiences; or else actions are motivated by an endeavour to escape sorrow, pain, fear, guilt, humiliation and other forms of dukkha. Even great acts of self-sacrifice are but instances of ambivalence in which one level of feeling (e.g. love, religious dedication or a wish for self-esteem) wins out over antagonistic and less respected levels. Christianity and Islam, with their great emphasis upon Heaven and Hell (regardless of the ways in which Heaven and Hell may be interpreted), provide clear examples of the pleasure-pain principle occurring in high reaches of religious thought.

Compassion originates not as a philosophical or religious ideal but rather as a feeling which motivates us to help others and is experienced as a very wholesome and rewarding state of mind. In fact loud advocations of love and compassion as ideals often indicate that they are wanting as realities; the militancy of many Bohemian peace marchers, fundamentalist clergymen and communist and socialist zealots provide clear examples.[1]

If, however, we take the more conventional usage of the word 'selfish', which encompasses greed and egotism but excludes love (*mettā*) and compassion, then the term does not apply to

[1] One may postulate that compassion and allied feelings are divinely willed, but such an assumption immediately raises both the question of free will and the question of the origin of less wholesome feelings such as greed and hatred. Starting on an experiential basis, Buddhism acknowledges the reality of such feelings and proceeds from there. It is interesting to note in this regard that close observations of several species of higher animals suggest that love and compassion are not exclusively human.[2] [3]

[2] *National Geographic*, Vol. 128, No. 6, 'New Discoveries Among Africa's Chimpanzees', by Jane Van Lawick-Goodall (Washington, D.C., December 1965), pp. 802–831.

[3] *Arctic Wild*, by Louis Chrisler (New York, Harper, 1958).

the Buddha's teachings. As several quotations will demonstrate:

'Then, Lohicca, he who would say: "Suppose a Samana or a Brahmana has reached some good state (of mind), then he should tell no one else about it. For what can one man do for another? To tell others would be like the man who, having broken through an old bond, should entangle himself in a new one. Like that, I say, is this desire to declare to others; it is a form of lust." He who should say thus would be putting obstacles in the way of those clansmen who have taken upon themselves the Doctrine and Discipline. . . . But putting obstacles in their way he would be out of sympathy for their welfare. Being out of sympathy for their welfare his heart would become established in enmity, and when one's heart is established in enmity, that is unsound doctrine.'

—*Dīgha-Nikāya* I, 228–229 (No. 12 *Lohicca Sutta*)

When told that it is unbefitting for one who has renounced the world to spend his life exhorting other men, the Buddha replied:

Whate'er the apparent cause, Sakka, whereby
Men come to dwell together none doth fit
The Wise Man's case. Compassion moves his mind.
And if, with mind thus satisfied, he spend
His life instructing other men, yet he
Thereby is nowise bound as by a yoke.
Compassion moveth him and sympathy.

—*Samyutta-Nikāya* I, 206 (X; 2)

And again he said:

'Monks, it is because I observe these two results therein that I am given to dwelling in lonely spots, in solitary lodging in the forest. What two? Observing my own pleasant way of living in this very life and feeling compassion for future generations. These are the two results.'

—*Anguttara-Nikāya* I, 60 (II, 2; 9)

Once one of the monks lay ill but was ignored by the others

so intent were they on spiritual training. At this time the Buddha admonished them:

'Whosoever, brethren, would wait upon me, whosoever, brethren, would honour me, whosoever brethren, would follow my advice, he should wait upon the sick.'

—*Vinaya, Mahāvagga* 302 (VIII, 26)

And when the Brahmin, Sangarava, said that the life of a monk was of benefit to but one person, the monk himself, the Buddha replied that one who succeeds in his practice and attains Enlightenment will become a teacher of men and can lead many thousands to the same Liberation.[1]

The justification for the Buddha's great emphasis upon self-development and self-purification was explained in the Sermon on the Mount when Jesus said:

'Or how wilt thou say to thy brother, Let me pull out the mote out of thine eye; and, behold, a beam is in thine own eye? Thou hypocrite, first cast out the beam out of thine own eye: and then shalt thou see clearly to cast out the mote out of thy brother's eye.'

—*St Matthew* 7: 4–5

It has been said: Men can be forgiven for the things they have done in the name of evil, but who can forgive that which has been done in the name of good? The histories of Europe, Ceylon, Mexico and numerous tribal areas provide the most tragic examples of Christian atrocities committed by men apparently sincere in the belief that they were serving God. Likewise for the Moslem faith. More recently communists with apparently genuine convictions of the rightness of the socialist state have been equally ruthless. A more subtle but more common occurrence of this same phenomenon is seen in the everyday process of child raising. Parents convinced that their particular habits, ideals, mores and customs are the best too often attempt to mould their children into the same patterns. Sometimes the

---

[1] *Anguttara-Nikāya* I, 167–168 (III, 6; 60).

persuasions are deliberate, direct and suppressive; other times unconscious, covert and insidious. But in either case it is an attempt by one party to force its ways upon another. Sometimes this is done with relative success and harmony, but sometimes with tragedy and heartache to all concerned. Thus the Buddha advised:

> 'But, Cunda, that one who himself is in the mire should pull out of the mire another sunk therein,—this, verily, is an unheard-of thing. But that one himself clear of the slough should be able to lift out of the slough another foundered therein,—such a thing may well be. And that one who himself is not subdued, not disciplined, has not attained to the Extinction of Delusion, should cause others to become subdued, and disciplined, to attain to the Extinction of Delusion,—such a thing has never been known. But that one, himself controlled, trained, delivered from delusion, should lead others to become controlled and trained, lead them to Deliverance from Delusion,—such a thing may very well be.'
>
> —*Majjhima-Nikāya* I, 45 (No. 8 *Sallekha Sutta*)

ESCAPIST

Akin to the problem of selfishness is that of escapism. The label 'escapist' is one commonly used by critics of Theravāda Buddhism, and, as with selfishness, the problem must first be dealt with in terms of semantics. Again referring to the pleasure-pain principle, half of life is escapist in that it is an attempt to avoid dukkha (suffering). A man who takes aspirin does so to escape the pain of his headache, and a large part of obeying customs and rules is done to avoid either reproach and punishment or to avoid one's own feelings of guilt. Thus in this sense of the word, Buddhism is very decidedly escapist, for its primary concern is to free men from dukkha. However, in addition to their literal meanings the words 'escapist' and 'escapism' almost always bear connotations of cowardice or of shirking one's duty. Thus when asked whether or not his religion is escapist, a Buddhist is placed in a position where an answer to the affirmative will admit to an unstated and unwarranted value judgement.

If escapist means shirking one's duty, then let us examine the concept of duty. Duty and obedience receive little mention in the Pāli Canon and are not proclaimed as virtues.[1] In Buddhist teaching each being is free to act as it sees fit but should first be aware of the nature and consequences of its actions. Duty is not something which exists in nature but rather is a social construct more or less necessary for the preservation of family, tribe and nation. While in an absolute sense duty itself may not be real, from an experiential position what is real is the feeling or sense of duty which men acquire through social conditioning. Thus in World War I the German soldier was compelled by duty to kill Frenchmen, while the Frenchman was equally duty-bound to kill Germans. Likewise in the 1960s when an East German escapes to the West, in the eyes of the West he is a hero who undergoes dangers and hardships to realize a better way of life. But from the East German position the same man is an escapist, who for selfish motives has fled his duties to the people and the socialist state.

If a man should hold dual citizenship in two countries and finds that he must relinquish one of the two, it is easy to imagine that citizens of the rejected nation might find it difficult to be sympathetic and understanding of his choice. Such a reaction would result from ethnocentrism, provincialism and a lack of familiarity with the world beyond their own. Likewise, when a man experiences Nirvāna and chooses it in preference to samsāra, how are we, who know only the one world and not the other, able to criticize his decision?

For all that is said about one's duty to society, it is unusual to find a man whose primary concern is not his own prosperity and happiness. And when a man does loudly proclaim the virtues of duty, we may question to what extent he is only parroting contemporary mores, attempting to win social approval or

[1] *Sacred Books of the Buddhists*, Vol. IV 'Dialogues of the Buddha Part III' (*Dīgha-Nikāya* III), translated by T. W. Rhys Davids (London, Pāli Text Society, 1957), p. 181.

reacting to guilt feelings which have resulted from the exploitation of one's fellow men. Psychiatrically it is known that those who most strongly adhere to the concept of duty suffer from compulsive personality structures. Such persons fear their own feelings and spontaneity, and thus their compulsiveness, excessive morality and preoccupation with duty are but defences used to control their own mistrusted feelings.[1] It is man's socially acquired sense of shame or guilt followed by his desire to avoid (i.e. to escape) this feeling that gives the sense of duty such powerful control over human behaviour.

If there is a higher duty than social mores, it is not duty *per se*, but compassion. For it is compassion that inspires us to help others regardless of the boundaries of culture, race, nation or species. The virtue performed by compassion is thus spontaneous and genuine rather than forced, premeditated or dutiful. Again if we consider the decades of tireless service to humanity as lived by the Buddha and the other arahants, how can we say they did not perform their 'duty' to the world?

7. THE MOTIVE AND THE MEANS

Throughout this essay three important matters have come into focus. First is the emphasis which Buddhism gives to experience as the basis of both knowledge and spiritual progress. Second, from this experiential background emerges the pleasure-pain principle as the primary concern of life. Thirdly, Nirvāna can be known and understood only by direct experience, and since it can only be known in this way, neither myself nor any of the readers of this essay (unless there be arahants among you) have any certainty that it is real.

With these facts in mind let us turn our attention to two remaining problems that need consideration concerning Nirvāna. First, why should one deny oneself many of life's comforts and joys and endure years of effort and discipline to attain something which may not exist? Second, if Nirvāna is realized only by the abolition of all cravings and desires, what about the

[1] *Modern Clinical Psychiatry, op. cit.*, pp. 62–63.

238

desire for Nirvāna itself, the very thing which makes us seek Nirvāna; is not this, too, a selfish desire?

The problem is not one of attachment to Nirvāna *per se*, but rather it is a problem of being attached to the thought or *idea* of Nirvāna. Thus the Buddha comments on the mind of one who is spiritually untrained and undeveloped as follows:

'He recognizes Nirvāna as Nirvāna. Having recognized Nirvāna as Nirvāna he thinks of Nirvāna; he thinks in (the idea of) Nirvāna; he thinks (of self as) Nirvāna; he thinks: "Nirvāna is mine", he is satisfied with Nirvāna. What is the reason for this? I say that it is not thoroughly understood by him.'

Then in contrast he speaks of an arahant, one for whom Nirvāna is a reality:

'He directly knows Nirvāna as Nirvāna. From directly knowing Nirvāna as Nirvāna he does not think of Nirvāna, he does not think in (the idea of) Nirvāna; he does not think (of self as) Nirvāna; he does not think: "Nirvāna is mine." He does not delight in Nirvāna. What is the reason for this? I say it is because it is thoroughly understood by him.'
　　　　　—Majjhima-Nikāya I, 4 (No. 1 *Mūlapariyāya Sutta*)

Perhaps the two above questions are best answered by letting the Pāli Canon speak for itself. In the *Majjhima-Nikāya* we find the following dialogue between the Buddha and the wanderer Māgandiya. The latter has made the accusation that the Buddha 'is a destroyer of life' to which the Buddha replies:

'Māgandiya, the eye delights in material shapes, is delighted by material shapes, rejoices in material shapes; it is tamed, watched, guarded and controlled by a Tathāgata, and he teaches a Doctrine for its control. Was it on account of this, Māgandiya, that you said: "The recluse Gotama is a destroyer of life"?'

'Just on account of this did I say, good Gotama: "The recluse Gotama is a destroyer of life." '

(As for eye and material shapes, the same is then repeated for sounds, smells, tastes, touch and mental states. The Buddha then continues:)

'What do you think about this, Māgandiya? Suppose someone formerly revelled in material shapes cognizable by the eye; agreeable, pleasant, desired, enticing, connected with sensual pleasure, alluring. After a time, having known the coming to be and passing away of material shapes and the satisfaction in them, and the peril of them and the way of escape from them as it really is, getting rid of craving for material shapes, suppressing the fever for material shapes, he should live devoid of lust, his mind inwardly calmed. What have you, Māgandiya, to say of him?'
'Nothing, good Gotama.'

(And again the same is repeated for sounds, smells, etc.)

'Now I, Māgandiya, when I was formerly a householder, endowed and provided with five strands of sense-pleasures, revelled in them: in material shapes cognizable by the eye, agreeable, pleasant . . . in sounds cognizable by the ear . . . in smells cognizable by the nose . . . in tastes cognizable by the tongue . . . in touches cognizable by the body, agreeable, pleasant, desired, enticing, connected with sensual pleasures, alluring. I had three palaces, Māgandiya, one for the rains, one for the cold season, one for the hot weather. During the four months of the rains, being delighted in the palace for the rains by women musicians, I did not come down from that palace. But after a time, knowing the coming to be and passing away of sense-pleasures, and the satisfaction in them and the peril of them and the way of escape from them as it really is, getting rid of the craving for sense-pleasures, suppressing the fever of sense-pleasures, I lived devoid of lust, my mind inwardly calmed. I saw other beings not yet devoid of attachment to sense-pleasures who were pursuing sense-pleasures: they were being consumed by craving for sense-pleasures, burning with the fever of sense-pleasures. I did not envy them: I had no delight in those things. What was the reason for this? It was, Māgandiya, that there is this delight which, apart from pleasures of the senses, apart from unskilled states of mind, attains and remains in a god-like happiness. Delighting in this delight, I do not envy what is low. I have no delight in that.'

—*Majjhima-Nikāya* II, 503–505
(No. 75 *Māgandiya Sutta*)

And to the monks he spoke:

'The eye is burning, visible objects are burning, eye-conscious-ness is burning, eye-contact is burning, also whatever is felt as pleasant or painful, or neither painful nor pleasant, that arises with eye-contact as its essential support, that too is burning. Burning with what? Burning with the fire of craving, with the fire of hate, with the fire of delusion; I say it is burning with birth, ageing and death, with sorrow, with lamentation, with pain, grief and despair.'

(And likewise for sounds, mental states, etc.)

'Monks, when a noble follower who has heard sees thus, he finds aversion in the eye, finds aversion in forms, finds aversion in eye-consciousness, finds aversion in eye-contact, and whatever is felt as painful or pleasant, or neither painful nor pleasant, that arises with eye-contact for its essential support, in that too he finds aversion.'

(And again for sounds, etc.)

'When he finds aversion, passion fades out. With the fading of passion he is liberated. When liberated there is knowledge that he is liberated: he understands: "Birth is exhausted, the holy life has been lived, what was to be done has been done, of this there is no more beyond.'

—*Vinaya, Mahāvagga* 34 (I, 21)

Another version of the same theme occurs in the *Saṁyutta-Nikāya*. Here the Buddha explains how the causal law of dependent origination leads to birth and suffering. Suffering inspires one to trust in the Dhamma, and this in turn gives rise to joy. Joy results in rapture; rapture produces serenity, and serenity results in happiness, which in turn makes for concentration. From concentration arises the knowledge and vision of things as they really are, and this makes for repulsion. Repulsion creates passionlessness, and passionlessness results in Liberation.[1]

Thus the scriptures quite clearly provide the solution to the two previously stated questions. One does not realize Nirvāna by becoming obsessed with the quest for a transcendental ideal. The Buddhist approach differs from that of certain of the Bhakti schools of Hinduism, for in Bhakti writings we are told that man finds divinity only when his whole being cries out in fervent emotion for the Divine, as one whose head is held under water craves in desperation for air. In contrast the Buddhist approach is one of confronting each state of consciousness with the close scrutiny of insight and mindfulness, and in so doing perceiving the unsatisfactory nature of such states and then relinquishing them for this reason alone. Unwholesome mental conditions are abandoned because of their own inherent defects and dangers, not at the bidding of supernatural revelation nor because a reward is promised in a hypothetical life to come. Nor is there a problem of denying oneself present happiness without any compensation. The rewards are immediate. Each forward step is a goal warranted by its own intrinsic merits. And this is so, even though all we can say of Nirvāna is that those who have walked the path before us have said that if we follow the course to its maximum possible realization, then something occurs which is beyond all description; a Something well worth knowing. Nirvāna is found by fully understanding the pleasure-pain principle, stripping it of the delusions it gives rise to, and thus putting oneself beyond its influence.

Thus we have resolved St Augustine's dilemma (page 221). Desire is not conquered by repression, nor by prayer, nor by ideology; for such techniques do not circumvent our lingering

[1] *Samyutta-Nikāya* II, 30–31 (XII, 3; 23).

thirst for satisfaction. They cannot resolve the ambivalence which they themselves have created. Rather the solution is given by the Buddha when he says that desire is overcome by foreseeing its result, 'penetrating it by insight and seeing it plain'.[1] Seeing it plain is seeing its pain, and desire is thus wilfully abandoned because of what it is in and of itself.

The essence of Buddhist practice rests upon the empirical facts of Samsāra—one's own experience. Faith in something which nobody has been able to experience and testify to is unnecessary; rather there must be faith in one's ability to master one's cravings and faith in the worth of the effort. An essential aspect of the Dhamma is mindfulness, the first of the seven factors of enlightenment (page 226). In simplified language it is repeatedly and persistently taking a good hard look at things, especially at oneself and one's own feelings in particular. It is the maximum possible degree of self-honesty and consequently one of the most difficult of all things to achieve.

While mindfulness which results in insight is the keynote of liberation, the problem is really more complicated than that. It is complicated because each human being is complicated. Each of us has many distinct and diverse levels to his psyche, and each of these levels must be dealt with in a manner appropriate to it alone. Our states of consciousness are continually changing from hour to hour, minute to minute, second to second. There is no single rule of practice to apply to all persons at all times. Thus the Buddha repeatedly emphasized that training can only be done now, in the immediate present.

'How is the solitary life perfected in detail? It is when that which is past is put away; when that which is future is given up, and when, with regard to present self-states that we have got, will and passion have been thoroughly mastered. It is thus that the solitary life is perfected in detail.'

—*Saṁyutta-Nikāya* II, 283 (XXI; 10)

And again:

[1] *Anguttara-Nikāya* I, 264 (III, 11; 110).

Do not hark back to things that passed,
And for the future cherish not fond hopes:
The past was left behind by thee,
The future state has yet to come.

But who with vision clear can see
The present which is here and now,
Such a wise one should aspire to win
What never can be lost nor shaken.

—*Majjhima-Nikāya* III, 187
(No. 131 *Bhaddekaratta Sutta*)

With this we are now prepared to discuss one final problem regarding the Dhamma, and that is the apparent contradiction between the ideals of love and compassion and the ideal of non-attachment. The words 'love' and 'compassion' do not represent two single entities but rather a whole spectrum of feelings which differ from each other in ways so subtle as to often defy description. Love and compassion can be extremely pleasant and meaningful, and they can be effective antidotes to greed and hatred. Yet at other times they can carry us to unrealistic extremes or lead to frustration if situations prevent their expression. Thus the correct application of love and compassion (and also of detachment and equanimity) is a matter of judgement and timing as determined by one's particular state of mind at a given moment. While logically and philosophically compassion and non-attachment may be contradictory ideals, when one comes to actually living and practising the Dhamma no conflict arises.

Despite the existence of dukkha (sorrow and discomfort) which is both inherent in and generated by passion and craving, there still remains the obvious fact that there is a level of pleasure in these states or at least an expectation of pleasure. And it is primarily for this reason that we find it so very difficult to relinquish them. The solution is not one that can be proved by argument, logic or science. It can be proved only by oneself and to oneself. That is to fully and mindfully note the nature and quality of those pleasures which are associated with lust and greed. One must behold them in their true form free of any social, religious or personal assumptions as to their merits and demerits. In the same manner one makes the same impartial and penetrative observations of equanimity, happiness and mettā. On the basis of their own inherent features these latter pleasures (equanimity, etc.) are seen to be more wholesome, more meaningful and more truly satisfying than the pleasures of passion and greed. Furthermore, the very presence of greed, hatred, jealousy or lust excludes the possibility of the higher feelings existing at that same moment. Thus again one finds a true incentive to abandon desires. There is no saviour but oneself; the Dhamma simply invites us to come and see. It points the way, but we must follow.

To a six-year-old child, adult existence often appears dull, spiritless and uninteresting. He is incapable of appreciating most adult interests, and if deprived of playthings, playmates and stories, he will most likely lapse into apathy or depression. But ten years later he is an adolescent with an entirely different set of values and interests. He no longer cares for the childish things of the six-year-old; yet still adult life looks rather blank and pointless when compared with dancing, dating and drag races. Adult values will come in time and with them a natural loss of interest in adolescent pleasures. Thus the layman who finds it difficult to sympathize with the quietude and solitude of a Buddhist monk may reflect upon how his own life appears in the eyes of younger generations. Buddhism is pointing the way for maturation beyond that of the usual social norms. We advance to progressively higher and higher pleasure levels until we reach a state where even pleasure and happiness are transcended. In the *Culasuññatā Sutta* the Buddha furnishes an explicit example beginning with the village life of a lay person and proceeding through a monk's life of solitude in the forest and then continuing on up through the highest states of jhāna; each level being successively relinquished for a more rewarding one, with Nirvāna as the end.[1] And in the *Anguttara-Nikāya* the Buddha is quoted:

[1] *Majjhima-Nikāya* III, 104–108 (No. 121 *Culasuññatā Sutta*).

'There are two kinds of happiness, O monks; the happiness of the householder and the happiness of the ascetic. But the greater of the two is the happiness of the ascetic.

'There are two kinds of happiness, O monks; the happiness of the senses and the happiness of renunciation. But the greater of the two is the happiness of renunciation.'

—*Anguttara-Nikāya* I, 80 (II, 7; 1–2)

And from the *Dhammapada*:

If by forsaking a lesser happiness
One may behold a greater happiness,
Let the wise man renounce the lesser
Considering the greater.

—*Dhammapada* 290

The journey to Nirvāna is not a sudden one. A thorough and harmonious restructuring of one's being can only come with time and patient endeavour. Thus we read the Buddha's words:

'Just as, brethren, the mighty ocean deepens and slopes gradually down, hollow after hollow, not plunging by a sudden precipice; even so brethren, in this Dhamma-discipline the training is gradual, it goes step by step; there is no sudden penetration of insight.'

—*Udāna* V 5; 54 (*Sona*)

And again:

'By degrees, little by little, from time to time, a wise man should remove his own impurities, as a smith removes the dross from silver.'

—*Dhammapada* 239

8. THE BUDDHIST INSTITUTION

In the preceding chapters our discussion of Nirvāna has led us to touch upon nearly all other features of the Dhamma—karma, rebirth, ethics, insight practice, aesthetics and epistemology. To complete the picture let us say a few words about Buddhism as a social institution. From the time of the Buddha until the present day, Buddhists have fallen into two major groupings. By far the larger group is the lay people, who for all practical purposes are much like lay people of any other religion except for their belief in Buddhist tenets. Among the laity one finds a wide range of individual variations in the extent to which they understand and practise the Dhamma. It is not unusual to meet both male and female lay Buddhists whose knowledge, discipline and meditation excel those of most monks and nuns.

The monks at the time of the Buddha were not priests. That is, they had no ecclesiastical functions, took no part in rites, ceremonies or ritual and were discouraged from practising astrology, fortune-telling and magic. The purpose of instituting the monastic order was twofold. First, it was intended to provide an environment and a way of life most conducive to progress towards Nirvāna. It free one of the usual cares and obligations of lay people and provided maximum opportunity for training, study and meditation. Second, it was a means of preserving and propagating the teaching. A study of the Vinaya Rules, by which all Theravādin Buddhist monks are bound, reveals that these rules are not primarily moral precepts. Rather they are standards of discipline conducive to one's psychological development or else regulations necessary for maintaining the harmony, preservation and integrity of a large and growing social body.

Thus from its very conception the monastic order had two missions; one was to learn and practise the Dhamma. The other was to preserve this knowledge and give it to all who wished to hear. Though magic and ritual have since become a part of nearly every Buddhist sect, we still find nations, such as Thailand and Ceylon, where the original purposes of the order are still recognized as the primary ones. One need not be a monk or nun to realize Nirvāna. The suttas list at least twenty-one persons who reached the goal while still laymen.[1,2] But for

[1] *Anguttara-Nikāya* III, 451 (VI, XII; 131–151).
[2] Commentary to the *Dhammapada* 142.

one seriously intent on spiritual progress, if he can free himself of social obligations, gain family permission (from his parents if young or from his wife if married), and can meet the other standards necessary for admission to the Order (freedom from debt and freedom from insanity and contagious diseases)[1] then the life of a monk or nun is the one which provides the best chances for realizing the goal.

[1] *Vinaya, Mahāvagga* 72–91 (I, 39–71).

THE PALI BUDDHIST SCRIPTURES

The canonical writings of Theravada Buddhism, composed in the Pāli language akin to Sanskrit, are known as the *Tipitaka* or Triple Basket. The three 'Baskets' are:

I   *Vinaya Pitaka* 'Book of Discipline',
II *Sutta Pitaka* 'Discourses',
III *Abhidhamma Pitaka* 'Special Teaching'.

Of these, II is of most general interest. Translations into English, mainly by the Pāli Text Society, exist of the *Vinaya* and most of the *Sutta Pitaka*, but of the seven books of the *Abhidhamma*, only four have so far been translated.

I. The *Vinaya*, translated in five volumes by I. B. Horner as 'The Book of Discipline', contains mainly rules for monks, including a list of offences for which they may be expelled or disciplined.

II. The *Sutta Pitaka* is divided into five sections called *Nikāyas*:

1. *Dīgha Nikāya* 'Long Section' (translated as 'Dialogues of the Buddha') consists of 34 longer discourses (Abbreviation: D).
2. *Majjhima Nikāya* 'Middle Length Sayings', contains 152 medium-length discourses (Abbreviation: M).
3. *Saṁyutta Nikāya* 'Conjoined Section' (translated as 'Kindred Saryings') contains a large number of short *suttas* (discourses) on related topics (Abbreviation: S).
4. *Anguttara Nikāya* 'Adding-One Section' (translated as 'Gradual Sayings') consists of numerous short *suttas* in eleven classified groups relating to things occurring singly, in twos, in threes, and so on up to eleven (Abbreviation: A).
5. *Khuddaka Nikāya* 'Shortish Section', partly translated as 'Minor Anthologies', contains 15 books of very varying character, including the (largely) ancient verses called *Sutta Nipāta*, and the *Dhammapada*, a famous anthology of 423 stanzas epitomizing the teaching.

III. The *Abhidhamma* is a systemic exposition in seven books:

1. *Dhammasangaṇī* 'Enumeration of Phenomena', translated by Mrs C. A. F. Rhys Davids (1900) as 'A Buddhist Manual of Psychological Ethics'.

2. *Vibhanga* 'Treatises' (in course of translation).
3. *Dhātu-Kathā* 'Discourse on Elements', translated by Ven. U Narada (1964).
4. *Puggala-Paññatti* 'Description of Individuals', translated by B. Law (1924).
5. *Kathā-Vatthu* 'Points of Controversy', translated by S. Z. Aung and Mrs Rhys Davids (1915).
6. *Yamaka* 'Book of Pairs' (not translated).
7. *Paṭṭhāna* 'Book of Origination' (in course of translation).

The reader interested in *Abhidhamma* is referred to *A Guide through the Abhidhamma Pitaka* by the Ven. Nyanatiloka, and the excellent *Abhidhamma Studies* by the Ven. Nyanaponika.

Different parts of the Canon are obviously of differing degrees of age and authenticity, and such points are much debated by scholars. But it is difficult to resist the conclusion that it is in the Pāli Canon alone that the oldest and most reliable information on the Buddha's life and teaching is to be found.

Some of the most important *suttas* are available separately in the Wheel series in new translations.

LIST OF ABBREVIATIONS

A.   *Aṅguttara Nikāya* (p. 249)

Bṛh. Up.   *Bṛhadāraṇyaka Upaniṣad*

Ch. Up.   *Chāndogya Upaniṣad*

D.   *Dīgha Nikāya* (p. 249)

Dhp.   *Dhammapada* (p. 249)

I.   *Itivuttaka* (part of *Khuddaka Nikāya*, p. 249)

M.   *Majjhima Nikāya* (p. 249)

S.   *Saṁyutta Nikāya* (p. 249)

Sn.   *Sutta Nipāta* (p. 249)

Tait Up.   *Taittiriya Upaniṣad*

Ud.   *Udāna* (part of *Khuddaka Nikāya*, p. 249)

INDEX

252